MAKING A REAL KILLING

LEN ACKLAND

Making a
Real Killing

ROCKY FLATS AND THE NUCLEAR WEST

University of New Mexico Press Albuquerque

Library of Congress Cataloging-in-Publication Data

Ackland, Len.

Making a real killing : Rocky Flats and the nuclear West / Len
Ackland. — 1st ed.

p.   cm.

Includes index.

ISBN 0-8263-1877-0 (cloth) ISBN 0-8263-2798-2 (paper)

1. Rocky Flats Plant (U.S.) — History.   2. Nuclear weapons
plants — Environmental aspects — Colorado.   3. Church family.
4. Golden Region (Colo.) — History.   I. Title.

UF534.C6   A25   1999

363.17'99'0978883 — dc21   99-6500

CIP

This book is dedicated to my parents

Eleanor L. (Yoder) Ackland

Jack F. Ackland

and my children

Seth, John, and Sarah

Contents

Preface and Acknowledgments

My childhood memory of the Rocky Flats nuclear weapons plant dates back to the mid-1950s, when my family would occasionally pass it during our frequent Sunday afternoon drives. Various routes existed from our home in Aurora, just east of Denver, into the mountains. A favorite was to go up Coal Creek canyon, which took us past what my parents simply called a "government plant." My father was a government employee himself, a middle manager at the U.S. Post Office in Denver, and my mother soon would go to work as a secretary for a U.S. Air Force intelligence unit at Lowry Air Base next to Aurora. Years later, in the early 1960s, I was a student at the University of Colorado at Boulder, eight miles north of Rocky Flats. The implications of this nuclear weapons factory eluded me, despite the Cuban missile crisis during my freshman year.

At the university I majored in history, a wonderful discipline for learning how to ask questions and seek accurate answers about the way the world really works. Journalism, the "first rough draft of history," as a *Washington Post* publisher once called it, interested me, but I didn't try it until I freelanced in Vietnam during 1968. The next year I attended graduate school at Johns Hopkins School of Advanced International Studies in Washington, D.C. I went mainly to study economics, because monetary interests underlie so much public policy, but my most insightful class was taught by adjunct professor Morton Halperin. Formerly a "whiz kid" who worked for Secretary of Defense Robert McNamara, Halperin knew how Washington operated. His class focused on understanding policy decisions by figuring out the players and then identifying the personal, bureaucratic, philosophical, and other interests they brought to the table.

It took a few twists and turns, including a stint as a researcher for the Tony Russo and Dan Ellsberg "Pentagon Papers" defense team, before I got my first paying job as a journalist in 1973 at an iconoclastic business weekly in Denver called *Cervi's Rocky Mountain Journal*. As a reporter, I heard a little about Rocky Flats but was busy trying to learn how corporate America operates. In 1975 *The Des Moines Register* hired me to do investigative business and labor stories. After moving in 1978 to the *Chicago Tribune*, I reported and wrote about the interrelationships among private industry, the government, technological developments, and the nuclear arms race. I began understanding the downsides and vulnerabilities inherent in computer technology. Complex, powerful computerized systems can be marvelous, as long everything works correctly. And technology, the application of scientific knowledge, can be used and abused.

Why, I began wondering, are we humans racing to create ever more sophisticated weapons able to destroy ourselves and most other species? In 1984 I had a chance to more fully examine the nuclear arms race after being hired as editor of the *Bulletin of the Atomic Scientists*, a distinguished Chicago-based magazine that has been a voice of concerned physical and social scientists since 1945. The *Bulletin* family, including board members, staff, and writers, educated me about nuclear weapons and the arms race. Without the knowledge they shared, I couldn't have envisioned this book. I thank them, particularly Vic Rabinowitch, Dennis Flanagan, Ruth Adams and the late Leonard Rieser. I am also grateful to the John D. and Catherine T. MacArthur Foundation's Program on Global Security and Sustainability for awarding me a research and writing grant in 1990 to begin researching the book. The University of Colorado at Boulder, where I joined the School of Journalism and Mass Communication faculty in 1991, has supported my work by virtue of its values and policies as a research university. My knowledge of environmental issues has grown through interaction with colleagues across several disciplines, particularly those people involved with the Center for Environmental Journalism.

My thanks go to Sarah Gilbert, Jennifer Stone Gonzalez, and Sergio De Souza, who as graduate students provided research assistance, and to Jad Davenport for his photography. I was aided by staff members of the Archives of the University of Colorado at Boulder Libraries; the Harry S. Truman Library in Independence, Missouri; the DOE Rocky Flats communications office; the Kaiser-Hill communications office; the *Denver Rocky Mountain News* library; and the National Archives branches. Rodney Ross and William Davis at the Center for Legislative Archives at the National Archives in Washington, D.C., helped me navigate that facility. Kandi

McKay Arce at Church Ranch was always cheerful in helping me find information. And Diane Willian at the journalism school assisted with secretarial tasks.

I thank all the friends with whom I had useful conversations about this book over the years. Seven deserve special mention: David Albright, Dianne Dumanoski, John Winsor, Marilyn Johnson, Richard Fineberg, Michael Krepon, and Larry MacDonnell. Fineberg, Krepon, and MacDonnell also generously reviewed and commented on portions of the manuscript along with Bini Abbott, Jane Bock, Carl Bock, Judy Danielson, Bill Lanouette, Stan Norris, Yvonne Pearson, Tom Rauch, Jim Ruttenber, Niels Schonbeck, Pam Solo, Ginger Swartz, and Jack Weaver. I am greatly indebted to Jerry Marsh, who thoughtfully critiqued the entire manuscript.

I appreciate everyone who spent time talking with me about their experiences at Rocky Flats or provided other information. A few of these people appear in the text and many more don't, since a book must be finite if it's going to be read. For that insight and much more I thank Elizabeth Hadas, my editor at the University of New Mexico Press and director of the press. Her enthusiasm, careful eye, and smooth control over the editorial process were a writer's dream.

Finally, I am deeply indebted to two very special people for helping make this book what it is. Charlie Church McKay, whose family has been involved with the land called Rocky Flats for more than a century and the plant called Rocky Flats for almost half that long, graciously and unconditionally gave me access to his family files. I thank him for this and for the many hours he spent being interviewed. The other person to whom I owe incalculable thanks is Carol Stutzman, my wife and most loving editor and constructive critic. She offered incisive criticism on my draft chapters and kept pushing me back to the narrative line when I strayed.

In writing this book I have sought to provide an accurate, interesting history that places Rocky Flats into the context of the nuclear arms race, the Cold War, and the aftermath. Whatever errors exist in the book are solely my responsibility.

Len Ackland
Boulder, Colorado
January 1999

Introduction to the Paperback Edition

Since the hardcover edition of this book was completed in 1999, Rocky Flats has continued to make news headlines. They focus primarily on problems involving the cleanup of this former nuclear weapons plant. At the end of the year 2000, for example, plant officials announced that ten workers cleaning up the major plutonium processing building had received excessive radiation exposure. Ominously, the officials were unable to identify the exact source of the exposure. The plant's lethal nature, as described in this updated version that includes a new epilogue, remains with us.

Len Ackland
May 2001

Prologue

It's early March, and Charlie McKay is driving his pickup truck slowly across the snow-covered pasture. His brother-in-law stands in the truck bed, slicing the twine holding together the hay bales and then throwing them off a flake at a time for the waiting cattle. McKay carefully examines the herd of white-faced Herefords to make sure that the new calves are healthy and that none of the pregnant cows are having trouble giving birth. "The first- and second-time mothers are the ones you have to watch," he explains. "They're more likely to have a hard time calving."

McKay's chore is typical for a Colorado rancher, but his pasture certainly isn't. It spreads around and across a high, treeless mesa called Rocky Flats, which juts like a diving board from the steep foothills of the Rocky Mountains just sixteen miles from downtown Denver. The pasture borders a U.S. government nuclear bomb plant occupying land taken from McKay's family in 1951. A barbed wire fence a couple of hundred feet from where he's driving bears square yellow signs warning "NO TRESPASSING — by order of the U.S. Department of Energy."

Sometimes heavily armed security guards wearing gray camouflage suits roar up the perimeter road inside the barbed-wire fence and stop their jeep across from McKay. "They'll be on their side of the fence and I'm over here fooling with the calves and feeding, putting salt down, and making sure everybody's fine and healthy," he says. "And these Rambo idiots will get out and lie down on the ground and crawl up to the fence and pull out their binoculars and start watching me." McKay wouldn't be hard to spot. In his late fifties, he's six feet, three inches tall and weighs 280 pounds, with a full head of white hair contrasting sharply with thick black eyebrows. "It's not

like I'm out here in some suspicious-looking vehicle," he says, clearly an-
noyed. "They don't know the difference between 'come here' and 'sic 'em.' "

Part of McKay's irritation stems from history and part from the fact that
his family still owns mineral rights, an access road, and water in ponds on
the ten-square-mile nuclear bomb plant site. Indeed, McKay, like his late
uncle Marcus Church before him, possesses keys to some of the security
gates and regularly goes onto the site. Now that the Cold War is over and
the plant no longer produces weapons, McKay is angry that he can't use the
land as he sees fit. A real estate developer as well as a rancher, he wants to
finally cash in on metropolitan Denver's growth boom with his Rocky Flats
property just as he has with his nearby holdings.

Three miles east of Rocky Flats, the Old West bumps into the New West
at McKay's "Church Ranch Corporate Headquarters," just off the busy
highway connecting Denver with the university town of Boulder. Adver-
tised by a green-and-white sign visible from the highway, the corporate
office is a modest, single-story ranch-style house. McKay and his wife,
Sadie, live in a similar house right next door. A couple of pickup trucks, a
small red tractor, and a two-horse trailer sit next to a wooden barn that has
withstood decades of Colorado winters. A faded sign on the wall reads
"Church Ranch Herefords, Since 1869." Chickens and ducks wander freely
among several work sheds, garages, a tiny guest house, a rusting horse-
drawn plow, and other old farm equipment. McKay has a keen sense of
history, and many of the buildings are numbered to go along with a historical pamphlet that his daughter and office manager, Kandi McKay Arce,
helped write.

The surrounding Church Ranch land is being developed as fast as Mc-
Kay can put together deals. Behind the rustic headquarters buildings are a
group of gray, three-story apartments. A U.S. Homes subdivision of huge
houses on small lots has sprouted across a field. And down the road, called
Church Ranch Boulevard, sit an office building, a gas station and conve-
nience store, a butterfly museum, and a movie theater complex. McKay, a
friendly workaholic who can't stand being idle, wants to make sure that his
family profits from the real estate activity filling in the thirty miles of
dwindling open space between Denver and Boulder. And he won't be satisfied until the Rocky Flats land is developed, too. "Rocky Flats deserves its
birthday party," McKay says, his broad face breaking into a grin. Like the
long line of family farmers and entrepreneurs before him, he views land as a
resource that must be developed to have real value.

A party celebrating the birth of Rocky Flats as a commercial or residential development isn't in the cards anytime soon. In 1995 the U.S. Depart-

ment of Energy, which oversees the nation's nuclear weapons production, labeled it the most dangerous weapons plant in the nation because of the health and safety risks the contaminated, deteriorating facility poses to the 2 million people of nearby metropolitan Denver. An accident could cause the catastrophe that nearly happened in 1969 during a raging fire in the plant's plutonium-manufacturing building.

For four decades Rocky Flats was a key facility in the U.S. nuclear weapons complex. Workers transformed plutonium from liquid to solid to metal to make nuclear bombs similar to the one that destroyed Nagasaki, Japan, in August 1945. That single bomb killed an estimated 60,000 to 70,000 men, women, and children immediately or during the first few months afterward. The Nagasaki fatality number doubled over the next five years as people died from radiation and other bomb injuries. With the development of hydrogen bombs in the mid-1950s, the plutonium bombs from Rocky Flats became the explosive detonators at the core of H-bombs. The plant manufactured the bomb cores, called "pits" or "primaries" in nuclear jargon and euphemistically called "triggers," for most of the 70,000 nuclear weapons produced for the U.S. arsenal. At the center of these bomb cores sit hollow plutonium shells about the size of grapefruits but weighing seven to nine pounds apiece. A typical one explodes with a force of around 20,000 tons of TNT.

During the Cold War, Rocky Flats operated from 1952 to 1989. Although the Energy Department "temporarily" halted the plant's plutonium production for environmental and safety reasons in 1989, the agency didn't formally abandon the plant's nuclear weapons mission until 1992. Today the facility still holds 14.2 tons of plutonium, about half of which is metal that could readily be made into nuclear warheads or bombs; the rest is in compounds or waste. Most of this toxic plutonium has nowhere to go. In addition, the site is seriously contaminated with other radioactive as well as nonradioactive toxic substances.

Like the horrendous explosions created by the small, hollow balls of plutonium it manufactured, the Rocky Flats story is much larger than itself. It is about the federal government and private firms employing what was once state-of-the-art manufacturing technology to create the most destructive weapons in history. It is about a community, its politicians, and its businesses, including media companies, initially seeking short-term economic gain, failing to ask questions, and now facing long-term environmental and health risks.

The saga of Rocky Flats and the end of the Cold War provide a rare opportunity to examine why the citizens of the world's greatest democracy

willingly participated in building huge nuclear arsenals capable of destroying the human species. The legacy of that nuclear arms race remains with
us. Tens of thousands of nuclear weapons still exist, about half of them in
Russia. Nations such as Iraq and Iran still want to acquire nuclear arsenals,
and nuclear weapons are possessed by nations such as India and Pakistan,
historical enemies.

On the ledger's positive side, the risk of global nuclear war has been
significantly reduced, due in part to the changed attitudes and actions of the
American people. During the "Nuclear Weapons Freeze" debates of the
early 1980s, many questioned the dubious assumption that nuclear weapons form a sound basis for national security. Some of the principal organizers of the national Freeze campaign had cut their teeth at Rocky Flats,
where large protest demonstrations began after the 1969 fire. The peace
movement's work in this country and abroad was part of a strange and
wondrous mix of circumstances, events, and motivations that changed the
world. Soviet leader Mikhail Gorbachev, whose country was reeling from
an ailing economy, took initiatives to which President Ronald Reagan responded positively. The Cold War's end was capped by the Soviet Union's
disintegration in 1991.

But the American public's role in helping reverse the nuclear arms race
has troubling implications for the future. Democracy's effectiveness lagged
decades behind the powerful political, economic, and technological forces
that created and insulated this nation's nuclear weapons establishment. A
doomsday arsenal of nuclear weapons was in place long before the media
and the public began asking questions and demanding honest answers. The
Rocky Flats story illustrates how this happened. It is a story of place and
people, many of whom came here not just to make a living, but to make a
killing.

ONE

Rich Pastures

The Home Place

The Church family's ranch lies in a shallow, wedge-shaped valley where the Rocky Mountain foothills begin flattening out into Colorado's arid eastern plains. Now being engulfed by housing and commercial developments, the valley was still rural in 1942 when forty-three-year-old Marcus Church, Charlie McKay's uncle, moved back from his ranch high in the Rockies. Although Denver was just fifteen miles to the southeast, the rapidly growing city of 325,000 hadn't yet lapped over the grassy ridge bordering the Church valley. Ridges and mesas also separated the ranch from Boulder, the small university town to the north.

From a nearby rise, Marcus could look at the snow-capped Rockies stretching like a giant dinosaur's backbone along the western horizon. This mountain range separates the continent into two drainage areas. Snow and rain falling on the Continental Divide's eastern side become creeks rushing toward the Atlantic Ocean or Gulf of Mexico. Snow and rain landing on the western flank flow toward the Pacific.

At the southern end of this jagged panorama, 14,000-foot Pikes Peak breaks the crisp blue sky. To the north, the towering mass of Longs Peak stops the eye. The violent but slow-moving granite and schist upheaval that began producing the Rockies about sixty million years ago drove heavy metals such as gold and silver closer to the surface. The mountain range, which reaches into Canada and New Mexico, breaks in diminishing waves to the east in Colorado. It forms rugged foothills, known as the Front

Range, which run from Wyoming in the north to the city of Pueblo in the south.

Giant reddish sandstone slabs, pushed up from an ancient seabed by the surging Rockies, lie north of Church Ranch along a section of the foothills above Boulder. Early settlers dubbed them the "flatirons," after the bottoms of old-fashioned clothes irons heated on woodstoves. The land formed differently south of the ranch. Distinctive flat-topped mesas and stony ridges called hogbacks separate this part of the Front Range from the plains.

Directly west of the ranch, bluestem and blue grama grasses creep up a gentle slope to a mesa four miles wide. The boulders dotting it are reminders that the mesa is part of an alluvial fan formed by debris washed out of the Rockies over tens of millions of years. Winter snows and spring rains supply enough moisture to grow deep-rooted native grasses. Coal Creek rushes out of a mountain canyon at the southwestern end of the mesa. Two occasionally dry, or intermittent, streams, Walnut Creek and Woman Creek, run off the mesa's sides and nourish tall grasses in deep erosion gullies. The Churches and the handful of neighboring ranchers once called the area Rich Pastures. People driving south from Boulder to the brewery town of Golden on the rutted, bumpy dirt road across the mesa top knew it better as Rocky Flats.

Marcus Church knew the mesa well. When he was growing up, his family owned most of the mesa top and thousands of adjacent acres. In checkerboard fashion, the family holdings reached three miles east to the "home place," the ranch where Marcus was born in 1899. As a kid, he led his younger brother, Perry, on expeditions to the mesa and gullies. They would catch frogs in the marshes, fish the streams, and hunt quail and rabbits. It was a wilderness playground.

It also was the pasture for hundreds of Church Ranch Hereford cattle. Young Marcus, like the children of ranchers and farmers everywhere, was taught the importance of hard work. His father and grandfather instructed him in the fields; his mother and grandmother stressed book learning. They all exuded pride in family and conveyed the lesson that the family's land was key to its success.

Marcus was a good student. He grew into a diligent, independent man rooted in the land, including the thousands of acres on Rocky Flats that the federal government would legally confiscate in 1951. Ironically, as elsewhere in the American West, that same government had opened the door to the family's ownership of the land in the first place.

Henry and Sarah Church

Marcus's grandparents, George Henry Church, who went by Henry, and Sarah (Miller) Church, came to Colorado in the summer of 1861, seeking adventure and gold. They had just gotten married that spring in Independence, Iowa, a farming community in the eastern part of the state. Henry, a tall, lean thirty-one-year-old, had arrived in Iowa eight years earlier from his family's farm in upstate New York. He had cleared wild prairie and timber, planted corn in the rich black soil, and made a decent living. Sarah, twenty-two, taught school and, until she got married, lived on a large farm with her parents and ten sisters and brothers.[1]

When the couple began courting in the late 1850s, lower prices for corn and wheat, stories of new gold finds in Colorado, and talk of impending war between the North and the South propelled many of their acquaintances west. The travelers included Elder Roberts, a geologist dismissed as the minister in Independence for declaring from the pulpit that the world hadn't been created in six days. "People did not want an infidel preaching to them," Sarah observed matter-of-factly in her reminiscences. Although descended from Dutch missionaries to Africa and herself a practicing Methodist, Sarah was not narrow-minded.[2]

Upon returning to Iowa, Roberts told the newlyweds about wide expanses and riches and advised them to see the West for themselves. "We decided to take his advice, tho my mother strongly opposed my going," Sarah recalled. "She said Henry could endure the danger of Indians and the hardships better without me, but I was delighted with the novelty of the journey. Many of our friends had gone two weeks before." Sarah didn't admit to any trepidation about the trip in the reminiscences she jotted down many years later.

The Churches planned to leave for Colorado in May and return by Christmas. They swapped their horses for four sturdy oxen and named them Buck, Bright, Tom, and Jerry. They bought a large-wheeled "prairie schooner," or covered wagon, and prepared food for a long journey. "We dried potatoes, first mashing them with plenty of cream and then making them into flat cakes like a large pancake, and drying them in the oven," Sarah recorded. "We carried potatoes that lasted us through." To occupy her time on the 800-mile, seven-week trip, she took a few books, including *Paradise Lost* and a book of Greek myths, as well as plenty of cloth and yarn for sewing and knitting.

The couple set out alone in May 1861, expecting to join other travelers after they crossed the Big Muddy, as the Missouri River was nicknamed. Approaching the town of Council Bluffs in western Iowa, the Churches ran into men who had quit the trek west. "They all advised us to turn back, said there was no gold and no farming as it never rained," Sarah wrote. "Just then it was raining on us every day, so we put on two new sheets to our wagon and said, 'It would be pleasant to be for a while where it never rains.'"[3]

After crossing the river, they joined four other wagons for the trip across the plains of Nebraska and eastern Colorado. The wagon trail followed the Platte River, its steady flow from west to east just hinting at the almost imperceptibly uphill route that would leave them a mile higher by the time they reached the base of the Rockies. Before long they felt the clamminess leave their skin as dry air replaced humidity around the 100th longitude, or meridian, in mid-Nebraska, the rough dividing line between the lush Midwest and semiarid West.

East of the 100th meridian more than eighteen inches of annual rainfall allow crops to be grown without irrigation. The sparse rainfall to the west led explorers to dub this area the "Great American Desert." Entering this dry region, Henry couldn't have imagined how much energy he would spend in coming years digging ditches to divert mountain creek water for livestock and crops.

Day after day the wagon wheels cut into the thin prairie mantle formed by soil washed from the Rockies. The ground's loose texture contrasted with the dense loam that nourished the neck-high tallgrass prairie that midwestern farmers had been transforming into the corn belt. Brown displaced green. June grass, little bluestem, and wheat grass grew in protective clumps and sent their roots on a wide hunt for moisture. Cottonwoods and willows were confined to the riverbanks.

The creatures inhabiting this semiarid ecosystem seemed as brown as the land. The travelers saw fleet-footed antelope, hawks that seemed to float in the air, lean coyotes, and endless prairie dog villages, whose entrance mounds looked like miniature volcanoes. Millions of bison, commonly called buffalo, still grazed the plains. They provided food, clothing, shelter material, and trade goods for Indians. Although the Churches didn't see any herds, they benefited from the animals' passing. Buffalo chips, wrote Sarah, "made a most excellent baking fire, keeping an even, uninterrupted heat."

The distant, wide horizon seemed frozen, despite the wagons' steady progress. An occasional storm and visits by friendly Indians broke the monotony for the Churches. During this year, 1861, just two years after the discovery of gold near Denver, the Indian tribes surrendered the bulk of their Colorado territory in the Treaty of Fort Wise. Most Indian leaders believed in negotiated settlements and most trusted the integrity of the United States. The massacre of peaceful Arapahos and Cheyennes at Sand Creek in southern Colorado was still three years away. The war in the northern plains that resulted in the 1876 battle at the Little Big Horn in Montana was in its early stages.[4]

Sarah Church's story of an encounter with Indians displays the prevalent ethnocentrism of white pioneers in the West. The Churches and their traveling companions were camped along the Platte in western Nebraska one morning when someone yelled, "The Indians are coming," Sarah recalled. "Looking we saw twenty or more all in their best calling clothes, as we soon learned, coming to buy 'White Squaws' for wives. The Squaws had no say in the matter and I, at least, was very much afraid of them so kept my distance. I saw they were in earnest conversation with some of the men, who seemed very much amused. Finally Pa [Henry] called to me and said, 'What do you think of it? This big Indian will give nine ponies and $100.00 for you and says he has more ponies and more dollars.' 'Well,' I said, 'You will never have a better offer and better close the sale.' "

The bantering ended with the arrival of a government agent, who said the Indians were quite serious about the negotiations. "He turned to the Indians, saying 'go back to camp, the white men do not sell their Squaws and they are mad at you.' " The agent then said, perhaps to impress the travelers, that earlier in the spring a similar encounter ended in gunfire and a woman was killed. "We broke camp early the next morning, but when we were ready to start they were all there to see us leave," Sarah wrote. "My admirer had a new red flannel band on his straw hat, his beaded moccasins and his finest leggings. He looked very sad." Unfortunately no Indian account of this encounter exists. But an instructive quote comes from a white man who lived twenty years with the Crow tribe. "The Indians liked to hear of the strange ways of white people," he remembered. "They wondered at these peculiarities, the same as white people wonder at the customs prevailing among Indians."[5]

Arriving in Denver in July 1861, the Churches found it "a town of perhaps 3 or 4,000 people with everything very new and somewhat surprising," Sarah wrote. "Perhaps this is partly because we have been on the plains away from people, houses, and even kerosene lamps until the streets at night look almost as bright as Fairy Land." Sarah's population estimate was close to the official census, which tallied 4,749 Denver residents in 1860, just two years after promoters from Kansas established two towns near the confluence of the South Platte River and Cherry Creek. Only the one named after Kansas Territory governor James W. Denver thrived.[6]

Henry and Sarah wasted little time before heading into the mountain canyons west of Denver to try their luck at mining. Near the settlement of Idaho Springs, they bought dozens of mining claims and worked through the summer and fall. The rich lode evaded them. Backtracking toward Denver, they traded their oxen for a ranch claim and log cabin near Mount Vernon canyon, the main wagon route from Denver into the mountains and the location of today's Interstate 70 highway.

Settling Down

Henry still dreamed of finding gold, but agreed with Sarah that a small herd of dairy cows would earn them a living in the meantime. Defying the chance of winter blizzards, they traveled to Iowa after the first of the year and returned to their Mount Vernon cabin in May 1861 with fifty cows and calves and a wagon full of milk pans and pails. They soon discovered that the garden area was small and rocky, the growing season short, and the cattle and calves sore-footed from the terrain. They moved to flatter grassland at the edge of the foothills a few miles northeast of Boulder. Shortly afterward, during a raging March 1863 snowstorm, Sarah gave birth to John Frank, the couple's only child. He would become Marcus's father.

A few weeks later Sarah's brother Lafayette Miller and his wife, Molly, arrived from Iowa. Sarah finally had another woman with whom she could share her growing unhappiness. "We do not like Colorado. Do not like living three and a half miles from a neighbor, do not like living so far from our old home or parents, brothers & sisters, and we decide that we will persuade the husbands to go home very soon and live in a civilized country," Sarah remembered. "We are so much happier just thinking about it." She never realized her desire to leave.

Lafayette and Molly Miller soon moved east, but only a dozen miles, to farm the prairie. After he died some years later, Molly donated land for a town and named it Lafayette. In the meantime, in late January 1864, Henry and Sarah decided to sell their place. An irrigation ditch Henry helped dig had failed to bring them enough water to grow crops or good pasture. Bad luck followed when a faulty chimney set the log house on fire and burned it to the ground.[7]

The couple stayed with friends while Henry sold their land and negotiated the sale of their remaining mining claims near Idaho Springs. The Churches disagreed about what to do next. Henry still fantasized about striking it rich and wanted to head for new "gold diggins." Sarah resisted. "I had seen new country enough and did not see how anyone could travel with a child in safety." She added, "It broke my heart to think of it, going any farther west was a terror."

Their plans unresolved, on a sunny April morning Henry and Sarah hitched up their wagon for a shopping trip to Denver, thirty-five miles to the south. Halfway there, they stopped in the late afternoon at a squatters' place on Walnut Creek and, as was the custom of the day, were invited to spend the night. The place wasn't much to look at — a dirt-roofed log house with corral fences connected to two sides of it, a few storage shacks, and a ramshackle barn. Except for the mountain backdrop, the spot was as treeless as the Kansas plains. The few cottonwood trees that had grown along the creek had been chopped down and stacked for firewood.

Sarah thought the place "wretched," but it gave her an idea. As they set out the next morning, she pointed out that open country ran all the way east to the Platte River. "Here's your uninterrupted range for cattle," she told Henry. She proposed that they buy the place and stay there temporarily until the mining claims sale was completed. Having put aside her thoughts of returning to "civilization," as she put it, Sarah hoped that "temporary" would become permanent.

The following week Henry rode back to Walnut Creek and paid the squatters $1,000 for the buildings and the right to the land, claimed under the Homestead Act of 1862. This act enabled settlers to cheaply gain title to 160 acres of land, one-fourth of a square mile, by living on and improving the land. Five years later, on September 8, 1869, Henry sealed his ownership at the U.S. Land Office in Denver by paying $200, or $1.25 an acre.[8]

Distributing land to homesteaders, along with controlling Indians, were the two key activities performed by the federal government in the frontier West, historian Patricia Limerick has noted. The activities were connected, of course, by the complication that the so-called virgin lands of the West were inhabited by Indians, who had to be removed for the land to be redistributed. From the beginning, the Church family and other successful settlers in the West were subsidized by the federal government.[9] But that reality wouldn't make the government's later taking of Rocky Flats land go down any easier for the Churches.

Homesteading in the vast semiarid region west of the 100th meridian was a challenging enterprise. Settlers had to find water, cultivate the hard sod, survive weather extremes, and market enough crops or livestock to pay off bank loans. By 1900 just one out of three homesteading families, or 400,000 of more than one million families, retained the public land they tried to occupy. Successful pioneer settlers like the Churches played an important part in the evolution of the West, a place where diverse cultures and interests interacted in complicated ways. For settlers, success usually depended on the wise use of resources — grass and water in Henry Church's case, once he reluctantly concluded that his fortunes lay on the hoof instead of in the mine.[10]

The land near Rocky Flats offered Henry excellent spring grazing for his cattle, but by the end of each summer the hot sun pushed temperatures into the high nineties and took its toll. In order to have enough grass left to cut and put up for winter hay, Henry had to limit the size of his herd. This ruined his ambitious plans to shift from dairy to beef cattle, which had a ready market in fast-growing Denver. Henry found his answer in the lush, high mountain valleys he had seen during his earlier fling with gold mining.

In late spring 1869, he drove his first herd of red-and-white Hereford beef cattle to the southwestern edge of Rocky Flats and up Coal Creek canyon, then over the Continental Divide and into a highlands basin known as Middle Park. Lying between the Divide and the rugged Gore Range, Middle Park was a long meadow above 8,000 feet in elevation. Toward the north end, near Grand Lake and the town of Granby, the basin was dissected by the Grand River (later renamed the Colorado), whose headwaters began just below the Divide. Small creeks cascaded from steep mountain slopes into the river, which expanded into the largest waterway of the Southwest by the time it reached Utah. One-armed geographer John Wesley Powell began his exploration of the Colorado River in Middle Park the year before Henry arrived there.

Henry Church also sought to improve his Front Range pastureland. A steady source of water was the missing ingredient. He decided to build a system of ditches and reservoirs. His first project was a reservoir fed by a ten-mile long, four-foot-wide ditch plowed out of the rocky soil by horses pulling dredges and laborers wielding picks and shovels. Bringing water from Coal Creek, the ditch, still known as Upper Church Ditch, cut across the top of Rocky Flats and wound along the land's downward-sloping contour to the reservoir northwest of the Church Ranch home place. Water is as precious as gold in the arid West, and its legal rights and use are staunchly protected. Even a century later, when the government operated its Rocky Flats nuclear weapons plant, it observed the Church family's water rights.

Henry had to buy the water rights from other Coal Creek users before digging his ditches. These rights were established under the doctrine of prior appropriation, or "first in time, first in right." Developed to prevent, or at least curtail, conflicts among miners, who needed water for their operations, this doctrine identified "senior" and "junior" water ownership rights. This meant, for example, that during a drought senior users might leave little or no water for the holders of junior rights. To resolve water disputes peacefully, special water courts were established, but arguments often led to violent confrontations before matters reached a court.

To minimize the inevitable conflicts over water diversions, Henry's strategy was not only to buy a person's water rights, but the land as well. To finance the purchases, Henry drew on his Iowa farming experience to create a lucrative business cycle based on growing wheat as well as cattle. By selling crops and cattle Henry increased his landholdings to about 1,500 irrigated acres plus 6,500 acres of pastureland on and near Rocky Flats. He built a second reservoir in the valley and an even more ambitious ditch that brought water from Clear Creek, which ran from a narrow mountain canyon into the town of Golden some ten miles to the south.[11]

Doing Business

The Churches' entrepreneurship didn't stop with ranching, ditch digging, and farming. Not long after they acquired the home place in 1864, the Overland Stage Company sought a stop for its Denver-to-Cheyenne line. The couple agreed to keep fresh horses and to feed and lodge passengers. At Sarah's urging, Henry tore down the log cabin and replaced it with a solid timber frame, twelve-room wood plank house. An 1866 photo shows Sarah and three-year-old Frank standing in the doorway of the house, a single-story living area attached to a two-story wing containing the bedrooms. A hitching post and large, hand-dug well with a roof extended on four posts dominate a barren front yard. An outhouse and other ranch buildings sit in the background. After the stagecoach closed the Church Crossing stop in the late 1860s, the ranch continued to run a café. Ox team drivers, called bullwhackers, driving wagons of baled hay and other goods to mountain towns and mining camps, regularly stopped for supper or breakfast.[12]

The Churches' concentration on farming and ranching enabled the family to ride out Denver's periodic economic slumps, such as the 1893 depression, caused when the bottom fell out of the silver market. At the time, thirty-year-old John Frank Church, soon to be Marcus's father, took responsibility for the family's cattle operations in the mountains, although he and his wife, Katherine, continued to live in a new house on the home place. Frank, as he was known, ended up having a mixed impact on the family fortunes.

A stocky, gregarious man who sported a bushy mustache, Frank had a limitless entrepreneurial zeal fueled by his desire to be as successful as his father. Once Denver's economy recovered at the turn of the century, Frank saw opportunity in the area's increasing urbanization. The Church Ranch found itself on a metropolitan transportation artery after an electric train line, the Denver and Interurban, began running in 1908 between Denver, Boulder, Broomfield, and other nearby towns. Its route map showed a stop at "Church," the home place. Praising the new train service, *The Denver Post* declared Boulder "a suburb of Denver." Frank and Katherine, a former schoolteacher, turned some of their land near the home place into residential real estate by creating a subdivision called Mandalay. Katherine, as practical as Frank was flighty, concentrated on the business side and kept the books.[13]

Frank became interested in politics and was elected to the Colorado state senate in 1922. But the legislature turned out to be a distraction from his business ambitions. After a single term he threw himself back into real estate, banking, and various ventures. He promoted a water project in Arizona that failed, then spent several years on Colorado's western slope, mining for gold. He arrived home from the mining venture in 1929, on the eve of the national stock market crash, with only a small pouch of gold to show for his efforts. During Frank's prolonged absence, Katherine had reestablished a dairy operation at the home place and their son Marcus, then thirty years old, had successfully expanded the family's mountain holdings near Granby, Colorado.[14]

Marcus Church

Marcus Church, the first member of the Church (and McKay) family to tangle with the federal government over Rocky Flats, was born on November 3, 1899. Typical of the Church men, Marcus packed more than two hundred pounds on a frame that extended over six feet. He graduated from the University of California at Berkeley in 1923 with a major in animal husbandry and married Anne Rice, a transplanted Oklahoman. The young couple moved to the Church mountain ranch in Middle Park, near Granby.

When they visited her family in Oklahoma, Church enjoyed pheasant hunting.[15]

Public land was still available for homesteading in Colorado, so in 1925 Marcus filed a claim for 640 acres of hillside property adjacent to the family property near Granby, bringing the total there to more than 2,700 acres. He raised several hundred head of both beef and dairy cattle on his land and nearby National Forest acreage, for which he had a permit to graze 270 head. His dairy provided milk and cream to tourists ascending in increasing numbers from the plains to Grand Lake each summer. By harvesting grass, Marcus could stack about 1,000 tons of hay each summer, enough to feed his herd during the winter instead of driving them over to Rocky Flats. He participated in his last cattle drive in 1927, shortly after the Moffat railroad tunnel was opened beneath the Continental Divide under Rollins Pass.

Personal and financial loss hit the Church family during the Great Depression. The biggest tragedy came when Marcus's younger brother, Perry, died in 1933 at age twenty-nine. On the business side, the general economic crash on top of his father, Frank's, mining fiasco and the sluggish pace of the family's subdivision development forced the Churches to sell more than 3,000 acres of the Front Range home place, including most of their irrigated land. Although Frank and Katherine retained just 104 acres of the home place ranch, they held on to about 4,000 acres on Rocky Flats. The family's mountain properties remained intact.

Marcus saw a lot of his father during the early 1930s, when Frank spent extended periods in the mountains. The two men decided head lettuce would thrive in the cool mountain summers of Middle Park. They hired Japanese workers to clear the sagebrush for a lettuce field and built a packing shed in the town of Granby so the produce could be shipped by railroad to Denver and other markets. Business was good, although cattle remained the family's main source of income.

Marcus always kept in close touch with his parents, visiting occasionally and writing often. After arriving back in Middle Park after one 1935 trip to the home place, he wrote them about the fate of two roosters he had been carrying in the bed of his pickup truck. Because the truck needed new tires, he stopped at "Pat's garage" in the Denver suburb of Arvada before heading into the mountains. "When Pat was about to finish I decided to run up to Joe's Place and get some lunch, and before I returned Pat threw the spare tire into the truck," Marcus wrote. "When I stopped in Idaho Springs I decided to investigate the roosters [*sic*] welfare, and found the tire resting on the sack. Results, one dead rooster. The other one withstood the pres-

Sarah Church, circa 1880. McKay Collection.

George Henry Church, circa 1880. McKay Collection.

Church Ranch home place, 1866. McKay Collection.

Marcus Church, pheasant hunting, circa 1950. McKay Collection.

Katherine Church with grandsons Perry and Charlie McKay (right), circa 1950. McKay Collection.

Marcus Church, 1972. Rocky Flats/DOE photo.

Charlie McKay feeding a few cows in a pen at the Church Ranch corporate head-quarters. He sold some former ranchland for the subdivision in the background. Photo by Jad Davenport, 1998.

The Old West meets the New West at the Church Ranch Corporate Center.
Photo by Jad Davenport, 1998.

Charlie McKay continues to raise cattle on his pastureland adjacent to
the Rocky Flats plant. Photo by Jad Davenport, 1998.

sure and he is very much alive now, especially early in the morning with his crowing."

Marcus and Anne returned to the home place in 1942, a little more than a year after Frank was killed in a traffic accident. The couple sold their mountain ranch for $80,000 and two hundred cows for $20,000 and moved into a one-story brick house at the home place. This same spot now serves as the corporate office for Charlie McKay, Marcus's nephew. Partly for symbolic reasons, Marcus immediately bought back fifty-five acres of his grandfather Henry's original homestead, one of the pieces of land sold off in the 1930s. He began rebuilding the cattle herd and farming operation. By the end of 1942, Marcus ran about 250 head of cattle on Rocky Flats and a couple of dozen head on 285 acres just south of Boulder. He also grew hay there. Well schooled in the need for water, Marcus paid $1,500 for a one-quarter interest in Rocky Flats Lake at the southern end of the mesa and used it to irrigate his adjacent fields. A few years later he would acquire the whole lake and turn it into a private reservoir and trout-fishing club.

Marcus left much of the land as open pasture and grew winter wheat on a rotating basis in other sections, planting one part and leaving the other fallow. A successful wheat crop depended on conserving one year's moisture for the next. Each spring he plowed the bare soil or stubble of the fallow land and then leveled off the plowed furrows with a disk or harrow. During the spring and summer he turned over this land a few times, destroying weeds in order to leave a mulch on the surface. Marcus seeded about the first week of September, giving the winter wheat a chance to germinate before frost. In the meantime, in July or August he harvested the wheat planted the previous year. A volunteer crop of winter wheat would often grow in the stubble of the freshly harvested acres, making good grazing for cattle. Marcus also planted and irrigated alfalfa and a little corn on his land.

Bombing Range

By the late 1940s, Marcus had resuscitated Church Ranch. His cattle operation expanded significantly after he and two neighbors successfully bid in 1946 to lease 54,000 acres, or eighty-four square miles, of rangeland from the real estate division of the U.S. Army Corps of Engineers. This prairie expanse was southeast of Denver and constituted the bulk of the Lowry Air Base bombing range. The land had been part of an incentive package Denver politicians used in the mid-1930s to convince the federal government that the city should be the site of its new base for the Army Air Corps, as the service was then called. The Lowry base was dedicated in February 1938 and named after Francis B. Lowry, a Denver native and pilot shot down and killed during World War I.[16]

In addition to grazing his own cattle on the bombing range, Church serviced the grazing needs of other ranchers. "Best grass in history, eighty sections untouched. Seeing is believing," declared his 1947 advertisement published in eight newspapers in Texas, New Mexico, and Arizona. He ran up to 3,500 head of cattle in summer, fewer in winter. During the winter he also pastured about seven hundred horses there. The animals were a good mix because the horses pawed through the snow to find grass.[17]

In 1948 the twelve-month lease was renewed, but the following year the government wrote Church that it needed nearly 14,000 of the 54,000 acres. Worried that the government would keep chipping away at the lease and leave him unable to make long-term plans, he requested that the Corps of Engineers give him a five-year renewal without opening the land to other bidders.

When several weeks went by without a response, Church decided to go the political route and had his attorney write Colorado's senior U.S. senator, Democrat Edwin Johnson. With tactical overstatement, the lawyer began the letter, "Mr. Church, your friend and our client, requests your assistance," and then spelled out the problem.[18] The senator responded promptly. "I have taken up this matter with the proper officials," he wrote in April 1949. Two weeks later the Corps of Engineers notified Marcus that the lease renewal was approved. "Needless to say, I am delighted by the decision, and I realize that it was through your intervention that this matter was so promptly and satisfactorily determined," Church wrote Johnson on May 11. "I appreciate your interest and sincerely hope that I will have the opportunity to personally convey my respects to you in the not too distant future."

The five-year lease, beginning in June 1949, charged Marcus and his partners just twenty-two cents an acre. This politically greased deal enraged El Paso, Texas, rancher Edgar Timberlake. He had been renting some of the government pastureland from Church for two years and saw no reason to continue paying a middleman. Upon learning of the lease renewal, Timberlake complained to the Corps that Church had violated the terms of the initial lease by, in effect, subletting the land.[19]

Asked about this by the Corps, Marcus responded that he was not simply furnishing grass but was offering renters a complete ranching operation by having his cowhands mend fences, return strays, and the like. When the Corps of Engineers requested that Church supply detailed records, he declined, instead turning once again to Senator Johnson for assistance. Johnson argued Church's case in an August 1949 letter to Major General Lewis A. Pick, Chief of Engineers. In October, Pick wrote Johnson that "after a thorough investigation" the Corps had determined that Church had "in no way violated the terms of his lease."[20]

Five years later, when Church's bombing range lease was up for renewal, he again went to Johnson for assistance, with the same positive results. By then Johnson and Church had something else in common. Each of them had become involved in the Rocky Flats nuclear weapons plant — Church by coincidence, Johnson by design.

TWO

Big Ed and the Bomb

Subsidized Individualism

United States Senator Edwin Johnson of Colorado, who would play a key role in the Rocky Flats drama, hadn't intervened in Marcus Church's wrangle with the U.S. Army Corps of Engineers out of friendship. Johnson wasn't acquainted with Church, although he knew the family name since he and Marcus's father, Frank, had served together in the Colorado state legislature in the 1920s. Regardless, Marcus was a constituent. And the fact that he went through a prominent Denver lawyer to ask the senator for help with the bombing range leases suggested the rancher possessed wealth, and perhaps clout. Johnson, a senior member of the Senate Military Affairs Committee, received quick action from the army engineers. The army didn't ignore senators with influence over military budgets.

Such constituent caretaking typified Johnson, a likable fellow who instinctively lived by the rules of politicking. He seldom saw a hand he didn't shake and had a reputation for personally answering more letters than any other senator in Washington. Known universally as Big Ed or the Big Swede, Johnson was a six-foot, two-inch, two hundred-pounder who sported a crew cut and always retained a slightly innocent, farm boy look.[1]

Raised on a Nebraska ranch, Johnson dreamed of becoming a railroad president. He was working up the ranks from telegrapher when, at age twenty-five, tuberculosis hit. His doctor prescribed a dry climate, so his wife, Fern, brought him to Colorado on a stretcher in 1909. Their first stop was a rest home near Fountain, north of Colorado Springs. Tough as a railroad spike, within months Johnson was back on his feet. He and Fern homesteaded in the untamed northwestern corner of Colorado. His Swedish-born father, Nels, came out from Kansas to help them build a one-room cabin with a rock cellar. The Johnsons prospered. In 1918 he won the race for county assessor and began an unbroken, highly successful thirty-eight-year political career, which would include three terms as governor and three terms as a U.S. senator.

Since his days as a member of the railroad union in Nebraska, Johnson had been a Democrat. That didn't bother the largely Republican voters of northwestern Colorado, who voted for the man, not the party. In 1922 they elected him to the state legislature to get something done about their lousy roads. He delivered. At the statehouse in Denver, Johnson also made a name for himself by taking on the Ku Klux Klan, which then dominated the Republican Party and thus the state's politics in the early 1920s. After its resurrection in Georgia during World War I, the Klan had spread north and west and took root in Denver in 1921.

The Klan fed on hatred of Jews, Catholics, and blacks, even though African-Americans constituted less than 3 percent of Denver's 250,000 residents. The organization also exploited legitimate public concern over the crime that accompanied the city's growth. The Klan's power peaked in 1924 when its members were elected governor, U.S. senator, and mayor of Denver and occupied a number of local offices. Opposition to the Klan grew and included public figures such as George Norlin, president of the University of Colorado. Johnson detested the Klan's herd mentality, symbolized by the way the group's legislative leader signaled his followers how to vote by placing a small flag on his desk either upright or tilted to one side. The organization's demise was assisted when newspapers exposed corruption in the Klan-dominated Denver police force in 1925.[2]

Johnson's opposition to the white-hooded racists didn't mean he was a progressive, as he would soon demonstrate by his treatment of Hispanics. Expediency marked his climb up the political ladder. During the 1934 gubernatorial race, he "was a conservative in the primary when he was running against Josephine Roche and a liberal in the general election campaign when he was running against Nate C. Warren," a Denver newspaper columnist observed. "He is essentially an opportunist."[3]

As Depression-era governor, Johnson again delivered, this time to the people of Colorado. Among other accomplishments, he brought in about $25 million in federal dollars to finance half of Colorado's first major highway network. He took unorthodox actions, like organizing jackrabbit hunts. And he exploited racism. In April 1936 he called out the National Guard to patrol the state's southern border with New Mexico to prevent the entry of "aliens, indigent persons, or invaders." He demanded that Mexican workers return to Mexico, saying Colorado jobs were for Colorado citizens. After less than two weeks, following protests from New Mexicans and many Coloradans, Johnson withdrew the troops. If anything, the episode convinced voters that he had their interests at heart. Seven months later they elected him to the U.S. Senate by a 2-to-1 margin.[4]

Johnson approached Washington, D.C., as local politics writ large. He enjoyed his Big Ed, maverick image. Studiously avoiding the capital city's social scene, he didn't own a dinner jacket and proudly referred to himself as a farmer. He carefully tended the political fields to benefit his constituents. Just as midwestern congressional representatives maneuvered for seats on the agriculture committees, Johnson managed to be appointed to the committees on mines and mining, public lands and surveys, interstate commerce, and military affairs.

Johnson embodied the peculiar relationship Westerners had developed with the federal government. He saw himself as a self-sufficient individualist, a man who had carved a homestead out of wilderness after overcoming tuberculosis. That the federal government had deeded him the public land for next to nothing was inconsequential. He had made the land produce; he had a right to it. Similarly, Colorado had a right to federal projects and federal dollars. These were the products of statehood, which the state received in 1876.

As historian Limerick observed, "The American West was the arena in which an expanded role for the federal government first took hold." From the outset, many federal dollars flowing to Colorado were connected to military facilities, beginning with the outposts and forts built before, during, and after the nineteenth-century Indian wars. The location of such installations wasn't always left to chance. In 1885, for example, the Denver chamber of commerce bribed an army major to get a military post located south of town.[5] Such crude tactics became less necessary, or perhaps more subtle, as Denver's railroad hubs made the city a destination point for more and more people and industries. After ballooning into the largest city between Kansas City and the West Coast, Denver was an obvious spot for regional facilities such as the Fitzsimons Army Hospital, built during World War I. The Great Depression's economic pressures pushed city officials to lobby more aggressively for military installations, conduits for jobs and money. Denver won the $40 million Lowry Air Base in 1937 after donating to the army more than 100 square miles of land for the base and a rural bombing range, which Marcus Church later leased for pasture.[6] World War II triggered an economic restructuring in Colorado and throughout the West. Between 1880 and 1940, western states developed what historian Gerald Nash calls a "colonial economy" based on the export of raw materials. That began changing during the war, when federal dollars, chased by private enterprise, bolstered the industrial and service sectors of the western economy. Between 1940 and 1945, the federal government invested about $40 billion in the West. Most went for the manufacture of ships, planes, and other weapons along with a vast network of military installations and more than 3 million military personnel.[7]

Denver got more than its fair share of federal dollars and experienced another boom like that stimulated by nineteenth-century mining. In late 1941, a Du Pont Company subsidiary opened the $20 million Remington munitions plant on 2,100 acres west of Denver. Its initial government contract amounted to $80 million, and peak employment reached 19,500 in mid-1943. In 1942 the army began producing napalm bombs and chemical weapons at its new Rocky Mountain Arsenal in the northeastern corner of Denver. General Charles Schadle, the Arsenal's commander, described the facility's location. "I helped pick the site after Colorado senators Eugene Millikin and Big Ed Johnson and Denver chamber of commerce officials showed us what was then an asparagus patch near the end of the High Line Canal," he said.[8]

The Arsenal was the first of many federal deals lubricated by Johnson and his colleague Millikin, a Republican oil executive and attorney who entered the Senate in 1941 when the governor appointed him to fill the vacancy left by the death of the state's senior senator. A balding, overweight, stoop-shouldered man, Millikin possessed a booming voice and acerbic wit, which he regularly exercised during floor debates. He once ridiculed Truman for a "third-rate burlesque performance." But he rose rapidly within the ranks of the Republican Party due to his uncanny negotiating ability. "Gene is a gumshoey sort of fellow," one Senate colleague observed. "He likes to move around very quietly in the background." A chain smoker, he often could be found engrossed in conversation outside the Senate cloakroom, since smoking was prohibited inside.[9]

During their overlapping fourteen years in the Senate, the bipartisan Johnson and Millikin team lassoed a number of military facilities for Colorado, including the headquarters of the North American Air Defense command (NORAD) and the U.S. Air Force Academy. They also exerted strong influence over post–World War II nuclear weapons developments, both in helping set policy and in securing production factories. In the nuclear arena their philosophy of national defense converged neatly with their constituents' desires to sell Colorado uranium and win federal facilities. Rocky Flats would be their big prize.

Civilian "Control" of Nuclear Energy

Johnson and Millikin contributed to the final shape of U.S. nuclear policy. After arriving in Washington in 1937, Johnson discovered the nation's capital to be far more than a deal-making bazaar where projects and funds are bartered in oak-paneled rooms. It was a heady place of power and global mission. And he felt part of it as a member of Congress. "No political institution in all the world or in all human history surpasses it, or ought to surpass it, in democratic procedures and nationwide prestige," Johnson said later. "The financial rewards are near zero but the reward of knowing intimately as close friends the political leaders of the world is a rich experience indeed."[10]

Among the political leaders who immediately attracted Johnson were the militant isolationists who shared his philosophy of self-sufficiency. This group, including Republican senators Robert A. Taft of Ohio and Michigan's Gerald P. Nye, maintained that the nation had to be well defended in order to remain above the international chaos. For many, air power was the weapon of choice. During his first year in the Senate, Johnson sponsored a bill calling for construction of 10,000 new warplanes and increased pilot training. His Senate colleagues rejected the bill as exceeding military needs. Two years later, after Nazi Germany's invasion of Poland in September 1939, Johnson firmly opposed U.S. entry into the war. He argued that the nation should remain neutral and help negotiate a settlement in Europe. He also fought against the draft. But once American troops were engaged in battle, he sponsored bills to provide them with pay raises and special benefits, such as free postage. He became chummy with Pentagon officials.

By the end of World War II, Johnson was chairman of the Senate's Military Affairs Committee, giving him a distinctive voice in the postwar debate over America's global role. The atomic bombings of Hiroshima and Nagasaki in August 1945 framed the debate. Authorized by President Harry S. Truman, the United States had dropped the "Little Boy" uranium bomb, equivalent to 12,500 tons of TNT, on Hiroshima on August 6. About 110,000 civilians and 20,000 soldiers died immediately or within the first three months, and the number nearly doubled during the next five years as the gravely wounded died and others succumbed to radiation poisoning. Nagasaki was hit three days later by the even more explosive "Fat Man" plutonium bomb, equivalent to 22,000 tons of TNT. Japan surrendered a week later.[11]

At the time, few people publicly questioned whether the atomic bombs should have been dropped. Decades later, opponents of the bomb argued that because Japan had been exploring surrender options, the A-bombs were not necessary to end the war and, indeed, were used mainly to try to intimidate the Soviets. Still, with American soldiers dying daily in summer 1945, it would have taken a president possessing extraordinary understanding and foresight not to order the use of a powerful weapon that promised to save American lives, regardless of how many. And in the modern age of total war, civilians were no longer off-limits.[12]

As World War II still echoed, Washington policymakers considered whether the military or civilians should manage the future of nuclear energy. This energy source already had proven to be a tool of vast destruction. But optimists saw its real promise in generating power for everything from atomic automobiles to power plants. One writer mused that atomic bombs could be used to melt the polar ice cap to provide "the entire world a moister, warmer climate." Somewhat more sober opinions were presented by observers such as University of Chicago president Robert M. Hutchins, who proclaimed in September 1945 that atomic energy could "usher in a new day of peace and plenty."[13]

The military had controlled nuclear developments during the war and saw no reason to change. The major challenge came from atomic scientists, some of whom opposed dropping the bombs on Japan and all of whom had chafed under the military's bureaucratic wartime controls. Concerned scientists agreed with Albert Einstein's warning that "the unleashed power of the atom has changed everything save our modes of thinking, and thus we drift toward unparalleled catastrophe."[14]

Organized into the Federation of American Scientists, the concerned scientists argued that genuine security in the postwar world required civilian control of nuclear energy along with strictly enforced international agreements. They contended the military and its excessive secrecy kept the public from understanding the danger of nuclear war, impeded peaceful uses of the atom, and damaged relations among nations. Congress became the battleground.

The advocates of civilian control struck first. Freshman senator Brien McMahon, a Connecticut Democrat, introduced a bill on September 6, 1945, calling for an atomic energy control board made up of cabinet officers and other federal officials. To counter the McMahon bill, the military drafted its own legislation and handed it to the friendly chairmen of the Military Affairs Committees of both chambers. Kentucky Democrat Andrew Jackson May in the House and Colorado's Johnson in the Senate introduced the military's bill, dubbed the May-Johnson bill, on October 4. Johnson said the military officers who oversaw development of the atomic bomb knew as much as anyone about what was good for the country.[15]

The congressional debate over nuclear decision making didn't engage the general public. Most people were busy reestablishing normal lives following the long war. The concerned scientists and their allies in the intellectual community succeeded in organizing a few demonstrations in spring 1946, encouraging some hard-line supporters of the military's May-Johnson bill to make compromises. The Senate leadership appointed Colorado's two senators to a special eleven-member committee designated to reconcile the differences between the May-Johnson and McMahon bills. Both Colorado senators were tied to the mining industry, which hoped to exploit the state's vast uranium deposits, and lobbied for appointment to the committee.[16]

Millikin again displayed his talents as a reconciler, or "fixer" as his detractors preferred, in drafting the Atomic Energy Act. He helped Republican senator Arthur Vandenberg of Michigan recast major sections of the bill, including the domestic uranium-mining provisions, to encourage private enterprise. These two senators carried the bill through the Senate-House conferences to come up with the act's final wording.[17]

President Truman remained in the background during the debate, which appeared to end with a victory for civilian control when he signed the Atomic Energy Act into law on August 1, 1946. This law formed the cornerstone of U.S. nuclear policy. It declared the federal government's monopoly over atomic energy, either for weapons or power, under the ultimate authority of the president as commander in chief. It established the civilian Atomic Energy Commission (AEC) to administer the nuclear enterprise. The AEC was headed by five commissioners, including a designated chairman, and a general manager. All were appointed by the president with the Senate's consent. The law also set up other new bodies, including the General Advisory Committee of nine civilian scientists. The Pentagon kept its hand in the AEC through the Military Liaison Committee, consisting of an unspecified number of military officers appointed by the secretaries of war and navy.

Congress reserved a crucial function for itself by creating the extraordinary congressional Joint Committee on Atomic Energy (JCAE), consisting of nine members from each chamber. The committee's jurisdiction included "all bills, resolutions, and other matters in the Senate or the House of Representatives relating primarily to the [Atomic Energy] Commission or to the development, use, and control of atomic energy." The JCAE's sweeping authority over atomic issues gave it the unique power to hold hearings, issue reports, and make recommendations on bills from either chamber. It possessed both authorization and appropriation power, unlike any other joint congressional committee. "The Joint Committee *was* Congress as far as atomic-energy matters were concerned," wrote George Washington University law professor Harold Green, who had served on the committee staff, and his coauthor.[18] And since Congress controlled the federal purse strings, the JCAE possessed inordinate influence in shaping the nation's nuclear weapons policy and its production complex.

Advocates of civilian control viewed the JCAE's inclusion in the Atomic Energy Act as a great victory. They cheered the act and all who made it possible. The editors of the *Bulletin of the Atomic Scientists* magazine, the voice of concerned scientists, noted that activist scientists had helped mobilize the public "against Army rule in science." The magazine did acknowledge that more needed to be done because "the American public has not yet become as alarmed with the prospects of nuclear war as the facts warrant." The *Bulletin* editors singled out McMahon for praise. "Thanks of the scientists go to Senator McMahon, the sponsor of the bill and untiring fighter for the principle of full civilian control of atomic energy."[19] What the scientists couldn't know then, and didn't even recognize at the time of McMahon's death in 1953, was that their hero would become instrumental in escalating the nuclear arms race they opposed.

Nor did they anticipate that the JCAE, the symbol of civilian control, would operate in a secret and unaccountable fashion, its members often combining their parochial interests with a militaristic view of national security. Johnson and Millikin epitomized the process. Colorado held two of the nine seats on the JCAE's Senate side, which was particularly influential because of that body's confirmation powers.

Senators Millikin and Johnson weren't well known on the national scene, unlike some colleagues such as the conservative Vandenberg or Democrats Richard B. Russell of Georgia, Harry F. Byrd of Virginia, and Henry "Scoop" Jackson of Washington. But each had his moment in the national spotlight. Millikin's time came after the Republicans won control of Congress during the 1946 elections and he was profiled in the *Chicago Tribune* and other newspapers. He headed the party's internal organization and was also chairman of the Finance Committee, "a job which rarely makes a celebrity of a Senator, but whose scope and power can hardly be exceeded," one reporter noted.[20]

Johnson would make headlines in 1949 when he became the first federal government official to reveal the U.S. intention to build hydrogen bombs. By and large, however, the two Colorado senators operated behind the scenes, which is where the nation's nuclear weapons policy was determined during the crucial 1947-to-1949 period.

The Arms Buildup Begins

Once the Atomic Energy Act went into force, the jockeying for control over the policies, facilities, workforce, and funding of the country's nuclear establishment began in earnest. In January 1947, as prescribed by the new law, the army's Manhattan Engineer District, which oversaw development of the first atomic bombs, turned over the weapons production complex to the AEC. The complex included facilities in thirteen states staffed by 2,000 civilian, 4,000 military, and 38,000 contractor employees. About half of the civilian and contractor employees worked on uranium bombs at Oak Ridge, Tennessee. The Los Alamos, New Mexico, laboratory ran a distant second with about 8,000 total employees, and Hanford, the Washington State plutonium production facility, came in third.[21]

Despite the number of employees and facilities, the complex was producing few nuclear bombs. Shortly after taking over, the AEC reported to President Truman in April 1947 that the nation's arsenal consisted of fewer than a dozen unassembled nuclear bombs. The sober report decried "certain serious weakness in the situation from the standpoint of national defense and security." It concluded that plutonium production was lagging and called for "a bold decision and a major undertaking."[22]

President Truman, whose ambivalence toward nuclear weapons was reflected by the distance he kept from nuclear strategy deliberations after the war, was not ready to sign off on such an undertaking. But the AEC's appeal for increased nuclear production coincided with Congress's broad efforts to reshape the nation's military establishment in light of growing Cold War tensions. Stalin was tightening the noose around the Central European countries that fell under Soviet influence after the war. Washington began interpreting conflicts everywhere, including anti-colonialist struggles such as the one occurring against the French in Indochina, as part of a worldwide communist conspiracy instead of recognizing the primarily nationalist roots of groups like the Vietminh. The result was the National Security Act, signed by Truman on July 26, 1947.[23]

Among its provisions, this new act transformed the War Department into the Department of Defense, made the air force independent from the army, and established the National Security Council and the Central Intelligence Agency. As the agency responsible for ensuring the nation's security, the new Defense Department began taking a more comprehensive look at the potential use of nuclear weapons to achieve military goals.[24]

Military planners drawn mostly from the air force began preparing lists of Soviet targets that should be attacked with atomic weapons in case of war. Strategic war plans were, of course, meaningless without the weapons to carry them out, and in July 1947 the nation possessed just thirteen atomic bombs. The AEC, military, and congressional JCAE all concurred that weapons production should increase. The AEC's general manager told the new director of the Hanford plant in Washington State that plutonium production would have to grow significantly within the next five years.[25] This goal required a large increase in the production of uranium, a dense metal that can be fissioned, or split, to release nuclear energy for power or bombs. It is also the building block for plutonium.

Uranium Can Beget Plutonium

On the periodic chart of elements on earth, uranium is the last naturally occurring element. Scientists named it after the planet Uranus. It carries atomic number 92, which is the total number of positively charged protons in the nucleus of each uranium atom. As in other atoms, the negatively charged electrons orbiting the nucleus match the number of protons. The nucleus also contains neutrons, with no charge. They, like protons, have an atomic weight of 1 each, in contrast to the virtually weightless electrons. Atoms of natural uranium contain 146 neutrons and 92 protons, adding up to an atomic weight of 238. Thus it is called uranium 238.

Uranium, like other elements, comes in different isotopes. Each uranium isotope has ninety-two protons, so all have the same atomic number. But isotopes contain varying numbers of neutrons and, consequently, have different atomic weights and slightly different chemical characteristics. Isotopes, such as uranium 235, can be unstable. The famous French scientist Marie Curie named these kinds of unstable elements "radioactive." They seek stability by emitting alpha particles (two protons and two neutrons), beta particles (electrons), gamma rays, and neutrons. In natural uranium, the radioactive isotope uranium 235 makes up just seven-tenths of 1 percent of the mass, while uranium 238 constitutes the other 99.3 percent.

German scientists discovered in late 1938 that they could bombard uranium atoms with neutrons to split the element into two other known elements. Borrowing a word from biology, they called this process fission.[26] Word of the discovery spread quickly, and scientists around the world confirmed fission in their laboratories. Many recognized that fissioning could release energy in accordance with Albert Einstein's famous formula: energy equals mass times the speed of light squared ($E = mc^2$). Tiny atoms possess enormous energy.

Scientists immediately speculated that since fissioning atoms released more neutrons, a "critical mass" of uranium 235 could produce a chain reaction. This would result in the release of an extraordinary amount of energy in an uncontrolled, explosive fashion — an atomic bomb. (In contrast, nuclear power reactors control chain reactions in order to steadily produce energy.) By 1940 scientists in England and the United States also theorized that neutrons captured by the nonfissionable uranium 238 would produce an element with atomic number 94. They speculated that isotopes of this element, which would be called plutonium, would fission like uranium 235.[27]

Scientists at the University of California at Berkeley transformed theory into reality in early 1941. Chemist Glenn T. Seaborg and his colleagues, building on other discoveries, created the phenomenal plutonium-239 isotope. It possesses a 24,065-year half-life, the period during which it loses half its radioactivity through emissions due to alpha decay and spontaneous fission. In March 1941 these scientists demonstrated that plutonium-239 atoms captured about fifty percent more neutrons than uranium 235 and would create more efficient atomic explosions. For more than a year after its discovery, plutonium had no name. To conceal the existence of this potential weapons material, it was referred to by the code name "copper." This caused trouble when copper metal was needed for some experiments. "For a while, plutonium was referred to as 'copper' and the real copper as 'honest-to-God' copper," Seaborg recalled.[28]

Finally, in March 1942, the scientists christened element 94 after Pluto, the most distant planet in the solar system. Scientists followed the tradition started when they named uranium. Neptunium, atomic number 93, came next and got its name from Neptune. Seaborg and his colleagues thought the name for element 94 was especially appropriate, given its extraordinary destructive potential. Pluto was the Roman god of the underworld. And the Seaborg group couldn't resist a little scientific black humor by skipping over the logical two-letter symbol "pl" and designating plutonium "pu."

Seaborg later said that he had expected an adverse reaction to the joke once plutonium's discovery was declassified at the end of the war, but that people simply accepted the olfactory symbol.[29]

Producing large enough quantities of plutonium for bombs required nuclear reactors. On December 6, 1941, the eve of the Japanese sneak attack on Pearl Harbor, a government-sponsored committee under the direction of Carnegie Institution president Vannevar Bush recommended an "all-out" effort for military research on chain reactions.[30] The reactor work soon moved from eastern universities to the University of Chicago, and the army created its Manhattan Engineer District, or Manhattan Project.

Guided by Italian-born physicist Enrico Fermi, scientists in Chicago built a reactor, known as a "pile" since it was made of uranium in a structure of piled-up graphite bricks. In a former squash court under the Stagg Field football stadium's stands, the scientists triggered the first controlled, self-sustaining nuclear chain reaction on December 2, 1942. Along with the chain reaction caused by the fissile uranium 235, the scientists learned that neutrons absorbed by the uranium 238 had indeed produced plutonium.

Four months later, the government broke ground in a remote region of Washington State for industrial-scale plutonium production reactors. This facility, called the Hanford Reservation, would also separate the plutonium from the uranium and other radioactive by-products. Although plutonium 239 and other plutonium isotopes are produced from uranium 238, the two elements possess different chemical structures and can be separated from each other by chemical means.[31]

In contrast, because isotopes are chemically almost identical, the separation of fissile uranium 235 from uranium 238 required a different, more complicated technique. The government's Oak Ridge, Tennessee, laboratory worked to separate enough uranium 235 for a bomb. Both separation approaches succeeded, although the scientists nearly missed having enough enriched uranium. The bomb dropped on Hiroshima contained 130 pounds of highly enriched uranium. The device tested in the New Mexican desert on July 16, 1945, and the bomb dropped on Nagasaki each contained about 13.5 pounds of plutonium. The natural uranium serving as raw material for these first atomic bombs came primarily from the Belgian Congo and Canada.[32]

After the war the U.S. government continued to depend on uranium imports for atomic bomb production. But by summer 1947, the heightened military, congressional, and AEC interest in building nuclear weapons created concern about the availability of foreign uranium and the vulnerability of supply lines in a crisis. The newly appointed director of the AEC's raw materials division, mining engineer John Gustafson, looked to the Colorado Plateau as a natural location for domestic mining and processing of uranium. This cracked the door for Colorado to enter the Cold War nuclear weapons business, an opportunity that the state would exploit fully at Rocky Flats.[33]

Nuclear "Weapons" Debate

This new AEC emphasis on domestic uranium sources delighted Colorado senators Johnson and Millikin. The nation's major uranium deposits were located on the Colorado Plateau, stretching over a vast expanse of rugged, arid canyonland in the Four Corners region of Colorado, Utah, Arizona, and New Mexico. The senators saw a righteous opportunity to aid Colorado's mining industry, which lawyer Millikin had previously represented. The catch was that Colorado uranium was lower grade than the ore imported from the Belgian Congo and Canada. Consequently domestic uranium hadn't been mined for itself, although it had been a by-product of mills processing vanadium, a metal used for preparing special steel alloys. The Colorado mills had secretly produced small quantities of uranium concentrates for the government during World War II. This ended after the war.[34]

Millikin had cleared the path for full-fledged domestic uranium mining by drafting language in the Atomic Energy Act of 1946 allowing private U.S. citizens and companies to sell uranium to the government. Still, profitable uranium exploration and mining on the Colorado Plateau depended on increased demand and higher prices. The AEC would soon provide them. In fall 1947 the AEC acquired a uranium-ore-processing mill in Utah and a vanadium plant in Durango, Colorado. The commission began reactivating other Colorado mills near the western slope towns of Naturita, Uravan, and Rifle. In order to successfully extract uranium from the low-grade ores of the Colorado Plateau, the AEC's Gustafson hired the Dow Chemical Company of Midland, Michigan, to conduct research into new processes. This was just one of several nuclear ties the government had with Dow in the years before the AEC chose the company to operate the Rocky Flats nuclear weapons plant.[35]

Under AEC guidance, the U.S. nuclear arsenal began to grow. By July 1948 the inventory amounted to fifty five-ton, Mark 3 Fat Man plutonium implosion bombs, quadruple the number on hand the previous year.[36] The AEC commissioners and staff were pleased with the progress. They drafted a letter to President Truman in January 1949, explaining that the AEC was producing more weapons than the Joint Chiefs of Staff had originally ordered in their 1947 long-term plan approved by the president.

But in the meantime, the Joint Chiefs had signed off on a new war plan, called TROJAN, identifying seventy Soviet targets requiring 133 atomic bombs — more than twice the number originally ordered. The military countered the January 1949 AEC letter with its own, stating that "the currently established military requirement for scheduled bomb production should be substantially increased and extended." This letter made clear the military leadership's conviction that nuclear weapons had become essential to U.S. national defense. The Joint Chiefs considered these devices a way to maximize firepower at a time of tight military budgets.[37]

Even as the military pushed for more nuclear weapons, the president's National Security Council provided no policy guidance about when and how nuclear bombs should be used. This reflected Truman's own reluctance to designate nuclear devices as just another weapon. He continued to hope that the United Nations, established in 1945, could oversee nuclear developments. Indeed, the U.S. government had officially pursued international control through the United Nations Atomic Energy Commission. A committee headed by then undersecretary of state Dean Acheson and the AEC's David Lilienthal in 1946 sketched out a global scheme for the peaceful development of atomic energy. This Acheson-Lilienthal Report was followed by a plan drafted by Wall Street financier Bernard Baruch aimed partly at retaining the U.S. atomic monopoly. The Soviet Union rebuked the Baruch Plan in 1946 and the international control effort couldn't be revived, although such control remained the "only official policy enunciated by the U.S. government relative to atomic weapons through the summer of 1948," according to military historian David A. Rosenberg.[38]

That same summer Truman was forced to confront nuclear policy issues after the Soviet Union blockaded the land routes to West Berlin. The United States responded by airlifting supplies to the city. Led by Secretary of Defense James Forrestal, the military used the blockade to renew its fight for custody of nuclear weapons, a responsibility it had lost to the AEC under the Atomic Energy Act. Truman argued against the military position at a July 21 meeting attended by AEC commissioners and top Defense Department officials.

"You have got to understand that this isn't a military weapon," the president said, according to AEC chairman Lilienthal's account. "It is used to wipe out women and children and unarmed people, and not for military uses. So we have got to treat this differently from rifles and cannon and ordinary things like that." Truman biographer David McCullough argued that this encounter showed the president's views about nuclear devices. "In times past Truman had spoken of the bomb as a military weapon like any other. In times past he had spoken of Hiroshima and Nagasaki as military targets," McCullough writes. "Not anymore. It was an extraordinary declaration, refuting absolutely—as Lilienthal understood—any thought that Truman was insensitive to the horror of the bomb or took lightly his responsibilities as Commander in Chief."[39]

During the next few years, the military repeatedly petitioned Truman for custody of nuclear weapons. The president, backed vigorously by Lilienthal, refused to reverse his decision. He and his national security advisers worried that if the military controlled nuclear bombs, the commanders and their civilian counterparts would then argue that the military should receive predelegated authority to drop them.[40]

As the internal bureaucratic tug-of-war continued, a theory about nuclear weapons took hold among national security analysts both inside and outside government. It was called "deterrence," based on the counterintuitive notion that nuclear weapons had to be built so they would not be used. The argument, articulated by Yale University political scientist Bernard Brodie, held that a country possessing nuclear weapons would be deterred from attacking another nuclear-armed power for fear of devastating retaliation.[41]

"Deterrence was mostly about psychology and psychology was about power relationships," explained Michael Krepon, president of the Henry L. Stimson Center in Washington. "If one side had more weapons, or more powerful weapons, the other could be placed at a disadvantage. Thus, deterrence theory put no cap on the number of weapons needed." The Pentagon's war planners were pragmatically concerned with matching U.S. nuclear weapons to Soviet targets and, later, to keeping an advantage over Soviet weapons production. In the absence of specific policy guidance, the military's war planners simply found more targets every time they looked. Trained and paid to identify targets, they always found somewhat more than there were bombs to hit them, historian Rosenberg points out. This maintained steady pressure for additional weapons production.[42]

In March 1949 the Military Liaison Committee to the AEC complained loudly to the congressional Joint Committee on Atomic Energy that the commission was not producing nearly enough nuclear bombs to meet military requirements.[43] In May a Joint Chiefs study chaired by Air Force Lieutenant General H. R. Harmon concluded that even if all 133 of the bombs stipulated in war plan TROJAN were successfully dropped on their Soviet targets, this wouldn't bring surrender. And the AEC hadn't come close to producing 133 nuclear bombs. The Joint Chiefs used the Harmon report to argue for considerably higher nuclear weapons production than could be achieved by existing or authorized plants. They sent the congressional joint committee a new list of weapons requirements on May 26, 1949.[44]

That same day, AEC chairman Lilienthal testified before the committee that current production was sufficient to meet national defense needs. His argument rested on the Joint Chiefs' earlier, 1947 assessment of future nuclear weapons requirements. Lilienthal contended that this earlier assessment represented strictly military criteria. He implied that bureaucratic interests and a desire for higher budgets drove the military's new estimates.[45]

Lilienthal perceptively saw the Joint Chiefs' new "requirements" as arbitrary and not based on strategic reasoning. The military's refusal to provide complete information about the basis for its war plans confirmed his suspicions. But Lilienthal, who opposed a national defense strategy dependent on weapons of mass destruction, soon found himself in the JCAE's gunsights. Most committee members shared the military's conviction that nuclear devices were nothing more than extremely powerful weapons. Led by Iowa Republican Bourke Hickenlooper, the JCAE instigated an investigation of AEC "mismanagement."[46] The congressional JCAE had become increasingly strident since January 1949, when Senator Brien McMahon took over as chairman after the Democrats swept Congress in the November election. McMahon argued for an ever larger nuclear arsenal. "There is a doctrine that we may reach a point when we have 'enough bombs.' To my mind, this doctrine is false," he wrote in July.[47]

The quixotic quest for international control over nuclear energy was the only obstacle to all-out U.S. nuclear weapons production. This goal had little chance in the new Cold War climate. Joseph Stalin's belligerent rhetoric and imperialistic behavior in Central Europe aided the opponents of international control, including those in Congress. Colorado's Senator Millikin was "one of the Republican leaders in the fight to keep the atomic bomb secret in the hands of the United States rather than surrender it to an international authority," the *Chicago Tribune* reported. Truman finally gave in. "I am of the opinion we'll never obtain international control," he told his top staff on July 14, 1949. "Since we can't obtain international control we must be strongest in atomic weapons."[48]

The die was cast. Without public debate, and even before the Soviet Union tested its first atomic bomb, the U.S. government decided that nuclear devices were "weapons" rather than irrationally destructive devices that should be strictly controlled if not abolished.[49] A new issue came to the fore — development of a hydrogen bomb, or H-bomb. The notion of a bomb based on fusing light elements instead of splitting the atoms of heavy elements had been around since the World War II Manhattan Project. The energy released when hydrogen atoms were fused was expected to be on the order of 1,000 times greater than that released by a fission atomic bomb. Physicist Edward Teller, a brilliant, single-minded Hungarian émigré employed at the government's Los Alamos laboratory, vigorously promoted an H-bomb effort both during and after the war. He gained support as the Cold War hardened.

The Soviet Union aided the H-bomb's advocates in August 1949 by testing its first atomic bomb, dubbed "Joe I" by the Americans. President Truman publicly revealed the Soviet test on September 23. That same day the JCAE began holding closed meetings in its private hearing room at the Capitol building. Committee members considered various alternatives for expanding the U.S. nuclear arsenal. General James McCormack described to the committee the potential destructive capability of a hydrogen, or thermonuclear, bomb. "If all of the theory turned out, you can have it any size up to the sun or thereabouts if you wanted," McCormack said. "I think one talks in terms of the super weapon as being one million tons or more of the TNT equivalent."[50]

Initial calculations indicated that Teller's first idea about how to make such a superbomb was unworkable. But mathematician Stanislaw Ulam would bail out Teller and other proponents of the "Super" in early 1951 with a solution that made feasible a different H-bomb design. In fall 1949, however, technical considerations constituted only part of the arguments taking place in secret at the highest levels of government.[51]

Opponents of the H-bomb project cast their arguments primarily in moral and strategic forms. They saw no rational need for the United States to build weapons capable of inflicting indiscriminate devastation on an even greater scale than atomic bombs. Outspoken opponents included the AEC's Lilienthal and physicist J. Robert Oppenheimer, who had directed the successful effort to build the atomic bomb and now was a top government adviser.

Teller and a few other prominent physicists favoring development of the new devices found eager allies in the military and JCAE. Committee chairman McMahon, for one, had come to believe that war with the Soviets was inevitable and that thermonuclear weapons were crucial to U.S. national security. By the end of October 1949, McMahon had begun "a campaign of letters and personal appeals to Truman to convince the President to authorize a crash program to build the Super," wrote historian Richard Rhodes.[52] That secret campaign was about to become public.

Big Ed's "Slip"

Senator Johnson of Colorado traveled to New York City to participate in a local, live television show on November 1, 1949. Called *Court of Current Issues,* the show debated issues of the day through a mock trial format. The question this day was: "Is There Too Much Secrecy in Our Atomic Program?" Two nuclear scientists testified "yes" and an FBI agent and Johnson argued "no." The senator began by explaining how his background and membership on the JCAE qualified him as an expert witness.

"In addition to that, perhaps I might say that while I am a Colorado farmer, in southwestern Colorado we have the largest deposits of uranium to be found anyplace in the United States," Johnson said in his deep-throated twang. "So I have been somewhat familiar with uranium, at least, for a long time." Turning to atomic secrets, he took after a favorite target. "Scientists all have a yen, like some old fisherwomen, to tell all that they know," he said, claiming incorrectly that this had enabled the Russians to build their bomb. Spies had provided assistance, but the senator didn't know that.[53] Johnson then dropped a bombshell of his own.

"Now, our scientists already have created a bomb that has six times the effectiveness of the bomb that was dropped at Nagasaki and they're not satisfied at all; they want one that has a thousand times the effect of that terrible bomb that was dropped at Nagasaki that snuffed out the lives of 50,000 people, just like that," he said. "And that is the big secret that the scientists in America are so anxious to divulge to the whole scientific world."[54]

With that, Johnson let the secret out and let the public in on the intense hydrogen bomb fight occurring inside the U.S. government. It took a couple of weeks for Johnson's disclosure to be felt because the television show was local. The nation's capital, and the rest of the country through wire services, heard about the hydrogen bomb on November 18, when the *Washington Post* published a front-page story containing Johnson's revelation of military secrets. President Truman angrily summoned JCAE chairman McMahon and Attorney General Howard McGrath to the White House and ordered them to stop the leaks of top secret information. But the damage was done. In the charged atmosphere created by the Soviet bomb test, public pressure increased for the United States to do anything necessary to preserve its security. The H-bomb seemed an obvious solution. Nuclear weapons were seen as the ace in the hole for the United States after the World War II demobilization.[55]

If Johnson hadn't leaked the H-bomb story, somebody else undoubtedly would have. He was just a bit player in the drama. But Johnson was personally stung by White House criticism that appeared in several news stories. He wrote a long, defensive letter to Truman on December 13. "I refuse to believe that a man with whom I had served in the Senate for years and who knows me intimately would use his high office to hold me up to public scorn without first extending the courtesy of hearing the facts from my own lips," he wrote. "On my oath, I most solemnly swear that never in my life, in New York or any other place, have I violated my trust as a member of the Joint Committee on Atomic Energy nor have I ever revealed anything imparted to me as secret or classified as security information," Johnson insisted.

The president, from his regular vacation escape at the Key West, Florida, naval base, responded with a chilly, one-sentence "Dear Ed" letter on December 17. "I read your letter of December 13th with a great deal of interest, and I appreciate very much your furnishing me with your views on the recent controversy about leaks of top secret information." By then the clamor for an H-bomb had picked up unstoppable momentum. "Thoughtful deliberation in the blinding glare of public opinion was now out of the question," as the official AEC history put it.[56]

At a high-level meeting on January 31, 1950, Lilienthal argued that a presidential statement favoring the development of an H-bomb would lead to a misimpression that nuclear weapons had become the nation's first line of defense. "Truman interrupted to say that a quiet examination of the issues would have been possible if Senator Johnson had not made his unfortunate statement. Now there was so much excitement over the issue that he had no choice but to go ahead," the history reported. Later that same day Truman announced that the United States was commencing an all-out effort to produce a hydrogen bomb. "It is part of my responsibility as Commander in Chief of the Armed Forces to see to it that our country is able to defend itself against any possible aggressor," Truman told the nation. "Accordingly, I have directed the Atomic Energy Commission to continue its work on all forms of atomic weapons, including the so-called hydrogen or superbomb."[57]

Amid the headlines, few observers recognized the profound implications of the H-bomb program. Among these few were the editors of the *Bulletin of the Atomic Scientists*, a magazine founded in Chicago in December 1945 to alert the public to the danger of a nuclear arms race. In the magazine's March 1950 issue, the editors stressed the "grave moral implications" of the program and called for reasoned public debate over hydrogen bombs and alternative approaches to national security. They blamed Johnson for shocking an unprepared public, terming his statement a "naive and monumental indiscretion."

Unquestionably indiscreet, the blunt Johnson was anything but naive. He knew what he supported—the crash H-bomb program. With it in place, Lilienthal resigned as AEC chairman, despite having been cleared of mismanagement charges by the JCAE investigation started the previous summer. The weapons advocates were just one step away from completely dominating the nation's nuclear establishment. Now they wanted one of their own to become chairman of the AEC.

Senator McMahon had a candidate in mind, his former law partner Gordon Dean, whom he had successfully pushed for AEC commissioner in 1949. But Truman appointed commissioner Sumner Pike, a Lilienthal ally, as acting chairman. The JCAE conservatives feared that Pike might be named the permanent replacement. Among them, Millikin and Johnson went after him for supporting uranium imports.

Borrowing from Winston Churchill's famous declaration, Millikin grandly pronounced on the Senate floor in May 1950 that he "was not sent to the Senate to liquidate Colorado." Johnson joined Millikin and the three other Senate Republicans on the JCAE to vote against Pike's reappointment as commissioner, the prerequisite for his becoming chairman. Once Truman let it be known that he would appoint Gordon Dean as AEC chairman, the conservatives backed off and Pike won reappointment as a commissioner.[58]

Millikin and Johnson scored political points in Colorado for attacking Pike's support of uranium imports. The points meant more to Millikin, who was in the midst of a tough reelection campaign. During the next few months, Millikin repeatedly played the uranium card. The Korean War, which began on June 25, provided him with another angle to call for increased uranium mining.

"It is to be assumed that if the Korean operation expanded into a real world war, one of the first enemy efforts would be to destroy our foreign sources of uranium supply," Millikin stressed to a state audience in August. Domestic uranium operations were vital to the nation's defense, he said, adding that mining and processing the low-grade ores of the Colorado Plateau wouldn't add much to the expense of weapons production since the "cost of raw materials is a very small part of the cost of the bomb."[59] Suddenly, however, Millikin and Johnson discovered that the nuclear weapons production they urged had aroused new desires among their constituents. And this time the senators didn't want to deliver.

No H-Bomb Plant for Colorado

Following President Truman's green light for the H-bomb program in January 1950, the JCAE lobbied hard to increase the AEC's $550 million annual nuclear weapons budget. The committee issued a report in March claiming that since World War II, just one-fortieth of the military budget had gone for atomic weapons. In June, Truman approved the construction of new H-bomb reactors. They would primarily produce tritium, a radioactive hydrogen gas, and plutonium. A month later he requested from Congress an additional $260 million appropriation for nuclear weapons production.[60]

The sum alerted chambers of commerce all over the country that nuclear facilities would translate into jobs and revenues. Aggressive lobbying prompted Truman to tell AEC chairman Dean that he had been contacted by delegations from Arkansas, Missouri, and several other states with regard to new locations for atomic energy plants. "This is a matter the Atomic Energy Commission itself will have to settle," the president wrote. "I hope you will place these plants where they will be most useful for the objective you are trying to obtain and that you will allow no pressure groups of any sort to influence you in their location."[61]

Local business groups seeking nuclear facilities contacted their senators and representatives. In early August the chamber of commerce in Alamosa, a southern Colorado town in the San Luis Valley, telegrammed Johnson and Millikin. The chamber urged the senators to help locate the H-bomb plant in the nearby Sand Dunes National Monument. The shifting channels of the Rio Grande, whose headwaters originate in the San Juan Mountains at the western edge of the valley, had created these rare dunes over the millennia. Wind blew sand deposited by the river up against the Sangre de Cristo mountain range on the valley's east border, sculpting sand dunes that spread over a fifty-square-mile area.

The Alamosa chamber made public its H-bomb plant campaign at a meeting of business and civic leaders on August 13. "Conjecture of local enthusiasts is that the plant installation could be situated at or near the national Sand Dunes monument area, of which about sixty-six percent is already owned by the government. Natural barriers, availability of water resources and a location that is as far removed as possible from the range of an enemy attack were major points outlined for the location of the project in the San Luis Valley," according to the local newspaper.[62]

Alamosa's efforts, followed by a similar campaign from the southwestern Colorado town of Durango, put Millikin and Johnson in a bind. The two senators had built their reputations on attracting federal projects. "Since Senators Millikin and Johnson are both on the Congressional Atomic Energy Committee, they could probably pull more wires on this matter than any other two men in Washington. But if they do, the senators said, they want Colorado to be interested in the hydrogen bomb plant for what it can contribute to the national defense and not for 'any fleeting financial gain,'" the Denver-based *Rocky Mountain News* observed.[63]

Johnson had responded earlier to the Alamosa chamber by telegram. "Undoubtedly the Sand Dunes area in most respects would be an ideal location for the proposed hydrogen bomb plant, but there are grave and inescapable dangers inherent in it. The location is a decision for the whole state to make. It is not a local matter entirely since it involves erection of a target which by its very nature invites military attack," he wrote.[64]

Johnson and Millikin also jointly sent a telegram to Colorado's governor, who supported efforts to bring the plant to the state. They warned that the reactors would be the "No. 1 spot" on Russia's target list and cited the "ever-present danger of an accidental blow-up, which very well might make a good part of Colorado uninhabited and uninhabitable." They added that if a state canvass showed that people really wanted the hydrogen bomb plant, they would go after it.[65]

Millikin and Johnson genuinely worried about the danger of nuclear reactors blowing up. Millikin asked about the safety of an H-bomb reactor during a closed JCAE meeting on August 24. McMahon responded that two schools of thought existed, with the General Electric Company, a reactor manufacturer, saying the nuclear reactors were safe. "Am I correct that there was a school of thinking that there was quite an element of danger of blowing up?" Millikin interjected. McMahon said yes. Millikin added, "The reason I raised this is that Colorado is interested in getting the installation, and Senator Johnson and I have asked that they should give careful thought to not only making themselves a target, but the danger of internal explosions. Of course, if the Federal Government wants to put it in Colorado, we would take it there as a patriotic duty, but so far as taking the initiative in the matter, we want to be thoughtful about what we are doing."[66]

The Colorado senators didn't need to worry. A military committee advised the AEC that the south-central part of the United States was the least vulnerable to Russian attack. A site location committee determined that this area provided good water and other resources. At the end of November the government told residents of Ellenton, a small town in rural South Carolina, that they would have to evacuate to make way for an H-bomb plant. Known as the Savannah River plant, this facility would produce both tritium and plutonium.[67]

Millikin suffered no political repercussions for Colorado's failure to get the H-bomb plant. The elections were over by the time the site was announced. Millikin, with open support from his friend Johnson, had handily defeated his Democratic opponent, John Carroll. The Colorado senatorial team was still intact and more powerful than ever.[68] "Millikin holds more key posts in the senate than virtually any other member," the Pueblo *Chieftain and Star-Journal* reported in a post-election roundup. The newspaper reminded readers that their senator was chairman of the GOP Conference Committee, former chairman of the Finance Committee, and now the ranking Republican member of that influential committee. The article noted that Millikin and Johnson both sat on the JCAE. "This is a very important committee assignment considering the fact that the Colorado plateau is the major source of domestically produced uranium."[69]

The Grand Junction *Daily Sentinel*, on the state's western slope, published a feature article on Johnson's pivotal role in the new Senate, made up of forty-nine Democrats and forty-seven Republicans. "Always unpredictable and utterly independent in his voting record, Sen. Johnson is customarily bracketed by press observers in the powerful conservative group which includes Democratic Senators George and Russell of Ga., Byrd of Va., and Republican senators Taft of Ohio and Millikin." As for Millikin, his reelection "is further evidence that in this bi-partisan 'team,' Colorado will wield in the next Congress an extraordinary influence in the affairs of the U.S. Senate."[70]

As if to underscore the point, the U.S. Air Force announced just weeks after the election that it was moving the nation's air defense headquarters, the North American Air Defense command, to Colorado Springs from Washington, D.C. "Senator Edwin C. Johnson said Thursday the transfer of the air defense command of the United States gives Colorado the unprecedented position of the 'air defense capital of the nation,'" *The Denver Post* reported. "The Senator said he has been working jointly with Senator Eugene D. Millikin, his Republican colleague, to bring the transfer about."[71]

Rocky Flats would be the next big federal apple they would pick, but the two senators wouldn't brag so openly about it. After all, they had vigorously and publicly argued an H-bomb reactor would make Colorado a target for Soviet bombs. A plant actually manufacturing nuclear weapons would make the state an even juicier target. But it would bring in substantial federal dollars and would be far less dangerous than a nuclear reactor facility — they thought.

THREE

A $45 Million Plant

"No Hint"

A cold spell dumped eight inches of fine powdery snow along Denver's Front Range in early February 1951. Instead of slowly melting and adding needed moisture to the soil, the snow blew off the Church Ranch land. "The ground is really getting dried out," Marcus Church wrote an acquaintance.[1] The ground that most concerned him was the 3,716 acres, about six square miles, that the Church family then owned on and around the Rocky Flats mesa. He used most of the land, and another 960 adjacent leased acres, to graze cattle. Although rocky, the land was covered with native grasses. At six to eight acres per cow, he could pasture about 500 head. In addition he planted wheat on a few hundred acres, averaging some thirty bushels per acre, and grew a little corn and irrigated grass for hay.[2]

The Church Ranch was one of several farms and ranches dotting the Front Range between the towns of Boulder and Golden, the home of the Coors Brewing Company. Not all the operations were as large as the Church Ranch. Some were small farms, like the one owned by Rudy and Jean Zehnder at the southeastern base of Rocky Flats mesa. Rudy had been raised on this land, homesteaded by his family in 1913. Jean was a city girl still getting used to country life, including the lack of indoor plumbing. They raised a bit of everything, chickens, pigs, and a small dairy herd — whose milk would come under close scrutiny in a few years.[3] For unbeknownst to the Zehnders, the Churches, and their neighbors, Rocky Flats mesa was about to change forever.

If any of these farmers and ranchers picked up the afternoon *Denver Post* on Friday, March 23, 1951, they were greeted with the banner headline, "There's Good News Today: U.S. to Build $45 Million A-Plant Near Denver." Other local papers ran similar banners. Based on an Atomic Energy Commission (AEC) news conference Friday morning at the small, out-of-the-way Mayflower Hotel in Denver, the *Rocky Mountain News* reported that a "top secret atomic production plant will be constructed immediately in the Rocky Flats area northwest of Denver." The AEC also simultaneously announced this news at press conferences in Los Alamos and Washington, D.C.

"Officials at all three announcement points emphasized that no atom bombs or weapons will be fabricated here, and it was indicated only that some unspecified raw material or component part of the nuclear fission process will be produced at Rocky Flats," the *News* reported. The *Boulder Daily Camera* quoted AEC spokesman Dick Elliott declaring in Denver, "Atomic bombs will not be built at this plant." He had "no comment" when asked whether the plant would have any connection with development of the H-bomb and cited "national security" considerations in refusing to answer specific questions about the installation. Still, the media had no trouble figuring out the plant's general nuclear weapons mission. The day after the news conferences, both Denver papers reported that the plant would either produce plutonium, separate uranium 235, produce other bomb materials, or make crude atomic materials for use as "radioactive poisons" in dusts or sprays.[4]

Local news stories stressed that the new Rocky Flats plant would be the most costly industrial facility ever built near Denver. Its $45 million price tag exceeded the federal government's two World War II era installations—the $35 million Denver Ordnance Plant, since renamed the Federal Center, and the $41 million Rocky Mountain Arsenal chemical weapons factory. Denver's largest private concern, the Gates Rubber Company, valued its property at $44 million. The AEC announced it would hire some 2,000 construction workers at Rocky Flats and said its permanent workforce would reach about 1,000. "News of the plant broke like a thunderbolt over the community," the March 24 *News* reported. "There had been no hint the AEC was considering the Denver area for a production facility, although anonymous inquiries . . . had been made in recent months about water supplies and land ownership in the area." While the "no hint" applied to Marcus Church and other area residents, it did not apply to Colorado's two U.S. senators, Edwin Johnson and Eugene Millikin. These men had known about the new nuclear weapons production plant since the previous fall and had been privy to the likely choice of Denver for several months. The facility was a central element in the military's plan to dramatically expand the nation's nuclear arsenal, a plan backed by both the congressional JCAE and the AEC. Truman's public endorsement of the H-bomb in January 1950, the beginning of the Korean War six months later, and developments in bomb-making technology had created an unstoppable momentum to increase nuclear weapons production.

A "Family of Weapons"

By fall 1950 U.S. nuclear weapons decisions rolled along two tracks. On one, planning for hydrogen bomb production proceeded, underscored by the AEC's public announcement in November that it would build the new H-bomb reactor facility on the Savannah River in South Carolina. Behind the scenes, however, scientists were having trouble figuring out how to make an H-bomb. "Facts have since developed that make the program seem less promising than it did one year ago," JCAE staff director William Borden wrote in a top secret memo to the committee chairman in December. In a more positive tone, he added, "The H program, by attracting additional top-grade scientists and adding to the sense of urgency at Los Alamos, has operated as a strong fertilizing agent . . . being largely responsible for the striking new possibilities in fission weapons."[5]

The "striking new possibilities" constituted the second track and involved design changes significantly increasing the efficiency and explosive power of fission bombs. These changes were coupled with the military's September 1950 request for new nuclear weapons. Along with bombs needed for a strategic air offensive against the Soviet Union, the Joint Chiefs for the first time called for smaller, tactical nuclear weapons. These included artillery-fired warheads and lightweight atomic bombs for direct support of ground troops in Western Europe. The military's plans meant "a greatly increased requirement for atomic weapons to supplement our conventional land, sea, and air forces," the National Security Council noted in a top secret memorandum to President Truman. He endorsed the plan on October 9.[6]

The upshot of both tracks, encompassing the H-bomb and the fission weapons, required the AEC to double the nation's nuclear weapons production capacity. In addition to the already planned H-bomb reactors, the agency wanted a continental U.S. nuclear test site, a new nuclear bomb assembly plant, and a new facility to process plutonium and manufacture the core nuclear components for fission bombs. Atomic Energy Commission officials determined that the weapons expansion plan would initially require an additional $1.05 billion appropriation from Congress for fiscal year 1951 on top of the $534 million already approved for the agency. Because Congress had essentially delegated its authority on nuclear issues to the JCAE, the AEC just had to persuade the eighteen senators and representatives on this friendly committee to go along.[7]

Commission chairman Gordon Dean and his staff traveled to Capitol Hill on November 30 to make their pitch to JCAE members. "I think we have developed a concept here of the family of weapons, which is a very intriguing concept," Dean told them. He asked Air Force Brigadier General James McCormack, Jr., the AEC's director of Military Application, to describe this new concept. McCormack reminded the congressmen that two years earlier the weapons scientists at Los Alamos had begun developing a lighter and smaller fission bomb. The bomb, called the TX-5 in its development phase, was now almost ready to be tested. Weighing just 3,200 pounds, one-third the weight of bombs in the stockpile, the TX-5 — known as the MARK 5 bomb when it went into production — could be carried by medium-sized bombers as well as navy bombers based on aircraft carriers. "This development has led beyond that," McCormack continued, "and we think has shown quite clearly that [a] bomb with an additional payment in terms of energy release from a given fissionable core can be much smaller than the TX-5."[8]

The key to a greater energy release, or "yield," from a fission bomb depended on the composition, structure, and configuration of its core, known as the "pit." While fissile material, plutonium 239 or uranium 235, lay at the pit's heart, it also consisted of other parts designed to enhance the chain reaction. The pit of the implosion bomb dropped on Nagasaki, for example, consisted of a solid plutonium sphere weighing about 13.5 pounds surrounded by a thick metal layer of uranium 238. The pit then was surrounded by high explosives. When detonated uniformly, these explosives set off an ingoing shock wave, or implosion, which compressed the plutonium into the supercritical mass required for a multiplying chain reaction. The uranium layer, which served as a tamper to smash the plutonium together, then reflected the escaping neutrons back into the plutonium. The resulting explosion was measured in comparison with thousands of tons of TNT — 22,000 tons in the case of Nagasaki.[9]

After World War II, weapons scientists at the Los Alamos laboratory experimented with various designs and materials for tampers, reflectors, fissile parts, and other pit components in seeking more efficient fission bomb explosions. Early on they increased the source of neutrons, to help maximize the chain reaction, by placing a golf-ball-sized part made of polonium and beryllium in the center of a pit so it would be crushed by the implosion and release neutrons. In the late 1940s the scientists came up with "levitation." The plutonium component was positioned on a cone or on thin rods, which left an air space between it and the tamper and chemical high explosives. Physicists described this as the hammer-and-nail principle. The farther away the hammer (the high explosive and tamper) was from the nail (the plutonium component), the greater the force when it hit, and the resulting high compression increased the chain reaction's efficiency.[10]

Another design change involved "composite" pits made with a combination of thin shells of plutonium and oralloy, the name given to enriched uranium containing a high percentage of uranium 235. Oralloy stood for "Oak Ridge alloy" after the facility that produced it. "We called this the super-oralloy bomb or S.O.B.," recalled Ted Taylor, a young Los Alamos weapons scientist at the time. This bomb was the largest fission device ever detonated, releasing energy equivalent to 500,000 tons of TNT.[11]

But the AEC officials testifying before the JCAE in November 1950 were talking about an even more significant development in fission bomb technology. Scientists had discovered how to "boost" the chain reactions in a fission weapon pit by inserting a small amount of fusion fuel—lithium and the hydrogen isotopes tritium and deuterium—into the center of the pit. These "thermonuclear boosted" bombs were not H-bombs but fission weapons that could achieve bigger explosions with smaller quantities of plutonium 239 or uranium 235. Scientists finalized the design for boosted weapons in October 1950.[12]

Advances in weapons designs provided the rationale for a nuclear test site within the United States. "With this family of weapons coming along and all the other possibilities, it is highly important that we have a continental test site located in such a place that it would be available to the Los Alamos Laboratory so they can go out, make an experiment, shoot it, and come right back, instead of having to wait long periods of time and have great cost," the AEC's Dean told the congressional joint committee during his November 30, 1950, appearance. Previously, he noted, the AEC considered nuclear tests "about once every two years" in the Pacific Ocean as adequate. Looking toward accelerated production, the AEC already had chosen a test site in the desert near Las Vegas, Nevada, Dean explained.[13] A nuclear bomb was exploded there eight weeks later, on January 27, 1951.

Along with the new H-bomb reactors in South Carolina and the Nevada nuclear bomb test site, the AEC's expansion plan required a new plant to assemble the high explosives and nuclear components. During World War II, Los Alamos fabricated components and assembled the bombs. After the war the Sandia base in Albuquerque, New Mexico, performed assembly work, and in 1947 the AEC built the Army Ordnance Plant in Burlington, Iowa, for final nuclear weapons assembly. In October 1950 the AEC's Division of Military Application recommended that the army's old Pantex Ordnance Works near Amarillo be converted to final nuclear bomb assembly and disassembly. The Pantex plant would begin operating in 1951.[14]

Finally, the AEC wanted a new, multipurpose plutonium facility. It would recover and recycle scrap plutonium, which was then being done on a small scale at Los Alamos. It also would manufacture plutonium and highly enriched uranium components and produce pits to complement the pit production at Hanford's plutonium finishing plant, which had been operating since 1949. General McCormack explained to the JCAE during the November hearing that the renewed emphasis on bomb design and experimentation would result in frequent new weapons models. The AEC required the "capability of converting the stockpile from old models to new models in a substantially shorter time than was previously possible." Los Alamos was taking at least eighteen months for such conversions. The AEC's proposed new production facility would cut the time in half. The facility also would produce a much larger number of nuclear pits by recycling outdated bombs and by using virgin plutonium produced by the nuclear reactors at Hanford in Washington State and Savannah River in South Carolina and the enriched uranium from Oak Ridge, Tennessee. The AEC staff code-named the new nuclear pit production plant Project Apple.

Project Apple "will enable the [Los Alamos] Laboratory to devote its efforts entirely toward research unhampered by responsibilities alien to that endeavor," AEC chairman Dean explained to Senator McMahon.[15] The laboratory would, however, retain an emergency plutonium component fabrication capacity. Project Apple quickly gained top priority for both the joint committee and the AEC. "I am wondering if that project shouldn't move forward with all possible haste," said Senator Henry "Scoop" Jackson, a Washington State Democrat, at a secret committee hearing on December 14. "I mean even getting it completed before the other facilities," Jackson added. Carleton Shugg, the AEC's deputy general manager, said the agency was moving "as fast as possible." He noted that the AEC had arranged emergency security clearances for the executives of the companies chosen to build the plant and to operate it.[16]

Dow Chemical Goes Nuclear

The AEC depended on private industry to run the nation's nuclear weapons enterprise. Although the Atomic Energy Act of 1946 authorized the AEC itself to operate facilities with federal employees, David Lilienthal, the agency's first chairman, thought private companies would do a better job. Similarly General Leslie Groves had enlisted some large companies to build the first complex under the Manhattan Project during World War II. Lilienthal argued that the government would benefit both from the companies' industrial expertise and the decentralization this approach offered. The AEC was to oversee the private contractors but not "meddle," said Lilienthal.[17]

In late 1950 the AEC picked Dow Chemical Company to operate the Project Apple plant after screening several companies, including Aluminum Company of America (ALCOA), National Lead Company, and American Cynamid. "This choice was based upon that company's very strong research, development, and production experience in the fields of inorganic chemistry and metallurgy, including the handling of toxic materials and the use of the complex devices and instruments associated with such operations," according to a confidential AEC account. It added that Dow had an "aggressive" technical organization.[18]

Dow, based in Midland, Michigan, was no stranger to government military work or nuclear energy. During World War II the chemical company manufactured magnesium for military conventional bomb casings. After the war Dow executives became interested in nuclear energy on several levels. As a large user of electricity, the company saw benefits in the cheaper prices promised by nuclear power. Dow organized a nuclear research lab and collaborated with Detroit Edison to explore nuclear power options.[19] On the raw materials side, Dow got involved in uranium milling on the Colorado Plateau. The company also was among those the AEC had considered to operate the new plutonium production reactors at Savannah River, but the Du Pont Company beat it out. And Dow was one of eight companies that in the fall of 1950 proposed the dual use of nuclear reactors to produce both power and plutonium.[20]

The AEC's commissioners selected Dow to run Project Apple on December 27. Over the holidays Dow executives traveled to Los Alamos to work out contract details with AEC officials from the agency's Santa Fe regional office, which would oversee the new facility. In early January, Dow's general manager, Mark Putnam, summoned seasoned Dow executive Francis Henry Langell to his Midland office and gave him the job of managing the Project Apple nuclear weapons facility. "It is classified, it is highly secret," Putnam said. "The site is yet to be selected."[21]

The AEC took the lead in choosing the new plant's site. And agency officials had learned from an earlier fiasco to pay plenty of attention to political considerations. Two years earlier the AEC sought a site for a nuclear reactor testing station and told some congressional representatives that Montana would be chosen. When the agency, after further examination, chose Idaho instead, angry JCAE members called a hearing to find out why the agency had flip-flopped. Although the decision stood, AEC officials were embarrassed.[22]

The politics underlying the Project Apple site selection were as straightforward as they were secret. Unlike the publicly announced search for an H-bomb reactor site, which had generated so much lobbying from communities around the nation the previous summer and fall, Project Apple was kept under wraps. This gave the AEC more discretion. And for the agency, everything pointed to Colorado as the best choice for this $45 million facility. With both Colorado senators sitting on the powerful congressional joint committee, the AEC couldn't go wrong by choosing this state. The commission would avoid contentious hearings. Moreover, key votes for future AEC budget requests were virtually guaranteed.

In addition, Colorado and the city of Denver, in particular, possessed attributes making its choice easy to justify. Metropolitan Denver, with a population of more than half a million people, had a good labor pool, an attractive climate, and big-city amenities, including ample housing for workers. This would let the AEC avoid the headaches of running "company towns" like those in Richland, Washington, and Oak Ridge, Tennessee, which had been chosen for nuclear facilities during World War II because of their isolation. The AEC recognized Denver "very early" as a good site for Project Apple, Dow's Langell recalled.[23]

Senators Johnson and Millikin didn't have to overtly lobby for Project Apple, which would mean jobs and income for the Denver area and would please their strong business constituency. Where the senators sat — on the JCAE — was much more important than what they said. As long as they didn't oppose it, the new plant was theirs. A few months earlier the senators had publicly opposed locating H-bomb reactors in Colorado due to their concerns about nuclear accidents. But this time they were convinced Project Apple posed no danger, a widely shared opinion. As two JCAE staffers noted, "There is one school of thought that it would be perfectly safe to put it [the Project Apple facility] on 16th Street here in Washington [D.C.], with which the authors do not disagree."[24]

"Isolation," but Housing, Too

Although the AEC wanted Denver as the Project Apple site from the beginning, the agency had learned how to avoid accusations of favoritism by at least going through the motions of an open selection process. On January 23 it commissioned the Cleveland-based Austin Company, hired as the project architect, to conduct a site survey using criteria set by the AEC and Dow. Austin was to report back to the AEC's Santa Fe regional office, which, with Dow's agreement, would recommend a site to an AEC review committee. In reality, Dow played a minimal role in the site selection process.[25]

The AEC set fifteen criteria for Project Apple's site, giving them a twist to ensure the desired outcome. A secret document identified four criteria as the more important: "(1) a dry, moderate, climate; (2) attractive living conditions and community facilities; (3) good transportation facilities; and (4) be well located from strategic invulnerability considerations."

Austin started the survey by looking at twenty-one locations in seven states: Arkansas, Colorado, Nebraska, Oklahoma, Kansas, Texas, and Missouri. "Of these, only the three Colorado locations [Denver, Colorado Springs, Pueblo] satisfactorily met the climatic conditions," according to the AEC. No surprise there. Five of the seven states are mostly humid. Amarillo, the only Texas site considered, is located in that state's hot, arid panhandle, which is hardly a "moderate" climate. On February 27 and 28, 1951, AEC and Dow officials met at Austin Company headquarters in Cleveland and gave their blessing to Denver as the Project Apple site. Dow's Langell, who attended the meeting, was pleased. "I knew that Denver would be a desirable place to live, it would be a place that would attract people."[26]

In fact, Denver had been attracting people since its clear choice as the facility's site quietly began circulating in federal government circles in January. One of the first recruits was William Cornelison, a thirty-eight-year-old former FBI agent working for the CIA in Washington, D.C. In late January 1951, about the time the Austin Company officially started its state-by-state site survey, Cornelison was visited by his old friend Ty Gillespie, a top Dow Company executive. Over dinner, Gillespie asked Cornelison to think about heading up the security department at a new Dow plant that would produce nuclear weapons. "Where is it?" asked Cornelison. "I can't tell you," Gillespie responded. With a laugh, he added, "I can only say it's west of the Mississippi, south of the Canadian border, and north of the Gulf of Mexico." The next day Cornelison called a friend at the AEC, who said the plant would be located near Denver. After checking with his wife, Cornelison told Gillespie he was interested in the position.[27]

Dow's choice of Cornelison gives a sense of the times. He was an old hand when it came to employee security. Indeed, the week following Cornelison's conversations with Gillespie he was in New York City, testifying against William Walter Remington, a former U.S. Commerce Department employee. Remington had been charged with lying under oath when he denied he had ever been a member of the Communist Party. Remington's case paralleled the better-known case against Alger Hiss, a State Department employee. During congressional loyalty hearings, ex-communists had accused both Remington and Hiss of passing classified material to the enemy. And each man, after denying the charges and Communist Party membership, was then charged with perjury and convicted in court proceedings. Cornelison, a North Carolina native who joined the FBI in 1935, had overseen the agency's investigation of Remington, who was convicted on February 7.[28]

As Project Apple lured Cornelison west, it helped send a Coloradan east. Weeks before the Austin Company's official site survey was completed, Senator Big Ed Johnson hired Colorado accountant Edward M. Keating in early February to serve as Washington liaison for Colorado companies interested in government defense contracts. Keating, a Boulder native, had been Johnson's executive secretary in Washington from 1937 to 1940 and then took a War Department job supervising food supplies. After returning to Colorado in 1947, he ran a tea and coffee store in Boulder and then an accounting firm in Colorado Springs.[29]

Johnson needed Keating's services again because, based on inside information, he knew Colorado's military business was about to pick up. In addition to Project Apple's imminent arrival at Rocky Flats, another unannounced military project was heading to Boulder. Since 1949 Johnson had been pushing the federal Bureau of Standards to move all of its military experimental work from Washington, D.C., to Boulder. His persistence had just paid off. In January 1951 the bureau won a $5.67 million AEC contract for a new Boulder laboratory that would build two large liquid hydrogen plants needed for H-bomb tests. One plant would be shipped to the Eniwetok nuclear test site in the Pacific, and the other would remain in

Boulder, where liquid hydrogen containers would also be built. Boulder's selection for the new laboratory wouldn't be made public until March, when it would be described simply as a "radio research laboratory."[30]

In the meantime the Austin Company came up with seven potential Denver-area sites for Project Apple. In early March a team of AEC and Dow officials quietly checked into Denver's Olin Hotel. "The hotel was in the middle of town near the capitol and was in fact an old ladies' home," Langell recalled. "But no one seemed to think it unusual for us to be meeting there." During the next few days the team visited the Red Rocks sandstone formations in the foothills west of Denver, Gunbarrel hill north of Boulder, and the army's Rocky Mountain Arsenal chemical warfare installation. By March 5 the team had narrowed the choice to two sites, the Arsenal and Rocky Flats.[31] High wind patterns eliminated two of the other potential sites, according to the Austin Company survey document. "It is desirable that the site be located to the leeward [downwind] of any densely populated area," the survey stated, without explicitly saying that this would prevent the dispersal of radiation from the plant. The survey contained a diagram showing high winds blew most frequently from the south.

The diagram grossly misrepresented reality. It was drawn from wind data at Stapleton Airport in northeast Denver, some twenty miles east of Rocky Flats. Measurements at Rocky Flats would have shown that prevailing winds blew from two mountain canyons to the west, at velocities frequently exceeding 100 miles per hour, and right toward Denver and its northern suburbs.[32] Such information should have eliminated Rocky Flats as a potential nuclear weapons plant site.

Aside from addressing wind, albeit incorrectly, the AEC neglected any other environmental or public health concerns. Following procedures established by the wartime Manhattan Engineer District, the agency did not even consider the underlying geological structure. And suitability for radioactive waste disposal was not a criterion for site selection.[33]

The AEC staff ranked Rocky Flats its top choice in a secret report sent to the five commissioners on March 20. Along with meeting the general Project Apple criteria, the report cited Rocky Flats as having particular advantages due to its easy access to electrical power, water, and gas. Also, "the relative isolation of this location, on a mesa about 1,000 feet above Denver in the foothills of the Rocky Mountains and about five miles from any residential area, makes this site very attractive from a public relations viewpoint because it will be known that radioactive materials will be handled at the plant."

But the very next paragraph contradicted the statement about the site's isolation. It referred to Rocky Flats' "apparent isolation" and lauded its proximity to residential areas needed to house workers. The report stated that Boulder, with a population of 20,000, was just seven miles away and the mesa also was close to Denver's suburbs. "A modern super-highway is under construction between Denver and Boulder which will not only improve access to this site but will probably spur the development of the area between Boulder and Denver." That prediction, which proved accurate, ignored the problem that such residential development would bring communities ever closer to the proposed nuclear weapons plant.[34]

After the Rocky Flats site was announced on March 23, the response from community leaders showed they were unaware that the plant posed any danger. "This is a wonderful thing for Boulder," said the city's mayor, J. Perry Bartlett. "It may bring some problems, but they are far outweighed by the advantages. We can be proud that Boulder is being projected more and more prominently into the role of serving the vital interests of America." Thomas M. Dines, president of Denver's United States National Bank, said the influx of workers "will mean that residential construction will have to be kept up and that banks will have to stay geared to handle the financing of added expansion for the city." And George A. Cavender, president of the Colorado Federation of Labor, said, "We're all happy to see the new industry located here."[35]

A few politicians worried that the plant would put pressure on their communities. Mayor Thomas Mills of Arvada, the Denver suburb closest to Rocky Flats, said, "The housing situation is rough here. We're completing one of our biggest projects — 133 small homes. But many of them already have been sold." He also warned population growth would necessitate the construction of "more schools and more water." The mayor of Golden, to the south of the plant, said, "There's been a big amount of new building, but there is very little of rental property."[36]

Few naysayers existed. One was *Rocky Mountain News* columnist Pasquale Marranzino. In a March 30 column titled "I Don't Want Any Atomic Plants," he wrote, "In a matter of months men of intelligence and purpose, patriotism and ambition, will begin tinkering with the scientific version of global Russian roulette — right in our own backyard." After acknowledging the anticipated economic gains, he wrote, "Philosophically, we drift back a few thousand years with eyes turned toward a heaven that holds nothing more than the drone of heavy bombers."

Whether or not the Rocky Flats plant would make Denver a prime target in nuclear war was an issue that could potentially have created community opposition. It was also probably part of the reason Senators Johnson and

Millikin didn't publicly take credit for bringing this federal facility to Colorado. Local reporters asked politicians if they were concerned about the new bull's-eye painted on Denver. Governor Thornton responded, "As to whether it will make us a more desirable target for atomic attack, I couldn't say — I'm not a military man." He then joked, "I'll be happy to move the Capitol to Gunnison [in western Colorado] if that proves to be the case." Boulder mayor Bartlett said his town's residents were discussing the danger and that he expected an acceleration in civil defense work. Everett Barnhart, Golden's mayor, said that in talking to people, he noticed "no special concern about becoming a potential target."[37]

Air force general Nathan F. Twining confirmed Rocky Flats would make Denver a target. "Naturally we will put fighters in the air and provide other standard ground protection," Twining said during a March 28 visit to Denver's Lowry Air Base. "Geographically and by reason of the mountain barriers, this section of the country would be much harder for an enemy to attack."[38]

Senators Johnson and Millikin tried to defuse the Rocky Flats target issue. In a telegram to local news media, the senators wrote, "We have been assured that the location selected is the best in the United States for the purpose and that because of its distance from potential enemies the hazards from enemy action are reduced to the minimum."[39]

Otherwise, the senators distanced themselves from the Rocky Flats decision. Although they could have added the plant to the long list of federal facilities they had landed for the state, they were uncharacteristically silent. Most contemporary media accounts overlooked the senators' obvious AEC connections and lumped them in with all the other politicians surprised by the AEC's site choice. An exception was the Pueblo *Chieftain and Star-Journal*, which mentioned the senators' prior knowledge in an article written by its Washington bureau. The April 3 story noted that both Johnson and Millikin sat on the JCAE and knew about the AEC's decision "a few weeks before it was announced." Even this article failed to point out the senators' influence over AEC decisions, an observation contained in stories about the H-bomb reactor lobbying six months earlier. The article did, however, remind readers that the previous fall "Johnson and Millikin opposed the selection of Colorado as [the] site for the H-bomb plant, which was recently located near Aiken, S.C. It would be a prime enemy target."[40]

The senators' most vocal public arguments against putting the H-bomb reactors in southern Colorado had rested on the target issue, even though their main concern had been fear of a catastrophic nuclear accident. Secrecy restrictions prevented Johnson and Millikin from trying to explain publicly the technical differences between the nuclear weapons reactors and the plutonium-processing and bomb fabrication plant to be built at Rocky Flats. So if they had taken credit for Rocky Flats, their southern Colorado constituents could have complained that the senators had shown favoritism toward Denver, the capital city in the state's north-central region.

In any case, the senators successfully sidestepped a potential political minefield, and public opposition never coalesced around the target issue. Perhaps people were soothed by the assurances from General Twining and others. Or perhaps people were intoxicated by the media coverage stressing the tangible benefits Rocky Flats would bring. Without public opposition, the AEC's last remaining task before beginning plant construction was to acquire the land.

Taking the Church Land

The AEC determined it needed approximately four square miles of land. As part of the site survey, government agents had discreetly looked into land ownership and prices in the Rocky Flats area weeks before the plant announcement in March. Public records revealed land in the area had most recently sold for about $15 an acre. At 640 acres per square mile, the site would total some 2,560 acres. "On that basis, the possibility exists that the required land might be acquired for about $50,000," the AEC's military division estimated, after conservatively adding nearly $12,000 to the price tag.[41] The land records also showed about half the land was owned by Katherine Church and most of the other half by George Lindsay and Frank Rodgers.

The U.S. Army Corps of Engineers' real estate division was responsible for acquiring the property. Marcus Church, then fifty-one years old, handled his mother, Katherine's, business affairs and leased the land from her at a nominal sum for tax and inheritance purposes. He must have scowled on learning about the Corps' role. The Corps of Engineers was the agency he had haggled with since the late 1940s over his Lowry Bombing Range lease. Now the Corps was after his family's land.[42] And Senator Johnson, who had been so helpful in the previous grazing lease negotiations, wasn't going to rescue Marcus this time. The Fifth Amendment of the U.S. Constitution allowed the federal government to condemn, or "take," land designated for legitimate purposes such as roads, dams, or national security. The government was obliged only to pay a fair price, or "just compensation," for the land.

After the AEC's public announcement about Rocky Flats, William Renner of the Corps' Omaha office contacted the Churches and other landowners. He explained that the government preferred to negotiate a satisfactory purchase price for the land instead of going to court. If agreement couldn't be reached, the government would initiate a condemnation proceeding and a court would decide on a fair land price.[43] With price the only point Katherine and Marcus could contest, they granted the AEC a three-month "temporary occupancy and use permit" on April 13. They also gave the agency permission to build a one-and-a-half-mile-long access road across Church land east from Highway 93, which runs along the foothills between Boulder and Golden.[44] This access road to the plant site would remain in Church family hands even after the government began operating the Rocky Flats plant.

Government surveyors concluded a few weeks after the Rocky Flats announcement that the originally proposed site included land with valuable mineral rights that would cost the government too much to acquire.[45] Consequently, on April 24 the site was shifted one mile south. But this move didn't completely resolve the mineral rights issue. For example, the Church family land on Rocky Flats was under lease to Shell Oil Company and Carter Oil Company, so the government eventually had to arrange with the companies not to exercise their leases.[46] Twenty years later, when the AEC decided to expand the plant's buffer zone, it didn't buy all mineral rights. This led to the peculiar, and sometimes confrontational, situation when Marcus Church, his nephew Charlie McKay, or their employees would enter the heavily guarded facility to gain access to the family's gravel- and clay-mining operations located on the plant's west side.

That all came later. In April 1951 the government offered Katherine Church $18 an acre for some 1,200 acres. The Churches rejected it out of hand. Marcus complained, "The government bid for the surface did not represent its true market value, and as far as the sub-surface bids, they were practically of a nuisance value only." While the Churches and government continued to debate the purchase price in court, the AEC contractors began moving their equipment onto the land Marcus used for cattle grazing.[47]

Negotiations between the government and the three main Rocky Flats landowners failed. On July 10, three days before the temporary use permit granted by the Churches was to expire, the U.S. Attorney filed a condemnation petition on behalf of the AEC. As the rationale for the taking, the petition simply stated that "it is necessary and advantageous to the government to acquire the lands . . . for use in connection with the Rocky Flats Area of the United States Atomic Energy Commission."[48] The same day

U.S. district judge William L. Knous issued an order granting the AEC immediate possession of the Rocky Flats site.

For Marcus, the first order of business was to take care of the couple of hundred cattle pastured on the site. He met David Persons, the AEC project manager, at the AEC's downtown Denver office, a converted garage at 13th and Glenarm Street. Marcus fumed that the AEC's offer for the Church land was ridiculously low. Persons replied, "Your real value is in the land that you have left, and the location of the Rocky Flats plant is a real boon to you in that it will enhance the value of the remaining land." He suggested the plant would attract other large companies and result in a valuable industrial complex. According to Church, Persons added that plant construction wouldn't be going full speed until September, so he saw no reason why the cattle couldn't keep grazing until then.

Marcus arrived home somewhat placated. But his wife, Anne, told him to call Wally Engstrom, the Austin Company construction manager in charge of building the plant. Engstrom told Church that during the previous night his cattle had knocked down some barrels that Austin had stacked at the site. The cattle had to be moved as soon as possible. "I removed them the next day," Church recalled.[49] His turbulent relationship with the plant had begun.

FOUR

Behind the Fences

◈

An Industrial Masterpiece

Shortly after July 10, 1951, when the Atomic Energy Commission (AEC) received permanent possession of the Rocky Flats land owned by the Churches and their neighbors, bulldozers began gouging out the foundation for "Building D," the atomic bomb assembly building. Francis Henry Langell, Dow Chemical's project manager for Rocky Flats, was pleased. For the previous seven months he had worked nonstop coordinating this project. He had to ensure that the multitude of tasks required for such a large industrial complex were completed and phased into the overall operation at the right moment. Dow's top executives had picked Langell to run Rocky Flats because he had repeatedly proven himself to be an exceptional organizer and manager.

A lanky, stern Ohio native who went by the nickname "Heinie," Langell had joined Dow in 1929 after earning a Ph.D. in chemistry from the University of Michigan. He worked out of Dow's headquarters laboratory in Midland, Michigan, where the company had gotten its start decades earlier by extracting and processing chemicals from brine deposited by salt water from an ancient sea. Among his early assignments, Langell helped build a pilot plant to extract brine from ocean water. Then he oversaw the construction and selected operators for the company's first seawater processing plant in North Carolina.[1] Over the years he gained a reputation for getting things done with dispatch.

"My main job with Dow has been to help design new plants, get them built, and then to operate them once we have got them built," he later explained. Before receiving the Rocky Flats assignment, he was working on special projects, including an assessment of the way nuclear energy might apply to Dow's operations.[2]

At a cost of $45 million, the Rocky Flats complex was larger than anything Langell had previously orchestrated. "It seemed like a big project," Langell reflected. But he had firm confidence in himself and in Dow's management, who "felt I could handle it or they wouldn't have assigned it to me. That gave me the confidence I needed sometimes when I would get a little low in the buggy for one reason or another."

Even when his Dow boss, Mark Putnam, explained that plutonium at Rocky Flats would pose unique problems, Langell hadn't flinched. "That didn't really worry me very much because in the course of my other work I had worked with chlorine gas. . . . We used sulfuric acid by the carload, tank carload, and we had worked with a lot of things that you had to understand and handle with care. So that phase of it really didn't jolt me very much," he later commented.

What impressed Langell was the Rocky Flats project's urgency. Having worked on military weapons plants during World War II, he was now caught up in the Cold War atmosphere. The Korean War and the reality of Soviet nuclear weapons made the dangers seem tangible. But Langell really became convinced that the Project Apple plant needed to get up and running as fast as possible after touring other U.S. nuclear weapons facilities in early 1951. "Frankly, I was pretty surprised," he said. "All this was highly classified and when I realized the state of the art, so to speak, as I saw it at Oak Ridge and Hanford and Los Alamos, I realized the necessity of getting Rocky Flats going in a hurry," he added. "There really was a great need for a place like Rocky Flats and the quicker the better, considering the world situation."

From experience, Langell knew that a successful project depended on a highly competent management team to whom he could delegate responsibilities. Immediately after receiving the assignment from Putnam in January, he phoned "Bunk" Bean, an old Dow friend, and invited him to become the project's personnel manager. Bean said he had just been offered another executive position within the company. "Well, hold up a minute," Langell implored. "We have got a job I can't tell you anything about, but I would like you to come along with us." Bean was intrigued. And just like the physicists who responded to similar calls that landed them at Los Alamos during World War II, Bean said yes, as did others. Several Dow officials in Langell's management group had previously worked on nuclear weapons.

They already possessed the special AEC "Q" security clearances required for all nuclear weapons employees. Langell himself received an emergency Q clearance just one week after getting his assignment.

Atomic Energy Commission officials and Langell determined that Project Apple required four major production units, which became identified as buildings A, B, C, and D. Building D (later 91, then 991) was the highest priority.[3] It would assemble nuclear bomb cores, or pits, from plutonium, uranium, and stainless steel components then produced elsewhere in the weapons complex. Scientists, engineers, and architects from Los Alamos already had drawn up Building 991's blueprint, which is the reason excavation could begin so quickly. While Building 991 would relieve Los Alamos once it began operating, the AEC's goal of expanding nuclear weapons production depended on the three other major Rocky Flats buildings. Two would handle uranium and the third, plutonium.

Pervasive Secrecy

By fall 1951 the Austin Company, the site architect that previously worked on secret AEC installations such as the Argonne National Laboratory outside Chicago, had subcontracted Rocky Flats work to some fifty local firms. More than 400 construction workers were already on-site, and the contractors employed hundreds of professionals off-site.[4] Engineers and architects in small shops around Denver designed the highly classified plutonium and uranium production buildings. Three large Denver plumbing and heating firms — McCarty and Johnson, Inc., Johnson & Davis Plumbing and Heating, and the Bell Plumbing & Heating Company — formed a joint venture that won a $2 million Austin subcontract in August 1951.[5] Their job was to design the vital piping, heating, ventilating, and air-conditioning for the plutonium and uranium production buildings. But company employees had to do their work in the dark.

"I did the mechanical design for Building 771," said Jim Stone, who got his first look at this plutonium-processing building decades later. "I never saw the site and never even knew the orientation of the site." He once asked which part of the building faced north. "Don't worry about it," his supervisor replied.[6] Stone and about thirty other design engineers worked at a south Denver shop in a large, open room with rows of drafting tables. The engineers, divided into five working groups, were strictly forbidden to discuss their tasks with anyone outside their group. "If you were jawing about the type of work you were doing, it would get you fired quicker than anything," Stone recalled. "You never took the work home, and you didn't even talk to the guy next to you."

"The philosophy was that everyone does his own little job, so you don't have the whole picture. I didn't get a good overview until I worked there in the '80s," he added. His later job would have far-reaching results, both for Stone and Rocky Flats. Troubled by plant operations, he blew the whistle to government agents. His tips contributed to the FBI's extraordinary 1989 raid on Rocky Flats.

In 1951 the FBI performed a very different function at Rocky Flats. "Everybody had to have a Q clearance," said Bill Cornelison, the plant's slight, intense, chain-smoking Dow security chief. "We'd submit [a prospective employee's] papers to the AEC, they would send them to the FBI, and the FBI would get back to the AEC, which would make the decision." Cornelison, who knew the FBI well since he formerly worked for the bureau, said the background check could take from a few weeks to several months and usually took longer once plant production started. He worked closely with the AEC's James A. O'Brien, a former Bureau of Narcotics investigator and army intelligence agent whom the agency appointed as its plant security chief.[7]

Following the lead of other AEC plants, Cornelison and O'Brien implemented a layered security system at Rocky Flats. Inside the facility, tasks were compartmentalized on a "need to know" basis to prevent a spy from obtaining enough details to harm national security. Employees were issued color-coded identification badges so they could enter only certain parts of the facility.

Barbed wire fences, guard post checkpoints, and an armed security force constituted the external counterpart to internal security. And overall security was bolstered by having all operational details kept secret from the media and, consequently, the public. Any operational information could be a "tipoff to Joe Stalin," the AEC's chief project engineer told reporters.[8]

The secrecy became more stringent as the construction tempo increased. In October 1951 a *Denver Post* reporter offhandedly wrote that a restricted media tour the day before "might be the last semi-public view of the installation." He also repeated the assertion from plant officials that "workers on the project will be safer than downtown office workers who have to cross busy streets on their way to lunch."[9]

By January 1952 the AEC and Dow had clamped a tight secrecy lid on Rocky Flats that would go virtually unchallenged by the media and public for the next seventeen years. A whitewashed guardhouse was visible from rutted, unpaved state highway 93 running along the foothills between Boulder and Golden. U.S. Government Property, Enter on Official Business Only warned a wooden sign on the dirt entrance road running east over the mesa top.

"The forty-one-million-dollar Rocky Flats plant of the Atomic Energy Commission will start producing — whatever it will produce — shortly after it is completed — whenever that is," began a January 28 *Rocky Mountain News* story. An accompanying photograph showed the guard shack and a group of temporary wooden buildings in the distance. The photo's caption ended with a dare. "There are also a couple of fences and a row of guards in between — care to investigate?"

Nobody did. A wartime atmosphere pervaded the country, fed by part fact and part fiction. Soviet nuclear spies were a reality, as proven by Klaus Fuchs, a wartime Los Alamos scientist exposed in 1950 as a Soviet spy. The Korean War had turned public concern into alarm. Wisconsin Republican senator Joseph McCarthy and his allies exploited public fears. The House Un-American Activities Committee subjected suspected communist sympathizers to rump trials. National security was being preserved at all costs, often including the abandonment of democratic procedures.

Cattle Can't Talk

Out of public sight and accountability, the Rocky Flats plant complex took shape. Authorized personnel would turn off state highway 93, be cleared at the guard post, and drive a mile east on the dirt access road to another security check at a ranch-style barbed wire fence. This fence surrounded the industrial area of less than 400 acres, two-thirds of a square mile. Behind this perimeter fence, dirt streets that would soon carry domestic names such as First Street, Central Avenue, and Cactus Avenue ran past a few temporary wooden buildings to the four major production buildings dispersed around the site. The initial utilities also were temporary. Tank trucks brought water from Boulder, a train locomotive generated steam to heat the buildings, and the Public Service Company of Colorado strung up temporary power lines.[10] The modest skyline of downtown Denver could be seen in the South Platte River basin sixteen miles to the southeast.

The security area lay on the east side of the mesa, where the land began sloping down to join the prairie. Ravines carved out of the mesa's edge by countless spring runoffs served as ideal locations for the plant's production buildings. Building 991, a two-story reinforced concrete structure about the length and width of a football field, was just nearing completion in January 1952. The gray structure sat at a ravine's bottom so that its roof paralleled ground level, making it invisible from state highway 93 a couple of miles to the west.

This nuclear bomb core assembly building would begin receiving radioactive materials in February, just a few weeks after its originally scheduled completion date. This timing delighted AEC officials in Washington. Atomic Energy Commission chairman Gordon Dean gave an upbeat report to Colorado senators Johnson and Millikin and the other members of the congressional Joint Committee on Atomic Energy (JCAE) on January 9. "The Rocky Flats facility, just outside Denver, is being constructed to relieve Los Alamos of [its] production, modification, and inspection work load pertaining to nuclear weapons parts and it is contemplated that within a year this facility will assume [the] production engineering work load from LASL [Los Alamos Scientific Laboratory]."[11]

The military, which was the AEC's client, and JCAE members were pressing hard for more nuclear weapons. In January the Joint Chiefs again had raised significantly the number of prospective Soviet nuclear targets — putting the number at 5,000 to 6,000. As target numbers escalated, so did the need for weapons — a dynamic that helped drive the nuclear arms race. President Truman on January 17 approved the Chiefs' recommendation for a fifty percent increase in plutonium production and a 150 percent expansion of uranium–235 production.[12]

Building 991's February testing began a new phase at Rocky Flats, requiring workers with different skills. "The first thing we wanted was technical staff like chemists and metallurgists," said Chuck Arnbrecht, who began working in the Dow Rocky Flats personnel office in March 1952. A tall, square-jawed Colorado native whose grandparents had homesteaded near the town of Loveland, Arnbrecht had returned to his home state a few months earlier after serving in a Marine Corps rifle platoon in Korea.[13]

Next on Dow's hiring list were highly skilled industrial workers. "We spent lots of time bringing in tool and die makers and machinists from the upper Midwest," Arnbrecht said. That was familiar territory for Dow. Detroit's automobile plants, Milwaukee's farm and construction machinery factories, and Chicago's machine shops regularly had provided talented workers for Dow's far-flung chemical plants.

While recruiting brought many skilled workers to Rocky Flats, Dow hired most production line employees locally, Arnbrecht noted. Many were construction workers kept on to work in the production buildings they had just completed. Langell had successfully pursued such a hiring strategy on his previous projects, including a Dow plant in Texas built by the Austin Company in 1939.[14] This strategy added a bonus at Rocky Flats. Because the construction workers already possessed the AEC's special Q security clearances, they could be shifted into production jobs without delay.

Construction work on the other three major Rocky Flats production buildings accelerated in spring 1952. In July the construction workforce peaked at 2,800. That same month the AEC appointed retired admiral Gilbert C. Hoover as the commission's new field manager at Rocky Flats. He soon discovered that his job included maintaining good relations with the plant's neighbors, especially Marcus Church.

Church was still stewing over the low price the government offered for his family's Rocky Flats land. He had taken the issue to court. Meanwhile the security fence around the plant's perimeter separated Church's remaining cattle pastures north and east of the plant from those on the southwest side. He repeatedly complained to Dow and AEC officials about having to drive his cattle around the plant. When Dow began setting up its off-site radiation samplers and needed to go into his pastures, Church saw an opportunity to cut a deal with the company.

"To make sure we didn't contaminate anything, we got samples of grass and water from around the plant and took it back to the lab to keep records on it," said Bill Cornelison, Dow's security chief. "Marcus would get mad that people were tramping on his grass and doing this and doing that."

"So one day Mike Carroll [another plant employee] and I went over to Church's home and knocked on the door," Cornelison recalled. "The first thing I said to him was, 'Mr. Church, everybody over at Rocky Flats thinks you're a son of a bitch. Do you mind if we come in and talk to you for a while?' He said, 'Come on in.' I think he was taken aback by it, really. We started talking to him and, hell, we made an agreement where we could do this and we could get what we wanted and he could run his cattle through our property. All he had to do is tell us and we'd open the gates for him and all that sort of stuff. Hell, we left as friends."[15]

Following that conversation, Church met at the plant on November 12 with the AEC's Hoover, Dow manager Langell, and Cornelison to formalize the deal. Church agreed to the samplers on his land, and the men assured him plant staff wouldn't inconvenience him. They said the plant would construct access gates on the north and south sides of the perimeter fence, allow Church to put his own locks on those gates, and permit him to drive his cattle across the plant's land.[16]

Years later, Cornelison laughed that a rancher moved his cattle through a top secret nuclear weapons plant. "Cattle can't talk. Why make big problems out of little ones? Church only did it three or four times," he recalled. "Nobody said anything, although it didn't get back to Washington, where they'd make a big deal out of it."

Bomb Production

Building C (771) was the plant's crown jewel. Dug into a rocky ravine on the plant's north side, this structure was about the size of a large airplane hangar, but two story and rectangular. It contained equipment to process plutonium into metal and then shape it into components for bomb pits, or cores. Plutonium, the key and defining element at Rocky Flats, required extra-special handling. Being radioactive, it emitted alpha particles that could do biological damage if inhaled by humans or other creatures. In some forms plutonium ignited spontaneously in the atmosphere. Less than a pound could "go critical," causing nuclear reactions that didn't explode but in a flash emitted radiation lethal to anyone nearby. Just a few pounds were needed for a nuclear bomb.

Langell and his team observed plutonium handling for the first time in early 1951 when they toured the Hanford plant, operated under AEC contract by the General Electric Company. The sprawling, 570-square-mile Hanford site contained nuclear reactors and other facilities, including a building that fabricated bomb pits. Langell was not impressed. "They are a company that knows how to make lightbulbs and things like that in great quantities, with remote control and all that sort of thing, and they felt that the way to do this job was to make it all automatic so that people don't have to do a lot of the things," he said. "Their philosophy is fine, I think, for what they are accustomed to doing, but for the small quantities involved and the probability of change in specifications and the various other things that one must consider, we felt that we must consider a little different approach."[17]

At Los Alamos laboratory, the next stop, Langell's team found an approach they liked. Workers processed, cut, and formed plutonium inside contained work areas called glove boxes. As the name implied, two heavy, long-sleeved rubber gloves reached through portholes into rectangular boxes that stood on legs about three feet off the concrete floor. Each box was about five feet long, four feet high, and three feet deep. Workers, often standing on steps, inserted their arms into the sleeves and looked through treated Plexiglas plastic windows as they performed tasks inside the boxes. They were safe from plutonium contamination as long as everything functioned properly.

"I was impressed by the amount of actual physical hand control that they kept over everything," Langell remarked. He hired Bud Venable, an MIT-trained chemical engineer who created the Los Alamos glove box system, to develop Building 771 for Rocky Flats. Venable and his staff designed a labyrinthine glove box system. Dozens of stainless steel glove boxes were welded together end to end to form rectangular tunnels inside the Building 771 workrooms. Series of glove boxes called "lines" were designated for particular tasks. Glove boxes were also stacked on top of each other for certain processing procedures. Conveyors inside the glove box system transported the plutonium from box to box and from line to line in many operations. Most were "slat" conveyors, resembling the caterpillar tread on a bulldozer but much longer, which ran along the bottom of the glove box. A few overhead chain conveyors were also used. The whole system was interconnected, which had advantages for material flow but later would have unforeseen consequences when fire broke out.

The glove box lines in Building 771 and less extensive lines in the other major production buildings constituted one safety barrier against worker radiation exposure and radiation release to the outside environment. The buildings' ventilation systems provided another barrier. "All the buildings were just the opposite of commercial buildings, where you want the dust and all kept out," said mechanical engineer Jim Stone. "At Rocky Flats you were trying to protect the environment, so the building was kept under negative pressure."[18] Just as atmospheric air currents move from high-pressure to low-pressure areas, a breach in the low-pressure plutonium production building was supposed to suck air in from the outside to contain the radioactive material inside the building. This theory would be tested at Building 771 during the plant's first major fire in 1957.

Two of the major Rocky Flats production buildings handled uranium. Building A (444) dealt with "depleted uranium," so named because it was left over after most uranium–235 atoms had been removed during the process of enriching uranium for weapons or reactor fuel. Depleted uranium essentially consisted of uranium 238. This uranium was used for the tamper/reflector surrounding the bomb's plutonium core. A few years later, Building 444 would also begin machining beryllium metal for a similar purpose.[19]

Building B (881) fabricated oralloy (Oak Ridge alloy) components for bomb cores. The oralloy, or highly enriched uranium, typically contained ninety-three percent uranium 235 by weight and was used extensively in contemporary bomb designs. Operations in the huge, two-story, concrete building included small foundries to melt and cast the uranium, machine tools to form and shape components, facilities to assemble the parts, equipment to recycle scrap uranium created during the manufacturing process, and associated chemical and radiography laboratories. Oak Ridge produced the original oralloy and shipped it to Rocky Flats as "buttons" a little smaller than hockey pucks, but weighing much more — similar to the way plutonium was later shipped from the Hanford and Savannah River plants.[20]

There were differences and many similarities in the way bomb parts were made from highly enriched uranium and plutonium. A major difference lay in how the materials were handled. Unlike plutonium handling, the uranium work didn't require an extensive glove box system to isolate it from workers and the environment. Uranium workers employed laboratory hoods, akin to rolltop desks, which were commonly used in hospitals and schools to isolate chemicals and other materials.

The plutonium and uranium buildings both used chemicals to separate and recover the metals from manufacturing scrap. Although different chemicals were used, the basic recovery operations in both "were similar in almost all respects," according to one study.[21] They also were similar in leaving enormous quantities of radioactively contaminated chemicals requiring disposal. Added to the liquid production waste were solid materials such as contaminated containers and clothing. Workers put much of this waste into drums and buried them, leaving a toxic legacy whose magnitude wouldn't be recognized for decades.

Production Workers Unionize

The entire Rocky Flats complex was tuning up by mid-1953. While some bomb assembly work had been done the previous year, Building 771 began processing its first plutonium in May 1953.[22] Within months all four major buildings would be fully operational. More than 1,000 full-time workers were hired. The wooden shacks disappeared. A local resident bought part of the temporary administration building and opened a bar on Highway 93 west of the plant.

The nation's mood was somber. Julius and Ethel Rosenberg were executed for espionage in June. And in September the media reported that the Soviet Union had tested its first H-bomb.[23] Worker Pat Kelly shifted to Building 881's newly completed chemistry laboratory in September. Since his hiring seven months earlier, the twenty-seven-year-old Kelly had been calibrating instruments in a temporary lab set up in a garage. He would see these instruments operate, but only to the degree allowed by the building's tight security.

The Denver Post reported the selection of Rocky Flats
on its March 23, 1951, front page.

Colorado Senator Edwin "Big Ed" Johnson played a key role in winning the Rocky Flats plant for his state. Photo by Harry Rhoades, *Rocky Mountain News.*

Right: After a 1974 expansion of the buffer zone, the plant site covered more than 10 square miles. *Rocky Mountain News* illustrative drawing.

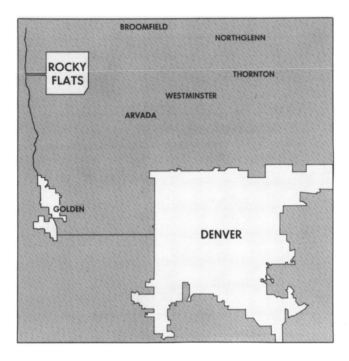

The plant site, located on a mesa sixteen miles northwest of Denver, was called "isolated" by a selection committee in 1951. *Rocky Mountain News* drawing.

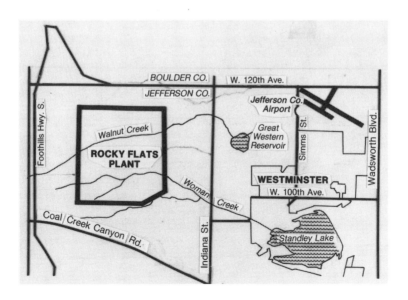

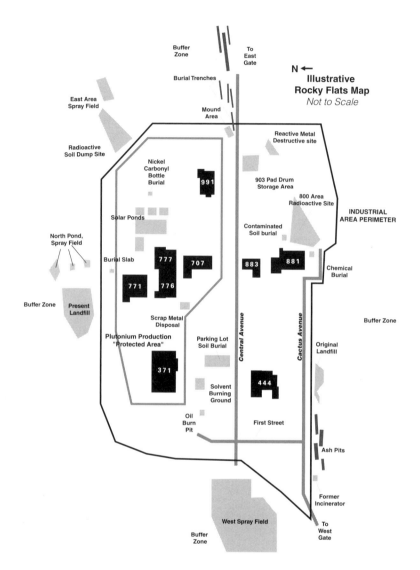

The plant's industrial area, occupying 384 acres, was located in the middle of the site. This illustrative drawing shows only the major production buildings, the heavily guarded plutonium production area, and waste sites identified by plant staff in 1990. Drawing by Michael Campbell.

This guard shack at the road entrance to the plant was completed in January 1952. Security measures continued to increase. *Rocky Mountain News* photo.

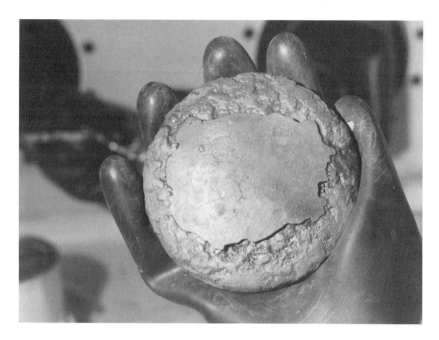

This "button" of pure plutonium metal weighed more than a pound.
Rocky Flats/DOE photo, 1974.

Plant worker holding a "button," as seen from inside a glove box.
Rocky Flats/DOE photo, 1981.

Thousands of barrels of nuclear waste were stored outside.
Many corroded and leaked. Rocky Flats/DOE photo, 1962.

For safety reasons, employees worked on plutonium through glove boxes, stacked or welded end to end in "glove box lines." Rocky Flats/DOE photo, 1980.

A burned-out glove box after the nearly catastrophic 1969 fire
in Building 776–777. Rocky Flats/DOE photo.

A protester in a skeleton mask at an April 1978 demonstration.
Photo by David Cornwell, *Rocky Mountain News.*

Protestors at an April 1978 demonstration outside the plant's west gate tossed a ball representing planet Earth. Photo by David Cornwell, *Rocky Mountain News.*

Demonstrators gather near Indiana St. outside the northeast corner of the plant in August 1978. Photo by Frank Murray, *Rocky Mountain News.*

Aerial view of plutonium-processing Building 771, in the right foreground. Site of a major 1957 fire, the Department of Energy called this building the nation's most dangerous in 1995. Rocky Flats/DOE photo, 1986.

The plutonium production "protected area" is guarded by barbed wire fences, guard towers, and a heavily armed security force. The structure is Building 371, a $215 million facility that never operated as intended. Photo by Steve Groer, *Rocky Mountain News.*

A plutonium storage vault in Building 707.
Photo by Mel Schieltz, *Rocky Mountain News.*

Jack Weaver (far right) and two coworkers during inspection of the
plutonium storage vault in Building 707. Rocky Flats/DOE photo, 1988.

Rocky Flats guard waves EPA mobile investigation unit into the plant during the June 1989 raid by the FBI and other federal agencies. Photo by George Kochaniec, Jr., *Rocky Mountain News*.

Jim Kelly (right) and Dennis Wise of the United Steelworkers Union discuss Energy Secretary James Watkins's January 1992 media briefing. Photo by Hal Stoezle, *Rocky Mountain News.*

Workers excavate the Trench 1 nuclear waste burial site, which is covered
to prevent wind dispersal. Rocky Flats/DOE photo, 1998.

The sealed door to an "infinity room" in Building 776–777.
Photo by Robert Del Tredici, 1994.

Building 881 was located on the southeast side of the plant's industrial area. Kelly and his fellow workers weren't allowed to drive their cars into this area. They parked outside the perimeter fence, after having their picture identification badges checked at the plant entrance off Highway 93 and driving more than a mile down the access road. They then passed through a second guard post, checked in at the administrative building, and were bused to one of the outlying production buildings. The ID badges were color coded and numbered to show which of the four production areas (A, B, C, or D) workers could enter.

Like the other major production buildings, Building 881 was partly underground and surrounded by an eight-foot-high chain-link fence topped by barbed wire.[24] Arriving at the guard shack outside the building's chain-link fence, Kelly and the other workers had to exchange their ID badges for another badge. "That way security kept track of who was in the building and made sure that you had the right clearance," said Kelly. "But then, inside, even though I had a clearance for the building, if I wanted to go into the machining area, I had to go through another guard station and get another badge."[25]

The security measures didn't bother Kelly, a straight-talking second-generation Irish Catholic and U.S. Navy veteran. From his new-employee orientation sessions the previous February, Kelly knew he was making parts for nuclear weapons. He wasn't concerned about radiation exposure, at least not then. "I felt that if I did things right, I'd be okay," said Kelly, who previously worked in Wyoming coal mines. He considered his new job safer than mining, and "it never bothered me to work in a coal mine." Besides, the pay at Rocky Flats was higher. He started at $1.85 an hour, below the plant average of $2.31 but still a good wage in those days.

Kelly was bothered, however, by Dow's discrimination against hourly workers as opposed to salaried, or managerial, employees. "About the third week I was there, I got strep throat," he recalled. "But I kept going to work because I couldn't afford to lose money. Finally my boss told me I had to go home, but to check out at medical first. The doctor says, 'Are you hourly or salary?' I said, 'Hourly, why?' He said, 'If we send you home and you're salary, you get paid. If hourly, you don't get paid.'" Kelly wasn't the only unhappy worker at Rocky Flats. Secrecy and security notwithstanding, the facility was a large industrial complex. Dow's Langell ran the plant from the top down. He appointed production managers who came to be described as "building czars" and reported directly to him.[26] Disagreements naturally cropped up between management and labor. Workers wanted a union to represent them in workplace grievances and in negotiations over salary and benefits. But Rocky Flats was owned by the government's Atomic Energy Commission, which originally banned unions throughout the nuclear weapons complex to prevent strikes from disrupting production.

Under pressure from unions and Congress, the AEC modified its nonunion policy in 1952. The commission permitted unionization, but only through a single bargaining unit instead of the various craft unions and industrial unions common at many companies. This allowed the AEC, and its federal successor agencies, to remain a "ghost at the bargaining table," as one Colorado labor leader put it.[27]

The first union election at Rocky Flats was set for March 1953, a month after Pat Kelly began working there. About 1,000 production workers were eligible to vote on representation.[28] Kelly actively supported the union campaign, which was not surprising given his background. His father, John, had been a Wyoming coal miner and union leader before President Franklin D. Roosevelt appointed him postmaster in Hanna, Wyoming. Pat Kelly had graduated early from high school, joined the navy as a teenager, and served three years in the Pacific during World War II. After the war he returned to Wyoming, took a job in a coal mine, and soon was an officer in the United Mine Workers local. He left the mines and was working as a soils technician in the U.S. Bureau of Reclamation laboratory in Cody, Wyoming, when in 1952 he learned about Rocky Flats from a sister in Denver.

Kelly believed the Congress of Industrial Unions (CIO) could best represent the production workers at Rocky Flats, where "chemical operator" was a common job title. But the American Federation of Labor (AFL), through the Denver Metal Trades Council, which represented craft employees such as plumbers and electricians, won the election. This was three years before the AFL-CIO merged. Kelly became active in the council and soon was elected president of one of its units. But he continued trying to bring a stronger union into the plant, an effort that paid off years later.

The Kelly name would become synonymous with the labor union movement at Rocky Flats. Dow hired Pat's younger brother, Jim, in 1956. The two men would play a singular, often controversial role in the plant's history. Jim, in particular, frequently found himself squeezed between the interests of workers, politicians, and the activists who eventually confronted Rocky Flats. But the rights, salaries, benefits, and health and safety of workers always remained the Kelly brothers' top priorities.

FIVE

Neutrons Trotting Around

"Radio-active Stuff"

Marcus Church knew radioactivity must be important. Why else would Rocky Flats plant officials offer to cut cattle gates into their perimeter fence in exchange for putting some little monitoring boxes in his pasture? But Atomic Energy Commission (AEC) managers had assured him in 1951 that the plant's presence would draw other companies to the remaining Church land. Surely radioactivity couldn't be much of a hazard if the officials made such promises. Church was curious about it but not worried.

His attitude came through in a December 1953 letter he wrote to his sister, Ruth McKay, who lived in the Chicago suburb of Evanston with her husband and two young sons, Charlie and Perry. Church told her a pretrial meeting would soon be held over the price the AEC would pay for the Rocky Flats land it took from the family. The meeting "can bring up such things as radio-active stuff that fall into the classified category and can't be talked about, so I anticipate a rather interesting session," he wrote. The session reassured him that the AEC and Dow had everything under control. But the land price dispute would drag on until April 1955, when the family was awarded $69,323 for its 1,228 acres. This price, $56 per acre, was triple the government's original offer in 1951. Meanwhile Marcus and his mother, Katherine, had used an AEC down payment to buy another 640 acres (one square mile) near the plant and become sole owners of the small Rocky Flats lake, also known as Smart Reservoir.[1]

While Church reacted nonchalantly to the question of radioactivity, some other Westerners, particularly in Utah, were worried. Utah was downwind from the Nevada site where nuclear bomb testing started in January 1951. Residents became worried about radioactive fallout when some cattle and sheep near the testing range suffered strange burns and fell ill. In March 1953 the AEC commenced its fourth series of tests, labeled the Upshot-Knothole Operation and consisting of eleven nuclear bomb explosions. Critics complained that the AEC was not taking public health hazards into account. The chairman of the University of Utah's physics department, a former director of the federal Brookhaven nuclear laboratory in New York, was among the local residents expressing concern about radioactive fallout.[2]

Such reactions must have disappointed AEC officials, who had been waging a public relations campaign, including pamphlets and movies, that was conceived before nuclear testing began in Nevada. Atomic Energy Commission staff and military officers had met in Washington, D.C., in December 1950 to devise their PR strategy. They focused on "the question of exploring radiological safety aspects in order to make the atom routine in the continental United States and make the public feel at home with atomic blasts and radiation hazards. . . . It appeared that the idea of making the public feel at home with neutrons trotting around was the angle to get across," according to a meeting summary.[3]

Criticism before the March 1953 Upshot-Knothole nuclear test series was nothing compared to the questions raised during and immediately afterward. The ninth explosion in the series was dubbed "Harry." Triggered at dawn on May 19, it had a yield of 32,000 tons of TNT, half again as large as the Nagasaki bomb. The AEC test crew in Nevada miscalculated the wind direction and a cloud of radioactive particles and dust began blowing east toward towns, including Saint George, Utah. Because of a similar problem a month earlier, the AEC was ready, and monitors began erecting roadblocks less than two hours after the shot. Still, most drivers were simply told the cloud might cause "radioactive fallout." At 9:30 A.M. an AEC official warned residents of Saint George to take cover. Schools canceled their morning recess. Dozens of contaminated cars were washed and cleaned at AEC expense. The local congressman passed along the complaints from residents to the AEC, but agency experts said radiation exposure standards were not exceeded and the Saint George fallout was an aberration.

Reports from Utah sheep ranchers of an unusually large number of deaths among ewes and lambs stirred a local debate over testing. The AEC issued a press release in June, saying that studies of the sheep deaths were under way and a committee to examine nuclear testing had been formed.

Behind closed doors, the AEC's contention that radiation didn't cause the sheep deaths was vigorously challenged by some experts. But this wasn't indicated by a commission report publicly circulated in January 1954. "Considering all of the information and data available, it is now evident that the peculiar lesions observed in the sheep around Cedar City in the spring of 1953 and the abnormal losses suffered by the several sheepmen cannot be accounted for by radiation or attributed to the atomic tests at the Nevada Proving Grounds," the report stated. Sheep ranchers were among the minority who didn't accept this conclusion. They filed complaints against the U.S. government, seeking $177,000 in damages for lost ewes and lambs, but a federal court rejected their claims.[4]

Perhaps stimulated by the sheep controversy in Utah, Denver's *Rocky Mountain News* submitted a list of thirty-four questions to the AEC in spring 1954. The answers ran on June 1, under the headline, "There's No Atomic Blast Danger at Rocky Flats." The newspaper's introduction stated "The [AEC's] guarded statement confirmed, by implication, that the installation is engaged in work on atomic weapons."

The newspaper's fourth question read, "There have been reports Rocky Flats is manufacturing a detonator, or some portion thereof, used in the atomic bomb. Is this true?" It was, but the AEC refused to answer, claiming even the disclosure of such a general description of the plant's mission could harm the nation's security. Instead the commission gave the standard response for questions it intended to evade. "Rocky Flats is a classified production plant and handles radioactive materials. . . . Further information regarding the function of the plant would be of value to unfriendly nations and cannot be disclosed under security regulations."

By claiming such a sweeping need for security, and thus secrecy, the AEC was able to duck the "radiation hazards" issue that the commission's public relations specialists had worried about at the December 1950 session. In the name of national security, the AEC felt free to tell citizens half-truths and lies. Responding to the newspaper's question about radiation sickness, the AEC stated, "The degree of radioactivity at Rocky Flats is small. However, in any work involving radioactive materials, precautions must be taken to hold exposure to a minimum. 'Radioactive sickness' is not a health factor at the plant."

The Denver-area media and general public seemed to separate the radiation from nuclear testing from the radiation present at Rocky Flats. This became clear in March 1955, when local papers reported that radiation from a new Nevada nuclear test series was drifting across the state. "No Cause for Alarm: Colorado Bathed by Heavy Fallout from Atom Blast," read the headline on the *Rocky Mountain News*'s front page. The AEC issued press releases assuring the public that the radiation was harmless, but two prominent University of Colorado medical school doctors, Ray R. Lanier and Theodore Puck, released a report on March 13 refuting the AEC.[5]

This was a perfect occasion for Big Ed Johnson to again defend the nuclear weapons enterprise. After retiring from the U.S. Senate, he had won the Colorado gubernatorial race in 1954. Governor Johnson angrily criticized the university doctors' claims that the testing fallout was dangerous and said they "should be arrested." The flap made news for several weeks, finally dying out with claims that the doctors' measurements had been conducted with contaminated Geiger counters. The articles about this radiation controversy downplayed Rocky Flats.[6]

Different Kinds of Radiation

Rocky Flats officials privately worried from the outset about potential radiation poisoning of workers and the community. "We recognized that working with radioactive materials, we have got to know what we have got and where it is at all times," said plant manager Heinie Langell. "So one of the very first departments that we set up was what other installations had called Health Physics, and we followed suit." The term health physics was a euphemism for "radiation protection," which both identified nuclear operations and implied that protection was needed against radiation hazards. Manhattan Project scientists had created the health physics description during World War II.[7]

At Rocky Flats, Langell appointed a Dow Company physician and Manhattan Project veteran to head the plant's health physics group. "The job of this group was to be sure that no one on the site and no one off the site is injured because of the fact that we are handling radioactive materials," Langell said. The danger radioactivity posed to living organisms was well known, if not fully understood, by the 1950s. Scientists knew that the earth exists in a sea of radiation. All matter emits energy in the form of waves or particles. The sun is the earth's major source of radiant energy, making life possible on this planet. The most common type of radiation it emits is called nonionizing, which includes everything from radio waves to visible light.

The sun and other bodies can also emit ionizing radiation, which can turn ordinary atoms into electrically charged particles called ions. The positively or negatively charged ions are highly reactive and can interfere with the natural chemical processes in living things. Radioactive materials, such as uranium and plutonium, emit ionizing radiation in identifiable patterns of alpha or beta particles, gamma rays, or neutrons.[8]

Shortly after scientists discovered radioactivity in the late 1890s, they found that prolonged exposure to x-ray machines caused reddened skin and, in hands, could damage skin and blood vessels severely enough to cause the loss of fingers. The scientists began shielding machines with lead to block the x rays, capable of penetrating human bodies. But short-term damage turned out to be the least of the worries. After World War I, increasing cancer deaths among researchers and radiation workers alarmed scientists about long-term radiation effects. Research on the damage caused by radiation sources outside the body—external sources—led the U.S. Advisory Committee on X-ray and Radium Protection to propose in 1934 the first limits on radiation "doses," the amount of energy actually absorbed by an organism. The 1936 Nobel Prize was awarded to a scientist who documented how x rays induce chromosome mutations.[9]

But radiation emissions also could come from radioactive atoms inside the body—internal sources—if radioactive substances were inhaled, ingested, or introduced through cuts. Researchers in the 1920s noted high cancer rates among European uranium miners, which were later traced to radon, a radioactive gas that is part of natural uranium's decay chain and emits alpha particles. When radon lodged in a person's lungs, the emissions could cause cancerous cell growth.

Then the devastating effects of internal radiation poisoning caused by alpha particles were documented in a 1924 report about a young New Jersey factory worker who used a radium mixture to paint luminous watch dials. An investigation found that she and her coworkers at the United States Radium Corporation plant licked the tips of their brushes to make finer points for painting the tiny watch numbers. Their bodies absorbed some radium, which is chemically akin to calcium and thus settled in the bone. There the radium's alpha particles bombarded cells in the skin, blood vessels, and bone. This caused ulcers, destroyed bone tissue, and caused bone cancer. At United States Radium, out of more than 300 workers, at least nine died between 1922 and 1924 and many others contracted cancer.[10]

Further studies of radium led radiation scientists to set the first dose limit for internal radiation in 1941. Chemists discovered plutonium the same year and, like radium, it was found to emit high-energy alpha particles. Once plutonium atoms entered a person's body, the alpha particle emissions could do potentially devastating damage when their energy hit living cells.[11]

Radiation emissions are measured in curies. One curie is the rate at which a gram (.04 ounce) of radium 226 disintegrates or decays as its atoms seek stability. A gram of radium 226 undergoes 37 billion disintegrations per second, emitting alpha particles and gamma rays. By comparison, a gram of plutonium undergoes only 2.2 billion disintegrations per second, measured as six-hundredths of a curie. Still, scientists soon learned plutonium's biological impact could be even greater than radium's.[12]

The "UPPU" Club

Plutonium was the source for both the first atomic bomb tested in New Mexico on July 16, 1945, and the bomb dropped on Nagasaki three weeks later on August 9. Workers at the Hanford plant in Washington State produced plutonium in nuclear reactors, separated it from the uranium and other fission products with a nitric acid solution, and sent the first shipment to Los Alamos in December 1944. Los Alamos had to further separate the plutonium from the acid solution, process it into metal, and shape it into the proper size for a bomb. The solid core of the Nagasaki bomb consisted of an estimated 13.5 pounds (6.1 kilograms) of plutonium. It would have been about the size of a tennis ball while weighing as much as a small bowling ball.[13] In building the bombs, scientists recognized that microscopic quantities of plutonium were dangerous to nuclear workers.

The Los Alamos workers initially handled the plutonium in wooden "dry boxes," the precursors of glove boxes, and wore respirators and protective clothing. But plutonium contamination was hard to detect. The "film badges" routinely used in nuclear facilities contained small strips of photographic film whose atoms were readily ionized by beta particles, gamma rays, and x rays. So film badges were relatively effective at detecting external radiation, which could travel significant distances through the air and penetrate human bodies. But alpha particles emitted by plutonium atoms traveled just 1.4 inches in air. Neutrons, too, were hard to detect.

To detect plutonium contamination, nuclear workers wiped one-inch squares of oiled filter paper across the surfaces of machines or tables and then tested them in an alpha counter. This crude detection method was called the "swipe method"; the pieces of filter paper were "swipes." Nasal swabs also were employed to spot exposed workers. And urinalysis could detect plutonium in a worker's body.[14] These same detection methods would be employed at Rocky Flats along with better methods developed in later years.

While wartime scientists knew plutonium was hazardous, in 1945 few details were known about the way plutonium behaved in the lungs and the rest of the body. Eager to learn more, in April that year scientists at several medical centers around the country began injecting small quantities of plutonium into patients who supposedly had life-threatening diseases. The scientists wanted "to determine the excretion rate of plutonium over time for known intakes" in order to set safe dose limits for nuclear bomb workers.[15]

Over the next two years medical scientists injected eighteen men and women with plutonium. Most, if not all, were not fully informed about what was happening to them, according to a Pulitzer Prize–winning series of articles by *Albuquerque Tribune* reporter Eileen Welsome in 1993. While the existence of the experiments had been revealed earlier, Welsome was the first to identify some of the victims and detail the experiments. Although the medical association between the plutonium and the victims' deaths is disputed, the public uproar over the experiments led to a government investigation and a 1996 government agreement to pay compensation to the victims' families.[16]

Studies in the late 1940s found plutonium to be from five to ten times more toxic than radium. While radium tended to spread throughout the bones, plutonium stayed on the bone surfaces, where it could damage actively dividing cells. Plutonium's damage to the lungs was even greater.[17] The Los Alamos laboratory sought to prevent exposure by insulating workers from plutonium by means of better glove boxes. Despite such improvements, nuclear weapons workers still got contaminated, as evidenced by many positive urine tests. Demonstrating a certain bravado common at secret nuclear weapons facilities, Los Alamos workers jokingly established a club in 1951. Playing on plutonium's scientific abbreviation, "pu," they called the club "UPPU" — "You Pee Pu."[18] Rocky Flats would soon have its own club chapter.

Plutonium Accounting

Dow Chemical's health physics group at Rocky Flats moved into action after the first plutonium arrived in February 1952 at Building 991, the newly completed nuclear core assembly facility ready to undergo shakedown testing. This plutonium already had been processed into metal, so it didn't require the extensive procedures needed when plutonium chemical processing started in Building 771 the following year.

Still, the plutonium, much more than the uranium used at the plant, required special handling. The health physics group was responsible for the employee film badges, protective clothing, and monitoring equipment inside the production buildings. To prepare for full-scale production, Dow's health physics group set up a system of outside air-sampling monitors to detect radiation releases from the plant. Ten air samplers were dispersed around the plant site itself and another fifteen off-site, which necessitated the fall 1952 arrangement with Marcus Church for the cattle gates.[19]

Plant manager Langell established two other managerial working groups before the plant began receiving plutonium and uranium. They were an "accountability group" and a "waste disposal group." The accountability group was a bookkeeping operation, Langell explained, responsible for knowing "what radioactive material comes into the plant, when it comes, how much comes in, what we do with it and how much goes out, and is there unaccounted-for radioactive material, and if so, how much?"[20] Plutonium was the main focus of this bookkeeping, and over the coming decades about 2,000 pounds — enough for more than 200 nuclear bombs — would become "material unaccounted for," or MUF in plant jargon.

Plant manager Langell's goal was to maximize the amount of radioactive raw material going into bombs and to minimize the waste. As a result, Rocky Flats was designed to be an efficient recycling operation able to reclaim as much of the valuable radioactive plutonium and uranium as possible. In Langell's words, "We don't want to lose anything of such value that we can possibly avoid losing."[21] Rocky Flats officials categorized potentially recoverable plutonium waste as "residues," in contrast to plain old waste slated for disposal. This distinction would become the subject of lawsuits in the 1980s.

The production waste at Rocky Flats consisted primarily of radioactively contaminated chemicals used to process the plutonium and uranium, and the oils used for the machines that cut and shaped the bomb parts. Added to this liquid waste were solid materials such as contaminated coveralls, containers, and rags. The AEC possessed ultimate responsibility for this waste, none of which was to be permanently stored at Rocky Flats.

Langell assigned a waste disposal group, headed by his longtime Dow colleague John Epp, to control the flow of waste and prepare it for off-site shipment by putting it into steel barrels. This task was performed primarily in auxiliary buildings constructed near the major production buildings.

Dow loaded the waste barrels into specially designed railroad cars and signed over the waste to the AEC on-site, just as it signed over the assembled bomb pits, which the AEC trucked to Pantex in Texas. Using the spur railroad track installed by the Denver & Rio Grande Western and the

Colorado & Southern railroads to connect the plant with their main tracks, the AEC shipped waste to the government's disposal site near Arco, Idaho. During 1954, the first year that Rocky Flats was in full weapons production, the AEC shipped 200 barrels a month of plutonium-contaminated waste to Idaho.[22]

A bottleneck in nuclear waste shipments quickly developed. Part of the problem was that the government's nuclear bomb establishment had never given waste a high priority, although "the dangers posed by radioactive waste were well understood" even during the Manhattan Project, an official history acknowledged. An AEC advisory board concluded in 1947 that radioactive waste disposal presented "the gravest of problems." Yet instead of addressing the issues, AEC officials took a public relations approach just as they did with nuclear testing. They claimed that waste disposal was under control and denied any problems existed. "The AEC's public relations efforts had resulted in a 'marked lessening of concern' by public regulatory officials over waste releases," the history concluded.[23]

The AEC's top priority was to meet the demands of its client, the Department of Defense, for more nuclear bombs. Dow was required to produce those bombs, regardless of the waste created. Heinie Langell took great pride in meeting the AEC's production quotas. "We at Rocky Flats were never the cause of any hold-up of delivery by the Commission to the Military," he said, while admitting the trade-off between bomb production and waste. "We didn't slack off on production. We decided to accumulate the excess wastes." This meant Langell and his staff had to get the waste "out of the road," in his words. He explained that this figure of speech meant that contaminated chemicals and other waste needed to be taken out of the production areas and stored in barrels.[24] Beginning in 1954 the plant started "temporarily" burying barrels on-site, a practice hidden from the public for nearly two decades. But the potential nuclear waste hazards were less direct than the radiation hazards faced every day by plant workers like Marvin Thielsen.

Marvin Thielsen

Following an FBI background security check and a thorough physical, Thielsen began working as a janitor at the Rocky Flats plant in June 1955. Short and built like an oil drum, the thirty-seven-year-old Thielsen had arrived a year earlier from South Dakota. It hadn't been a happy move. He grew up in that northern plains state and returned to farm there after being honorably discharged from the army in 1945. He loved the expansive land, even the harsh, subzero winter days when he could spend a little more time at the local café drinking coffee and sharing stories with his buddies. He could tell a good story.[25]

But Thielsen, like so many others, couldn't make a go of farming. A friend pointed him toward Denver, where he first found work as a laborer in 1954 and then was joined by his wife and their two young daughters. The following year he jumped at a Rocky Flats janitorial job, which offered better pay and a chance to move up the ladder. Within a year Thielsen was promoted to "assistant operator" in Building 771, the plutonium production facility, and began working on a glove box line through thick, arm-length gloves.

"They were like welder's gloves, made of stiff rubber," Thielsen said. "Working in them is like trying to thread a needle with canvas gloves on. It requires dexterity." The job also was risky because the gloves could be punctured by irradiated metal or glass slivers inside the boxes. Two years later, after a shard of glass sliced through a glove into his left index finger, Thielsen rushed to the building's first aid station. "You're lucky you didn't get something else hot; you'd have to cut that off," the nurse joked, using the slang word "hot," which stood for radioactive. She cleaned the cut and put a Band-Aid over it, and he returned to work.

"The contamination came up in a pee bucket count the next day," Thielsen said, referring to the urine test showing plutonium in his body. The company treatment record tersely summarized the incident: "Stuck piece of glass tubing into finger. Puncture wound, distal 2nd finger, left. Cleansed, wound scrubbed and portions debrided, Merthiolate, Band-Aid. Spect. count .027µg. Wound contaminated. Contamination not completely removed."[26]

The ".027µg" in Thielsen's accident report stood for .027 microgram, or millionths of a gram, of plutonium. This microscopic amount constituted more than half the maximum permissible "body burden" dose limit for nuclear workers. A body burden is the amount of radioactive material remaining inside a person's body and acting as an internal source of radiation.[27] Although body burden is still a common term among nuclear weapons workers, radiation standards in the 1990s are expressed as annual limits and usually measured in terms of rem, standing for "roentgen equivalent man." Radiation scientists developed this standard measure in order to account for the different biological effects of alpha, beta, gamma, and neutron radiation. Small doses are commonly measured in millirem, or thousandths of a rem.

Translated into modern terms, Thielsen's body burden was roughly 2 rem per year, which means he received five times more than the .36 rem of radiation an average U.S. citizen receives annually. More than half of the typical person's dose comes from natural "background" radiation from rocks and cosmic rays, and the rest is from human-made sources such as diagnostic x rays and the residue from atmospheric nuclear weapons tests. Today the recommended international standard for additional radiation doses is 2 rem for workers and .1 rem for the public.[28]

Thielsen didn't say anything about plutonium when his wife asked about the Band-Aid. He didn't want to worry her. He wasn't even sure how worried he should be himself. All he knew was that the plant doctor said he had received a heavy enough radiation dose to give him a "body burden" of plutonium and that he shouldn't get any more. Thielsen soon was transferred from Building 771 to a lower-exposure waste-processing building, but it would be years before he was moved out of the plant's "hot" side. And then, ironically, he would be assigned to work with beryllium, a nonradioactive but hazardous lightweight metal. Thielsen would contract an incurable lung disease. Radiation was not the plant's only dangerous by-product.

While the daily danger for workers stemmed from both radioactive and nonradioactive hazards, the overall quantity of plutonium processed at Rocky Flats constituted the greatest danger for their families and other Denver area residents. The risk was the chance that plutonium would be dispersed into the environment, either routinely or through an accident. The first major accident occurred in September 1957.

SIX

Expect a Fire, but Produce

Spooky Material

Jim Kelly never forgot his first look at plutonium. Until this sweltering August 1957 day, he hadn't even heard its name. For Rocky Flats employees who didn't work in Building C (771), plutonium was known only as "material C." Kelly had joined the plant's workforce a year earlier, at the urging of his older brother, Pat, who already worked there. Jim was a blunt-talking, wiry young man in his midtwenties who served in the navy after finishing high school in Hanna, Wyoming. At Rocky Flats, after working a year in the uranium-manufacturing buildings, he successfully bid for a higher-paying radiation monitor job in Building 771. He got his first look at the isolated, windowless, two-story reinforced concrete structure occupying a deep ravine on the production area's north side.[1]

"I had a feeling of wonderment," Kelly said. "It started in the locker room, where I put on these white coveralls, booties, and a surgeon's cap—which absolutely blew my mind. Why did I have to wear this goddamn doctor's cap?" Proceeding down a hallway, Kelly passed into an air lock, two sets of swinging double doors set a few feet apart so a worker could pass through one set and let it close tightly before passing through the second. He emerged on the plutonium-processing side of the building, the "hot" (radioactive) side. "It was an absolute 180 [degrees] from anything you'd ever seen in your life," he said. Kelly walked down hospital-like corridors, peering into rooms made of concrete blocks and crammed with machinery and workers. Miles of pipes hung from the ceilings.

At the south end of the huge building Kelly entered a room with a long glove box system and white-suited machinists and chemical operators. Kelly looked through a glove box window and saw a plutonium component the size of a billiard ball. "It was very shiny. It was very fucking spooky," he said. "This feeling came to me about this piece of plutonium. The system that this thing was encased in automatically told you that there was something bad about this stuff." He turned to supervisor Ernie Ray and said he had decided not to take the radiation monitor job. "I'll just stay where I am," he said. Ray smiled and replied, "It's not as bad as it looks. You'll be all right here." He added that Kelly could always transfer out if he didn't like it. After thinking about the job overnight, Kelly agreed to give it a try. "It was like a thirty-cent-an-hour raise, which was a lot of money in those days," he later explained.

Kelly's intuition about plutonium's nature was right on the mark. Plutonium not only is uniquely dangerous; its characteristics and behavior were not fully understood. Yet weapons scientists and engineers had figured out how to take a few pounds of plutonium metal, make it into a spherelike shape, and detonate it in order to create a nuclear explosion capable of killing tens of thousands of human beings at a time.

These bomb makers also knew plutonium had to be handled with extreme caution during the production process, for three reasons. First, microscopic particles of radioactive plutonium were extremely toxic if inhaled. Second, a small amount of plutonium — depending on its makeup, shape, and factors such as the presence of water — could create a localized chain reaction called a "criticality," which could be fatal to anyone within several yards. Third, plutonium metal, especially small chips or filings, was pyrophoric, meaning it could catch fire on its own in the presence of air.

Plutonium fires had flared frequently over the years at the Hanford and Los Alamos nuclear weapons facilities, but they had been kept small by workers who isolated the burning plutonium.[2] At Rocky Flats the first "major" plutonium fire, which the Atomic Energy Commission (AEC) defined as one costing more than $5,000 to clean up, occurred on September 30, 1955, during a routine operation. Plutonium chips ignited spontaneously and a glove box glove caught fire. Workers tried to extinguish the fire with carbon dioxide extinguishers. This not only failed to put the fire out, it spread contamination into the glove box line. Finally employees scooped up the burning plutonium, placed it in a steel container, and let it burn itself out. Sixteen workers were contaminated, none seriously. Workers decontaminated the burned area by entering it with protective clothing and respirators, scrubbing down floors and walls, and putting all trash in plastic bags. The decontamination cost was estimated at $9,500.[3]

A month later, based on this and other accidents, the AEC admitted it didn't completely understand plutonium's combustibility and hadn't been able to develop a foolproof way to extinguish plutonium fires. The AEC's Washington, D.C., headquarters issued an "Accident and Fire Prevention" bulletin to its facilities in October 1955. "Comparatively little is known regarding plutonium fire extinguishing methods that are reliable in all cases," the AEC bulletin stated. It spelled out certain approaches to avoid. "It is known, for example, that the rate of plutonium combustion may be markedly increased and, under some conditions, explosions may occur following application of water, foam, soda-acid, carbon tetrachloride, or dry chemical (sodium bicarbonate) 'extinguishants.'"

The AEC bulletin continued, "Until such time as further information becomes available from research into the causative factors of pyrophoricity of metallic plutonium, preventing and controlling plutonium fires must be determined by past experience coupled with use of educated judgment." The AEC gave four guidelines for preventing plutonium fires. The agency advised that the amount of plutonium metal kept in an area be limited, that plutonium be handled only where external fire hazards were minimized, and that in the event of fire the burning metal be isolated rapidly. Finally, the report concluded, "Expect to have a fire."[4] But the AEC's warnings about fire came as the agency was ordering Dow Chemical Company to produce a new kind of bomb core requiring even more plutonium. And fire safety at Rocky Flats, just like nuclear waste, took a backseat to production.

Hollow Pits

When Rocky Flats went into full bomb production in 1954, virtually all plutonium operations took place in Building 771. Plutonium arrived from the Hanford plant in the form of liquid plutonium nitrate carried in small stainless steel flasks packed in cylinders the size of truck wheels. Each flask contained about seven ounces (200 grams) of plutonium.[5] Using vacuum pumps, workers transferred the liquid from the flasks into a tall, thin glass cylinder inside a stainless steel glove box arrangement they called the "telephone booth." They added hydrogen peroxide. Its molecules attached to the plutonium molecules and created a solid, which precipitated out and dropped to the bottom of the glass vessel. Then this solid was moved through the glove box line and washed by alcohol, heated by hot air, and dried and converted to 1.1-pound (500-gram) batches of plutonium peroxide, or "green cake."[6]

Each batch of the green cake was put into a tray and moved by slat conveyor along a glove box line known as the "chem line" to the so-called G furnaces. The green cake was converted to plutonium dioxide and then heated in a stream of gaseous hydrogen fluoride to create plutonium tetra-fluoride, known as "pink cake." The pink cake was conveyed to a furnace and reduced to 10.5-ounce (300-gram) pure plutonium metal "buttons," somewhat smaller in volume than hockey pucks but more than double the weight. Later buttons weighed 500 grams (1.1 pounds) or more. In 1955, after Dow added a second plutonium-processing glove box line, Building 771 could produce 26.4 pounds (twelve kilograms) of pure metal a day, enough for three nuclear bombs. In the building's fabrication wing, small furnaces melted the buttons and the plutonium was cast into bomb parts, which then were precisely pressed, cut, and shaped.[7]

Once machined into their final shape, the plutonium parts were plated with nickel and removed from the glove box system. The nickel plating, which replaced the cadmium used on early atomic bombs, enabled the plutonium components to be handled without glove box containment. After plating, the plutonium parts were sent to Building 991, where workers assembled them and the uranium parts made in other buildings into the bomb cores, or pits. The pits were then shipped by truck to the Pantex plant in Amarillo, Texas, to be joined with conventional explosives and other parts and readied for bomb casings. To guard against unauthorized use of nuclear weapons, pits initially were stored separately from the remainder of the weapon and were to be inserted "in flight" just before the weapon was used. This changed in the late 1950s after designers developed coded locks that prevented a nuclear weapon from being armed without the proper code.[8]

By 1955 the AEC wanted to mass produce the hollow nuclear pit components, consisting of thin plutonium or uranium shells, which weapons designers had been developing and testing for years. These components, referred to in shorthand as "hollow pits," were required for production of thermonuclear "boosted" fission nuclear weapons since a small amount of fusion fuel was injected into the center of the fissile core. This new, hollow design used less uranium and more plutonium and created a more powerful explosion as well as a smaller, lighter fission bomb. The lighter weight was vital since fission bombs were increasingly being used as "primaries" to detonate the "secondaries" containing the H-bomb fusion fuel outside the pit. The United States created the world's first H-bomb and demonstrated its awesome power in the October 31, 1952, "Mike" test in the Pacific Ocean. This explosion equaled 10.4 million tons of TNT and was 500 times more powerful than the bomb that destroyed Nagasaki. Using hollow pits, new H-bomb warheads could be carried by missiles.[9]

The shift to hollow pits would be the most significant nuclear weapons design change ever to affect Rocky Flats. Along with more plutonium, this new design required more machining, more complex assembly procedures, and more extensive safety controls. It meant the Rocky Flats plant had to be expanded. So at the end of 1955, less than two years after full production began, a new construction project commenced. Initially estimated at $13.5 million, its cost would climb to $21 million over the next two years. Altogether it would add ten more buildings to the facility and modify three others. The biggest change was that Building 771's tasks would be divided up. Two new large plutonium production buildings, designated 76 (776) and 77 (777) and connected by a common interior wall, would take over the plutonium machining and manufacturing responsibilities. Building 771 would then essentially be a chemical factory specializing in processing plutonium into metal. It would transfer the plutonium metal to building 776, lying directly to its south, by way of an underground tunnel.[10]

Although Buildings 776 and 777 would be ready to undergo production testing in summer 1957, the AEC wanted hollow bomb pits sooner than that. The agency was under pressure from President Dwight D. Eisenhower and the military. In February 1956 Eisenhower approved a Joint Chiefs of Staff request for increased production of both very high yield thermonuclear weapons and small warheads suitable for air defense. By the fall navy leaders were calling for submarine-launched missiles to carry the lightweight thermonuclear warheads made feasible by hollow plutonium components, which in some designs would be assembled with hollow uranium shells in nesting doll fashion. In addition, growing signs that the Soviet Union was developing long-range missiles, to be demonstrated to the world with the 1957 *Sputnik* satellite launch, motivated the AEC to produce the new components as quickly as possible. Dow's contract with the AEC required the company to begin producing hollow pits in spring 1957, but the construction pace for the new plutonium buildings was behind schedule.[11]

By early 1957, in order to meet existing bomb production quotas, Building 771 already was handling several times more plutonium than its design allowed. This led to severe crowding of machinery and personnel. Accidents were inevitable. The first major one occurred in June, when gases built up in the tank where hydrogen peroxide was being used to precipitate liquid plutonium nitrate into the "green cake" solid. The resulting explosion shattered the glass precipitation vessel and blew the side off the steel containment vessel. Two workers were heavily contaminated with radiation. The next major accident came three months later.[12]

In response to AEC pressure, Dow officials turned Building 771's Room 180, about half the size of a low-ceiling basketball court, into a development laboratory for hollow pits. Workers hurriedly constructed a glove box line in Room 180's northeast section so a "Special Products Group" could machine plutonium into various shapes. Unlike glove boxes formed from solid stainless steel sheets with holes cut in them for glove ports and windows, the glove boxes in this room consisted of stainless steel frames with thick plastic panels used for the walls. Many of the panels were made of transparent Plexiglas, which allowed workers to easily see inside the glove boxes. While this design was used in a few other limited plutonium operations that required visibility, it was usually avoided because the plastic was flammable. The AEC's earlier warning against building up such material in plutonium production areas was ignored in Room 180.[13]

By this time Rocky Flats plant manager Heinie Langell was confident he and his staff could safely handle plutonium. He had more than three years of plutonium production experience under his belt and relatively few accidents had occurred for an industrial plant this size. Besides, as a chemist and chemical factory manager, Langell had handled dangerous, toxic materials before. He had even worked with pyrophoric substances, those materials such as magnesium — and plutonium — that could ignite spontaneously in air.

During World War II, Langell supervised Dow factories that made airplane wheels and other military equipment out of lightweight magnesium. When machining magnesium, "You had to be specially trained in how to handle chips and their dust, and so forth, to avoid fires," Langell said, adding that Dow had experienced serious fires because magnesium in some forms oxidizes immediately with oxygen in the air and ignites. Working with magnesium required "a neat, clean, good housekeeping plant," Langell said, which was the same standard he instituted for working with plutonium at Rocky Flats. The plant also had its own fire department.[14]

Although Langell knew that a safe, efficient plant maximized productivity, calculated trade-offs occasionally were required. For above all, Langell prided himself on achieving the production quotas set by the AEC. If that meant that Building 771 had to temporarily be stretched to its limits until the new plutonium-manufacturing buildings could begin operating, so be it. He and his staff were sure they could handle it.

On the night of September 11, 1957, Room 180 contained 137.5 pounds

(62.5 kilograms) of plutonium, a typical amount for the research and development work under way there. Most of the plutonium was in its metal form. Some plutonium was about to be consumed by fire. And some was about to be vented into the environment through the building's tall smokestack.[15]

Exactly how much plutonium was released is still disputed. The fire's cause is not. A storage box in the middle of the room's glove box system held about twenty-two pounds (ten kilograms) of plutonium in six different containers. One steel can held plutonium "skull," a thin film left over from the mold where the molten metal was cast. Sometime before 10 P.M., the plutonium skull ignited spontaneously. While plutonium burns without visible flame, something like a charcoal briquette, it emits intense heat and brilliant white light. Before long a Plexiglas glove box caught fire.[16]

The Fire

Shortly after 10 P.M. on Wednesday, September 11, plant guards Earl Irvin and Robert Anderson were making a routine tour of Building 771 when they smelled a pungent odor, like burning rubber. They entered Room 180 through its double doors and found it filling with smoke. They saw small flames leaping from burning glove boxes. While Anderson ran to get a carbon dioxide fire extinguisher, Irvin called the Rocky Flats fire department. It was 10:10.[17]

Fire Lieutenant Verle "Lefty" Eminger and two other firemen arrived within minutes in Pumper No. 2. Due to concerns about water causing a plutonium "criticality" chain reaction, Building 771 contained no sprinkler system. While the two firemen unreeled the pumper's hose, Eminger, wearing a thick coat and asbestos gloves, rushed to the hall outside Room 180, where several night managers and employees had gathered. Inside, flames had burned through the glove boxes and were out into the room.

Seeing the extent of the fire, Eminger suggested fighting it with water. But production supervisor Bob Vandegrift and Bruce Owen, the building's night radiation monitor, said no. They worried about how much plutonium was burning and feared a criticality. So Vandegrift donned a bulky, self-contained Chemox breathing apparatus like Eminger already wore and the two men entered the room carrying carbon dioxide extinguishers. The fire was so hot, they could only get within a few feet of the glove boxes. They emptied the extinguishers and returned to the door for a large carbon dioxide cart, which they pulled into the room. The carbon dioxide had no effect.

Flames lapped at the ceiling of the room. As Eminger and Vandegrift unsuccessfully fought the fire, a nearly fateful decision was being made elsewhere.

Building 771's extensive ventilation and filtering systems were designed to prevent plutonium from escaping into work spaces or the outside environment. Exhaust ducts leading to filters on the building's second floor were built into the glove box lines, and separate ducts led from the rooms themselves. While room air went directly through the ducts into the main filter bank, the glove box air went through a two-step filter process. This air, contaminated from the plutonium production process, was first sucked by fans through so-called booster filters, intended to capture most of the plutonium particles. The air was then pulled by four huge exhaust fans through the main filter bank, known as a filter plenum. This bank of filters was like a wall running nearly the entire width of the building's second floor. It was more than 200 feet long and made of a steel frame with square slots where paper filters were inserted. This filter plenum held 620 filters, each of which was two feet wide, two feet tall, and one foot thick. They were called high-efficiency particulate air (HEPA) filters. The exhaust fans sucked the air through the filter bank and vented it through an exhaust tunnel leading to the 152-foot-tall smokestack.[18]

The almost fateful decision was made by Building 771 supervisor Bud Venable, who was telephoned at home by a plant employee at 10:23 P.M. Apprised of the situation and worried that the flames in Room 180 were endangering firefighters, Venable ordered the fans to be run at high speed. At this maximum speed of 200,000 cubic feet per minute, the fans successfully pulled smoke out of Room 180 through the air ducts. But they also pulled the fire into the second-floor filter system. At 10:28 P.M. a worker spotted smoke in the main filter bank. Hot gases began building up.

Meanwhile the fire raged down in Room 180. "At this time, the complete room in [the] right hand corner near [the] lathe was on fire and looked as though the fire was going toward the air ducts in that corner," Lieutenant Eminger later wrote. Since carbon dioxide wasn't working, he again suggested using water. The firemen had already strung a one-and-a-half-inch-diameter fire hose with a fog nozzle along the west hall to the door of Room 180. Radiation monitor Owen still objected to water because of a potential criticality, but Vandegrift decided the nozzles could be aimed at glove boxes ahead of the fire and not into the burning boxes.

Eminger and Vandegrift pulled the hose into the room. Eminger, down on one knee and holding the nozzle control handle in his left hand and the hose in his right, "directed the open fog nozzle to the ceiling of the room 3 or 4 times and the flame was down," he said. The men felt the temperature drop. Seconds later small fires ignited on the floor in the same area. Made more aware of a potential criticality, Eminger adjusted the fog nozzle to produce less spray. Several minutes later flames were no longer visible.

Sure that the fire had spread to the filters on the second floor, Eminger and Vandegrift decided to inspect the filter bank. But just as they reached the doors to leave Room 180, an explosion knocked Vandegrift to the floor and sent Eminger sprawling through the double doors. Other workers in the hallway also were knocked down. Nobody was seriously hurt. Owen ordered everyone to evacuate the building. It was 10:39 P.M.

The explosion occurred on the intake side of the second-floor main filter bank, so some of the contamination was blown back into the building. The explosion was probably caused by the sudden combustion of volatile gases and dust that had accumulated on the filters, which hadn't been changed in four years.[19] The explosion's force twisted the plenum's steel frame, destroyed dozens of filters, and dislodged a lead cap at the top of the smokestack. From that time on, unfiltered contaminated air escaped the building. Luckily, however, the explosion shut down the exhaust fans.

If the fans had continued running at high speed, much more plutonium would have been sucked through the ducts and released into the Denver area. In theory, the fans should have stopped running long before the explosion. Heat-detecting equipment installed in the filter bank was supposed to automatically shut down the exhaust fans in the event of fire. But the sensitive equipment previously had been disrupting normal operations and slowing production, so it had been disabled, according to Dow Chemical's long-secret report on the fire.[20] This wouldn't be the last time in the plant's history that safety would be sacrificed to production, with serious consequences resulting.

Following the 10:40 P.M. explosion, the filter bank was ablaze. A complete electrical power outage in the building occurred at 11:10. Except for the flames, the second floor was immersed in smoke and blackness. For the next three hours firefighters pumped some 30,000 gallons of water onto the plenum. They "knocked down" the fire at about 2 A.M., meaning flames were no longer visible, but they didn't fully extinguish it for a few more hours. On the building's first floor, workers placed emergency battery-powered lights in the hallways and rooms. Several small fires had reignited in Room 180, which was periodically checked by the firefighters, including guards and other employees who had been phoned and ordered to report to the plant. The fire was declared officially out at 11:28 A.M. on Thursday.

Radiation Contamination

The only thing normal about plutonium fires was the way flammable objects such as plastic, rubber gloves, and paper air filters burned. The plutonium metal itself didn't give off flames, but burned so intensely it could melt steel. Moist air could cause the plutonium to reignite. And the fine plutonium oxide "ash" particles, which were extremely toxic if inhaled, could contaminate clothing or skin. So the firefighters not only needed protective clothing and self-contained breathing equipment; they needed to be carefully checked for radiation afterward.

The plant's radiation staff set up a decontamination site in Building 774, the nearby waste-processing facility that had a shower and health-monitoring station. Employees relieved of firefighting duties showered and were checked for skin radiation. If positive, they had to scrub again. "For some reason, the most highly contaminated spot I had was my left ear," recalled plant guard William Dennison, who helped fight the fire. "Before it finally came clean, I thought I was going to scrub my ear clear off."[21]

The firefighters also were given nose and throat swabs to check for internal poisoning. If the swabs came up positive, the employees were given pint-sized urine bottles to bring samples back for testing. Of many dozens of workers tested, positive indications of plutonium were found in eighty-eight nose and throat swabs. Over the next few days plutonium showed up in three fecal samples, two blood samples, and one urinalysis. Still Dow Chemical's medical director at the plant concluded, "For all practical purposes, the plutonium contamination resulting from the fire is negligible."[22]

Determining worker contamination was infinitely easier than trying to figure out the amount of radioactive material dispersed from the plant site. One problem was that the smokestack radiation monitors stopped functioning after the filter plenum explosion Wednesday night and didn't become operational until a week later.[23] Another problem involved estimating the amount of plutonium that had accumulated in the ducts and on the filters due to routine operations and was then released during the fire. Most important was to determine how much of the 137.5 pounds (62.5 kilograms) of plutonium in Room 180 went up the smokestack.

Dow Chemical Company's official investigation report, completed in October 1957 but classified "Secret" by the government until 1993, stated that 18.3 pounds (8.3 kilograms) of plutonium were unaccounted for after the fire. However, "this is not an estimate of the amount released," said health physicist Paul Voillequé. He and other scientists who have studied the fire agree that the bulk of the material unaccounted for (MUF) ended up in the waste from the Room 180 cleanup and simply wasn't measured. Based on Voillequé's reconstruction of the fire scene and calculations, he estimated that the plutonium release ranged from 1.8 ounces to 1.1 pounds (fifty to five hundred grams). The high end exceeded that in several earlier studies but was much lower than the estimate used in the lawsuit rancher Marcus Church filed against the government and plant operators in 1975.[24] Even a small amount such as 1.8 ounces (fifty grams) of plutonium was hazardous if dispersed in microscopic quantities over a populated area and inhaled by people. For example, the safety exposure limit for a Rocky Flats worker at the time was just 500 billionths, or .0000005, of one gram of plutonium.[25]

Some Denver area citizens who closely followed Rocky Flats in the 1990s remained skeptical of the low plutonium release figures. At their urging, the Colorado Health Advisory Panel continued to oversee soil sampling studies until the late 1990s. To date, none has found evidence of high plutonium releases.

Fire Cleanup

Jim Kelly was awakened by a phone call about four hours after the fire was discovered and ordered to report to work. Arriving at the plant around 3 A.M. Thursday morning, he parked outside the security fence, punched in at the time clock, and boarded the employee bus for Building 771.

"Halfway down the hill is where I ran into the real world. The people already there had established a clothes-changing area—half a mile away from the building," Kelly recalled. "I changed clothes and went down to the building." When he got close enough to see the smokestack, which was illuminated by a spotlight, a fellow worker noticed Kelly's wide-eyed look. "You're a new guy—what do you see different, Jimmy?" Norm Messoni asked. Kelly said he didn't know. "Had it ever dawned on you that there ain't supposed to be smoke coming out of stacks at Rocky Flats?" Messoni asked.[26]

Cleanup crews, covered from head to foot and wearing respirators, already had begun moving through the building's first floor to get preliminary readings on the extent of contamination. Smoke and air drafts had spread plutonium particles throughout the building. As a radiation monitor, Kelly carried a "peewee" detector, consisting of a headset, a heavy battery-powered instrument, and a cable for the handheld probe. Decontamination formally began on Friday, September 13, two days after the fire ignited. Workers literally inched their way through the building, using absorbent chemical solutions, scrapers, and scrubbers to clean everything from floor to ceiling. They placed contaminated material in plastic bags and removed the bags from the building. The cleanup crew started with the offices, locker rooms, and other areas on the normally nonradioactive side of the building and then moved to the "hot" production side. Room 180 was sealed off for the time being.[27]

The Building 771 workers pitched into the cleanup with an energy boosted by the fear that their jobs were at stake. The word was out that top AEC and Dow officials thought the building was too contaminated and might have to be abandoned. But Dow's building superintendent Venable wasn't going to let that happen. "Bud Venable was the only man in captivity who believed you could clean it up," said Kelly, who came to know his boss very well. "771 was his baby. He wasn't about to throw in the towel. Venable figured that if 771 was done away with, eventually Rocky Flats would dissipate, that they would build a new 771 building and it wouldn't be built here."

Venable wasn't known as the Building 771 "czar" for nothing. Plant manager Langell had brought him to Rocky Flats from Los Alamos because of his glove box expertise. Venable, a chemist, had made the plutonium operation happen. He also was the man who had made the nearly fatal decision during the fire to run the exhaust fans at high speed, hastening the fire's spread to the main filter bank. He wanted to rectify the mistake.

A rugged man who wasn't slowed down by the wooden leg he walked on due to a childhood injury, Venable threw himself into the Building 771 cleanup. He inspired the workers. "He was back there on a ladder scrubbing pipes like the rest of us," said Kelly, whose task was to monitor the radiation. "We'd get back to the locker room and I'd hear him scream, 'Kelly, get your ass over here and give me an OK on my stick,' and I'd go monitor his wooden leg for him."[28]

The combined efforts of Venable and the plutonium workers paid off. Dow's October 7 fire investigation report estimated that plutonium processing could recommence in Building 771 by December 1, 1957. Investigators initially estimated the loss in equipment and material plus the cost of cleanup as $392,000. That figure would escalate to $818,000 after other losses were calculated, including $120,000 for nuclear material and $40,000 for filter replacement. Because Room 180 was being used for research and development when the fire occurred, it was not considered essential for production and would be cleaned up later. Indeed, it wouldn't be fully decontaminated until April 1960.[29]

The 1957 fire had major consequences, but not the kinds that might have been expected. On one level, just as the firefighters had successfully contained the fire, the AEC and Dow Chemical contained outside scrutiny of their operations at Rocky Flats. The AEC's Washington, D.C., headquarters issued a brief, two-page AEC "serious accident" report in November 1957. The report, which didn't name Rocky Flats, quickly summarized the fire facts but did conclude with a hint of deeper problems. "When these facts are viewed in retrospect, it appears (by hindsight) irrational that facilities were ever designed in such a manner as to permit hazards from a relatively insignificant amount of material [plutonium] to so strongly influence the chain of events which led to a major loss."[30] The deeper implications of this rare, if qualified, AEC admission were ignored, although Dow took a few corrective actions at the plant. Some of the shocking details about dangerous production practices at Rocky Flats, such as glove boxes made entirely of Plexiglas and equipment overcrowding, were contained in Dow's secret seventy-eight-page fire investigation report. But the public body with access to this report, the congressional Joint Committee on Atomic Energy (JCAE), was more concerned about nuclear weapons production than about broad public safety and health issues. And the intense push for new hollow pit plutonium bombs, which contributed to the conditions leading up to the Building 771 fire, also enabled the AEC and Dow to continue weapons production at Rocky Flats. When the fire occurred, the two new plutonium-manufacturing and assembly buildings — 776 and 777 — had just gone into operation. A backlog of plutonium metal from Building 771 meant that bomb production in the new buildings didn't miss a beat.

On another level, the 1957 fire raised safety awareness among Rocky Flats workers and caused both divisions and solidarity among them. "The '57 fire was the first experience about what happens if plutonium burns. How widespread it can be. How vicious it can be," said Jim Kelly. He noted that until the fire, the plant workers in the uranium production buildings knew nothing about "material C," the code name for plutonium. "I can only imagine how the people in [Buildings] 44 and 81 were visualizing the incident." Those other workers referred to Building 771 as a "hellhole" and worse, Kelly said. "771 became a very evil monster to the rest of the plant. And that enhanced the camaraderie of the people in 771. The people in 771 became a community in itself because it was under attack from everybody." Everybody except the media and general public, that is. The fire was a classic case where those who knew didn't tell, and those who didn't know didn't bother to ask.

Business as Usual

The local newspapers didn't completely ignore the September 11 fire. The day afterward, on Thursday, the afternoon *Denver Post* carried a front-page story under the headline, "Atomic Fire Causes $50,000 Loss." The story quoted a plant spokesman as attributing the fire to "spontaneous combustion" in a processing line. "The AEC spokesman declined to describe further the 'processing line,'" the unbylined story continued. "He said radioactive materials were located in the building, but would not describe their relationship to the fire." The *Rocky Mountain News* carried a brief account of the fire on page forty-six of its Friday morning edition.

Neither paper carried a follow-up in their hefty Sunday editions, even though any journalist curious about "spontaneous combustion" and radioactive materials could have easily looked in the newspapers' clippings files and found references to plutonium and uranium. But the journalists, the paid "watchdogs" of democracy, had been muted by the aura of national security surrounding the plant. And the public, caught up in a Cold War panic that accelerated three weeks after the fire when the Soviet Union launched its *Sputnik* satellite on October 4, didn't press for answers about the fire.

The *Boulder Daily Camera* didn't even deem the fire worthy of mention four months later when it ran an upbeat story about the facility. "Completion of a $21,000,000 expansion marked 1957 at the Rocky Flats atomic plant eight miles south of Boulder," began the story, obviously based on an AEC Rocky Flats' press release. The article included assurances from the plant's AEC spokesman that "there have been no personal casualties or community effects resulting from the use of radioactive materials. As was announced in June 1957, two Dow workers were injured as a result of an explosion in the plant. Both of these employees continue to work at Rocky Flats plant." The story contained no reference to the fire. But the article gave the AEC spokesman the final word. "For Rocky Flats plant," the spokesman said, "1957, and for that matter, 1958, could be characterized as 'business as usual.'"[31]

Business as usual for the AEC meant nuclear weapons production was untouchable. Agency officials had learned they could employ claims of "national security" to conceal mishaps. Insulated by secrecy, the AEC was unaccountable to the general public. The main body that should have represented the public, Congress, had delegated its broad responsibilities to its atomic energy committee, the JCAE. And the JCAE had historically collaborated in the AEC and military quest for more nuclear weapons and all of the expensive planes, artillery, and other equipment needed to deliver them, particularly when the politicians' home states and districts shared in the contracts.[32]

Business as usual for the Denver community after the 1957 fire meant enjoying the benefits of an ever-growing Rocky Flats plant — valued as a $65 million facility after the expansion — with 1,575 employees. A *Denver Post* article in January 1958 lauded the plant as "one of the biggest investments in Colorado. The annual payroll is $9.5 million and another $4 million is spent locally each year for goods and services." And Denver, which had come to be known as "little Washington" due to all its federal offices and employees, was booming. Newspapers and broadcasters were community boosters. Growth fattened their profits along with the rest of the business community.[33]

The Denver metropolitan area's population, which totaled 563,000 in 1950, was climbing rapidly and would reach 916,000 by the next census in 1960. The oil industry, including exploration, service, and production companies, had started establishing offices in the city. The city's skyline crept upward. In 1958 the twenty-eight-story First National Building joined the Denver Club Building and Mile High Center high-rises. More and taller skyscrapers as well as suburban shopping malls were on the way. Historians Thomas Noel and Stephen Leonard describe Denver's metropolitan area as growing like bunches of grapes. And one of the big bunches was Jefferson County, whose northwest corner contained Rocky Flats.[34]

Marcus Church liked the growth and considered his family's future prosperity tied to land development. In 1955 he was appointed to the board of directors for Industries for Jefferson County, the same group his nephew Charlie McKay would be active with years later. The organization's goal was to promote business and increase the tax base. The board met Tuesday mornings. "We met frequently at the Jefferson County Planning Office and this was my introduction to the planning field and it gave me an opportunity to visualize potential development," Church recalled. "This in turn caused me to analyze the basic requirements for the Church lands if they were to be made merchantable as a potential development area."[35] Church had already leased some of his remaining Rocky Flats land to sand, gravel, and clay companies. He was talking with other board members about developing a small airport east of Rocky Flats. And he continued to raise cattle and plant crops. In the fall of 1957, after the fire at the plant, Church planted winter wheat on land he leased nearby. The following year he harvested thirty-five bushels per acre.[36]

Neither Church nor his neighbors knew that Rocky Flats officials had found plutonium from the 1957 fire outside the plant's boundaries. A 1970 AEC report conceded, "Environmental sampling following this fire showed detectable amounts of plutonium on vegetation collected off-site out to a distance of 8½ miles."[37] But this AEC admission came only after another huge plant fire forced the agency to respond to public concern. By then Rocky Flats had produced thousands more nuclear weapons, had pumped hundreds of millions more dollars into the community, and had created many more environmental and health problems.

SEVEN

Arms Race and Waste

Mayor of Rocky Flats

Marcus Church knew little about the 1957 fire at Rocky Flats but figured he would have heard if anything really bad had happened. So he made the plant an industrial backdrop for his fledgling commercial land development efforts from the late 1950s through the 1960s. In one brochure, pitching his "Rocky Flats Industrial District," Church wrote enthusiastically, "Dow Chemical has a major plant within the area employing several thousand people."[1] He sought to improve transportation to the area in order to make it more attractive to companies looking for plant sites. An early victory came when he and other local entrepreneurs, including the Coors Brewing Company family in nearby Golden, convinced Jefferson County to build a small airport just east of Rocky Flats. The August 1, 1959, groundbreaking was special for Church on two counts — the event itself and the presence of his favorite nephew, Charlie McKay.[2]

Church, about to turn 60, was beginning to think about posterity. He and his wife, Anne, didn't have children. But they were the aunt and uncle of his sister Ruth McKay's two sons, Charlie and Perry, who were growing up in the Chicago suburb of Evanston. Charlie, born on June 1, 1940, particularly enjoyed spending summers in Colorado, riding horses and tractors and doing chores for his uncle. "My uncle Mark was not anybody to mess with," McKay recalled admiringly. "He was tougher than nails. I remember riding with him in his brand-new white Mercury Marquis and he wanted to get to the other side of some plowed ground to run off trespassers, so we went shooting across there." McKay, who as a kid was tall and skinny and wrestled in the 103-pound weight class in high school, idolized Marcus Church. He would carry on his uncle's ranching and development operations after Church died in 1979.[3]

In the summer of 1959, just before entering the University of Arkansas, McKay hitchhiked to Colorado in time for the airport groundbreaking. "It was a hot, windy, dusty day," McKay remembered. "Half the people left, and Joe Coors had an old Ford station wagon with a cooler full of pony [beer] cans. He passed one to me and I thought I was really a high roller, standing there."

While McKay went on to school and then into the construction business in the Midwest, Church put his energy into developing the family land around Rocky Flats. He hired an engineering company to do detailed site planning and applied to the county for commercial and industrial zoning for part of his land. He was encouraged when a division of the Ideal Cement Company built a plant off Highway 93 northwest of the Rocky Flats facility. Church organized a business meeting and tour of this new cement plant in May 1961. Afterward he wrote his sister, Ruth, that the invitation to the meeting "was signed by Marcus F. Church, Mayor of Rocky Flats, President, Rocky Flats Development Corp., and Chairman of Board of Rocky Flats Chamber of Commerce. A one-man operation up to now, so [I] invited three other land owners," he wrote.[4] Typing out letters on an old Underwood, Church kept in touch with his sister more frequently after their mother, Katherine, died in October 1960, leaving them her 3,100 acres of land and other property. The total would have been 4,300 acres if the government hadn't taken one-fourth of the family's land for Rocky Flats. Soon the government would demand more land.

In the early 1960s Church converted the garage of his ranch-style brick home on Wadsworth Boulevard into an office. He put in an acoustic tile ceiling, a linoleum floor, and butternut paneling on three walls. He lined the fourth wall with cork to hang a large aerial map of the area, showing railroad tracks, power lines, gas lines, highways, potential highways, and mining sites. Yet Church was still having little luck attracting commercial land buyers, mainly because highway construction and a water project were moving slowly. "Sometimes I think eternity is not near long enough to get some of these projects on the road," he wrote his sister in May 1963. "Of course the real problem is that there is plenty of land everywhere and the Church land is really still too far out [from Denver]." At this juncture, Church didn't regard the AEC's Rocky Flats plant as retarding development, but as benefiting it. He hoped this large operation would be a magnet for other companies, as AEC officials told him it would.[5]

He wasn't alone in viewing the plant as just another big business. The newspaper in Boulder, where about a third of the plant's nearly 2,000 workers lived, covered the plant as if it were any ordinary, prominent company. The paper regularly carried articles about employee bowling leagues and the annual December "Snowflake Serenade" dances in the Glenn Miller Ballroom on the University of Colorado campus. "Snowflake Serenade to Be Held in Memorial Center," read a typical headline, this one on December 9, 1957. "More Than 1,200 Dow Employees and Spouses Expected to Attend."

The Front Lines

No swing bands played inside the Rocky Flats fences. A wartime atmosphere prevailed. The plant lay on the front lines of the Cold War, which was intensifying due to national and international politics. The harsh Soviet repression of the 1956 uprising in Hungary confirmed the communist regime's brutality. The following year, a month after the Soviet Union's October 1957 *Sputnik* launch, a U.S. blue-ribbon committee's report was leaked to the press. Titled "Deterrence and Survival in the Nuclear Age," the report suggested the United States was falling behind the Soviets in nuclear capacity and stated the evidence "clearly indicates an increasing threat which may become critical in 1959 or early 1960." The committee, dominated by corporate executives and known as the Gaither Committee after its chairman, Rowan Gaither, urged the government to spend $25 billion to build bomb shelters around the country and budget an additional $19 billion for nuclear weapons.[6]

President Eisenhower, who had appointed the committee, knew the report's assessment was inaccurate. But secrecy constrained him from releasing U.S. intelligence information showing the Soviets were in bad military and economic shape. Consequently Eisenhower, a Republican and decorated army general, was badgered for higher military expenditures by the "military–industrial complex," as he would label this consortium of powerful interests in his 1961 presidential farewell speech. Taking advantage of the Gaither Committee report, the Democrats accused the Eisenhower administration of fostering a "missile gap" — which didn't exist. "In a way [the charge] was not without its own justice: The Republicans had won in the past in no small part because they had blamed the Democrats for losing countries to Communism; in the early part of the Cold War, the Republicans had exaggerated the natural anxieties of the Cold War," David Halberstam wrote in his comprehensive account of the 1950s. "The result was that not only had the Democrats vowed never to be accused of being soft on Communism again, they were determined to find an issue that showed that they were, if anything, even more vigilant and tougher."[7] The purported missile gap helped Democrat John F. Kennedy take the White House in 1960.

Most Americans, including the managers and employees at Rocky Flats, accepted the notion that the United States had to win the nuclear arms race in order to defeat communism. The risky logic of deterrence — that massive arsenals of nuclear weapons had to be built to deter the other side from using them — went virtually unchallenged. A few groups, such as the annual Pugwash Conferences founded by U.S. and Soviet scientists in 1957, advocated alternatives to a balance of nuclear terror between the two "superpowers." They received little media or public attention. The prospect that deterrence might fail, resulting in global nuclear war, was ignored by the public, which didn't realize how close the world would come to that catastrophe during the 1962 Cuban missile crisis. "Better Dead Than Red" was the morbid motto of the day.

Despite the unifying Cold War mission at Rocky Flats, the relationship between workers and management mirrored that in other industries. The two sides regularly disagreed over wages, benefits, and working conditions in their contract negotiations. After the 1957 fire, workers began demanding more company attention to health and safety problems. "I think everybody's sensitivity to safety was magnified 100 times after the '57 fire," said Jim Kelly, who still worked in Building 771 and had become active in union affairs. "The rest of the plant, by the very nature of it being in the same place, became aware of the nature of the work."[8]

Penetrating Radiation

The Building 771 fire was the most dramatic event arousing worker concern about radiation, but not the only one. The fire coincided with the production changeover to new nuclear weapons cores, or pits, which weapons scientists began modifying almost as frequently as Detroit automakers changed models. Based on hollow plutonium shells, the new pit design forced Rocky Flats production managers to focus for the first time on penetrating radiation such as beta particles, x rays, gamma rays, and, eventually, on neutrons.

Scientists had long known that plutonium 239, the isotope constituting

93.8 percent of typical weapon-grade plutonium in a nuclear fission bomb, emitted some penetrating radiation as well as nonpenetrating alpha parti-cles. Another isotope, plutonium 240, which contributed 5.8 percent of the metal's mass, primarily emitted neutrons. But plutonium 241, although it made up less than half of 1 percent of weapon-grade plutonium, had a short half-life of just 14.4 years and thus was much more radioactive. Moreover, it emitted beta particles, one form of penetrating radiation.[9]

Dow and AEC officials didn't worry about penetrating radiation when Rocky Flats was built. The mass of the solid plutonium spheres, used in the pits of the nuclear arsenal's implosion bombs from 1945 until the design change in the mid-1950s, absorbed most of this radiation. In addition, in 1951 the AEC's safety standard for external radiation exposure was fifteen rem per year. "Based on these exposure guides and design factors, no radia-tion shielding was included in the Rocky Flats facility," according to a secret 1968 plant radiation study.[10] The glove box, ventilation, and filtering systems were designed primarily to contain plutonium 239's alpha emis-sions, which were dangerous if particles were inhaled or entered the body through a cut.

The switch to hollow plutonium shells increased the manufactured met-al's surface area, so its mass absorbed less penetrating radiation. In addition, the new design required larger quantities of plutonium. "This change in weapon design resulted in higher x-[ray] and gamma dose rates, which was noted primarily by a significant increase in hand exposure" to employees working through the glove boxes, the 1968 study noted. Managers sought better lead-impregnated gloves as the foundry, fabrication, and assembly operations began going online in Buildings 776 and 777 in summer 1957, shortly before the 771 fire.[11]

A significant impact on worker safety from the design change came from the undesirable isotope plutonium 241 and its decay products. Plutonium-241 atoms emit radiation as they seek stability and create the radioactive "daughters" uranium 237 and americium 241. The americium is particu-larly radioactive, and its gamma-ray emissions made the plutonium dan-gerous to handle. Americium not only built up in the plutonium that Rocky Flats processed and stored while awaiting fabrication; it also was present in the plutonium weapons returned to the plant for reprocessing and fabrica-tion into new bombs.

Building 771 began operating a special chemical-processing area in 1957 to extract americium from weapon-grade plutonium. But largely because of pits returned from the weapons stockpile, sixty plant workers were exposed to more than 3 rem of penetrating radiation in 1958, compared with just six workers in 1957. Plant officials recognized "the urgent need for additional radiation shielding to be installed in the chemistry operations," the plant radiation study noted. Thin lead plates welded onto glove boxes and extra-heavy one-eighth-inch leaded gloves on the americium line helped reduce the gamma radiation exposures.[12]

Worker Safety

Rocky Flats production workers didn't think enough was being done to ensure radiation safety, although in 1958 the Atomic Energy Commission (AEC) tightened its exposure guideline to no more than 5 rem annual accumulated dose, a third of the previous guideline.[13] The several hundred employees represented by Local 543 of the Chemical Workers union insisted that radiation hazards had not been adequately addressed. But their concerns weren't shared by the Denver Metal Trades Council, which, under AEC rules allowing just one umbrella labor organization to negotiate for workers at its plants, represented the Rocky Flats rank-and-file employees at the bargaining table.

Most of the council's executives didn't even work at the plant. And they pursued a cautious "don't rock the boat" approach in bargaining with Dow, according to one outside labor leader.[14] The Rocky Flats production workers, led by Jim Kelly's older brother, Pat, sought a stronger union. They turned to District 50 of the United Mine Workers of America, which was experienced with occupational diseases such as "black lung" among coal miners. This union began a campaign to represent the Rocky Flats workers and, after several votes by the affected workforce, would finally succeed in 1964.

Meanwhile Pat Kelly and other Chemical Workers union leaders had found different venues to raise safety concerns. They asked the statewide Colorado Labor Council in fall 1958 to pass a resolution urging stronger occupational disability and workers' compensation provisions at Rocky Flats. The resolution, which the council adopted, criticized the AEC for occupying "a unique niche in relation to having the authority to say 'union or no union in our plants.' It [the AEC] also seemed to have the clout to declare itself as immune from either federal or state compensation and occupational disease statutes."[15]

In early 1959 production workers at Rocky Flats joined the Oil, Chemical, and Atomic Workers and other unions from around the country in appealing to Democrat leaders in Congress to scrutinize radiation safety.

Some scientists and members of Congress were already criticizing the AEC for radioactive fallout from its atmospheric nuclear bomb tests. Pat Kelly and other leaders of Local 543 prepared a report arguing that workers at Rocky Flats and other nuclear facilities were subjected to radiation hazards whose long-term effects were not recognized by contemporary workers' compensation laws.

"Those who are familiar with [the] irradiation industry realize that the effects of radiation are insidious, accumulative, and hazardous, and that they may not become apparent for as long as fifty years from the original date of exposure," Kelly told a Joint Committee on Atomic Energy (JCAE) subcommittee hearing in March 1959. He said, diplomatically, that government-supervised nuclear operations "generally have been accompanied by utmost concern for the safety of employees" and gave the appearance of a good safety record. "But it is this very fact that the laudable record which harbors danger may lump into an unwarranted sense of security."[16]

Pat Kelly's testimony generated much stronger reaction at Rocky Flats than in Congress, which never passed adequate legislation covering nuclear workers. Plant manager Heinie Langell was furious at Kelly. "I no sooner got back and Langell calls me in. 'I'm going to fire you and your brother, Jim,'" Kelly recalled him threatening. "This could be intimidating, but I knew I had some rights. I wasn't going to bow to that kind of pressure. So I said, 'Go ahead, and I'll be waiting on the doorstep of the NLRB [National Labor Relations Board] tomorrow morning.'" Nothing happened.

"Heinie was a very capable, intelligent, basically fair person," Kelly said. "But he was nurtured under the Dow philosophy that the company is always right. They didn't want to be infringed upon in any way or told how to do anything. He was a Dow man all the way. Dow could do no wrong."[17]

For his part, Langell was proud of the plant's safety record. He presided at the plant's annual safety awards banquets recognizing outstanding workers, personally examined accident reports, and received a safety plaque from Colorado governor Steve McNichols for the plant's self-proclaimed record. While Langell disagreed with the Kelly brothers over radiation safety and other issues, he admired their dedication to worker rights. "I respect them and I believe they respect me," Langell once commented. He regarded the workers as part of the Rocky Flats family and believed they should be treated decently.[18]

But the worker "family" at the plant also had elements of a secret club. At least one of its initiation rituals flaunted the same radiation dangers its union leaders were publicly condemning. Twenty-one-year-old Jack Weaver got a taste of this in early 1962. Weaver was a tall, gangly young man raised in the farming community of Berthoud, about thirty miles north of Rocky Flats. After graduating from high school, he farmed with his father and did other work for a couple of years before taking a job as a laborer at the plant in September 1961. A few months later he successfully bid for a chemical operator opening in Building 771, the plutonium-processing facility.

In one part of Building 771 tanks holding plutonium solutions were kept in a room with stainless steel walls and a row of glove box windows. The room was so contaminated that workers who entered it had to put on extra protective clothing. One day a coworker said he would show Weaver how to take a sample from the tank. After watching through a window, Weaver thought it would be no problem. So he suited up, went into the room, and opened the tank's tap. The bottle began slowly filling.

"I hear this rap on the window and every window on the side of this room was filled with faces," Weaver said. "They're all pressed up against there and I think, 'They're here to watch this rookie do his thing,' and I figure, 'This ain't too tough.'" When the bottle was about three-fourths full, Weaver shut the valve. And just as he went to put the cap on the bottle, "Somebody hits the wall of this stainless steel room with a sledgehammer." He jerked, splashing the contaminated liquid all over himself. His next stop was the decontamination room. "But I was one of the lucky ones . . . because I never had to go to medical," Weaver said. "All I had to do was get scrubbed down in the building and go back to work. Some guys went to medical and had to get their chest shaved. That was the initiation in that building. It wasn't fun, wasn't pretty, and I never participated in that kind of thing."[19]

Weaver did, however, participate in the workers' struggle with Dow management. After Langell retired in the early 1960s, this conflict intensified, despite an effort by his successor to improve supervisor sensitivity to employee concerns. Managers were sent to Dow Chemical sessions they dubbed "Charm School."[20] But in August 1962 the plant's 1,500 production employees went on strike after negotiators couldn't agree on working conditions and wages in a new labor contract with Dow. The strike, which lasted twenty-eight days, would be the first of two resulting from stalled contract negotiations during the 1960s. Such labor-management disputes helped set the stage for Dow's eventual exit from Rocky Flats.

Strikes and company press releases provided the main fare for the media's plant coverage. A front-page *Denver Post* headline on April 10, 1963, read: "Good News, Rocky Flats to Expand Facilities." The paper reported that the plant would soon begin another $4.36 million in construction projects and would expand its workforce from 2,822 employees to 3,300 during the next year and a half. The story put the plant's annual payroll at $18 million and said the facility spent about $8 million yearly "in the Denver-Boulder area for equipment and supplies." The same figures were reported in similar stories in the *Rocky Mountain News* and the *Boulder Daily Camera.*

The numbers were provided on Tuesday, April 9, during a media breakfast and plant tour, the first time Dow invited journalists into the plant since the October 1951 tour a dozen years earlier. "Tuesday's limited press tour, a visit to the Health Physics Facility, Building 23, was not an 'open house,'" *Post* reporter Gene Lindberg wrote. He noted that health physics involved radiation protection and described a new "body counter" the plant had developed. "No veils were lifted as to what, exactly, goes on in the way of nuclear weapons production."[21]

Faith and Denial

While the media willingly left the Rocky Flats secrecy veils in place—in terms of products, health and safety hazards, and waste—Jim Kelly and his coworkers knew exactly what they were producing. They understood the devastating nature of nuclear bombs. Some of the workers had served in army units forced to witness bomb tests in Nevada at close range. Others had been in the navy and were among the thousands of servicemen ordered to participate in the nuclear bomb tests in the Pacific. One of Kelly's friends watched an H-bomb test at Bikini Island in 1954. "Just sitting around and talking to Norm about all of that was very scary. Very scary to have somebody that watched one, not just read about it in the paper," said Kelly. "To have a guy telling you what it was like, how unimaginable one of those things was, made you go home and not even talk to your family about it."[22]

The prospect of nuclear war seemed nearer when tensions between the United States and Soviet Union heightened after John F. Kennedy took office in 1961. The abortive U.S.-backed Bay of Pigs invasion of Cuba in April was followed a few months later by a confrontation between Kennedy and Soviet premier Nikita Khrushchev in Vienna. By year's end, Kennedy had revived the civil defense program. Nuclear bomb shelters, with their distinctive yellow-and-black radiation symbols, began popping up around the country.

"My kids were very small when every day you read in the paper about did you have your bomb shelter, your hole in the yard, put your food away?" said Kelly, who was married and eventually had four children. "Those of us who had families sat around at break out there talking about these little radiation detectors that people were selling to put in bomb shelters," he recalled. "Everybody was bringing in plans out of this book or that book about how to build a bomb shelter, how to build one if you had a basement, how to build one if you didn't have a basement. What kind of equipment you needed for survival of your family. It was something very real."

Kelly bought a small radiation detector, and he and his wife stocked canned food in the basement of their home in Arvada, a suburb just east of Rocky Flats. "We knew full well it was not something that would qualify as a bomb shelter, but they had also said things like a basement was better than no basement. If you had a house with a basement, you were a step ahead of a house with no basement. So everybody was talking about doing what they could do. None of us had any money. None of us who ever sat around like that had a dime to spend on anything we would have to go buy, so it was a matter of what we could do with what we had or what we could make ourselves," he said.

"I think the attitude of most [Rocky Flats] workers back then was that there would be a nuclear war sometime. I know that went through my mind," said Kelly. "I always looked at nuclear weapons that not only can you make them, but you can have them used on you. That was the terrible worry to me as my kids were growing up."

Despite this agonizing worry and his awareness of the destructive power of nuclear weapons, Kelly reconciled himself to his own bomb-building work in several ways. First, as a soldier in the Cold War, he had complete faith in his commander in chief — the president of the United States — a faith that became unassailable after Kennedy was elected. Kelly admired Kennedy, an Irish Catholic like himself and a friend of organized labor, and threw himself into the 1960 presidential campaign. "I believed so much in John F. Kennedy that I knew, and nobody could change my mind, that John F. Kennedy would never see a nuclear war that he hadn't put every fiber in him trying to stop," said Kelly, who named his second son after Kennedy.

The Cuban missile crisis in October 1962 put Kelly's faith to a test. He and some coworkers followed the developments on a transistor radio at work, and he discussed the dangerous situation with his wife. "Her family tended to be anti-Kennedy. They are from Nebraska. I tried to convey to my wife that no way would there ever be a nuclear exchange that John Kennedy hadn't done everything within his power to stop," Kelly said. "We kind of lived through that period that way. We were praying for John Kennedy as much as we were praying for anything else."

Kelly, like other members of the American public, had no idea at the time just how close the world came to nuclear war. In retrospect, the touch-and-go nature of the crisis has been emphasized by many historians, including two who edited tape recordings of the deliberations among Kennedy and his closest advisers in October 1962. The historians commented in 1997 on Soviet leader Nikita Khrushchev's decision to abandon his original goals and withdraw the missiles. "What would have happened, had Khrushchev not made this bitter choice, is awful to contemplate."[23]

Aside from Kelly's faith that President Kennedy would do everything possible to prevent nuclear war, he knew that he wouldn't personally be responsible for starting one. "I always hid behind the fact that I was not the guy who would make that decision. Somebody out there had to be pulling the trigger, but that would never be me," Kelly explained. "In my mind, I always told myself that would never be me."

Finally Kelly tried to convince himself that he and his coworkers weren't really making full-fledged nuclear bombs. "It was always some comfort, as morbid as it might seem, that that bomb as it left the plant — that 'unit' as they called it — couldn't go off," he said. Kelly was referring to the fact that the high explosives used to trigger the plutonium chain reaction were added at the Pantex plant in Texas. "I think every one of us liked to go home with the feeling that what we were doing wasn't hurting anybody." Later, in the mid-1970s, anti-nuclear protestors would cause him to rethink this.

Bomb Waste

Kelly and his fellow Cold War foot soldiers were efficient in producing nuclear weapons at Rocky Flats. And the U.S. Atomic Energy Commission and Dow Chemical measured the plant's success in numbers of weapons. Their relentless push for higher production levels, which contributed to the September 1957 fire, continued. Indeed, the Dow managers at Rocky Flats were eager to prove to the AEC that the fire hadn't seriously affected plant operations, despite the new challenges involved in making the hollow, thin-shelled plutonium and uranium components for the bomb pits. They even rushed a new production facility for uranium parts into operation before its roof was completed.[24]

While the hollow pits required less uranium, they needed more plutonium and many more components than the previous solid fissile core design. And because the components needed considerably more machining, rolling, forming, and turning, large quantities of lubricating oil were required to operate the uranium fabrication equipment and the machines in

Building 776, the new plutonium foundry and manufacturing facility. The equipment and bomb components also had to be washed with a toxic degreasing chemical called carbon tetrachloride, or "carbon tet." Thus production of the new bombs geometrically increased the plant's contaminated waste.

Radioactive waste and other waste were always the plant's unwanted byproducts. Rocky Flats shipped as much as it could by train to the AEC's disposal site in Idaho. For instance, in 1954, the first year of full production, the plant sent 200 barrels of plutonium-contaminated waste per month to Idaho from Building 771 and the 774 waste-packaging facility. The number increased to 300 monthly by 1956, and the next year 400 barrels a month left the plant. The amount of plutonium contained in these waste barrels was not carefully measured, a fact later blamed for the large amount of material unaccounted for (MUF) at the site.[25]

Almost from the beginning, Rocky Flats created more radioactive, toxic, and mixed waste than it could ship off-site. Burial was the most expedient way to dispose of this excess waste. Combustibles, including work clothes and contaminated oil, were first burned in incinerators and open pits and the ash buried. Neighbors occasionally saw the smoke, but didn't think anything of it. Noncombustibles were usually put into steel drums before burial, although some liquids were simply poured onto the ground.[26]

Over the years plant managers used a total of 178 waste sites within the plant's boundaries. Among the major sites was the hillside behind uranium building 881 on the plant's south side, where officials supervised the dumping of everything from uranium-contaminated drums to volatile organic chemicals and sludge, which eventually seeped into the groundwater. On the east side the plant used heavy equipment to dig out a series of eleven trenches, some as large as fifty feet by three hundred feet, to dispose of both full and flattened drums contaminated with plutonium or uranium and other waste. About 55,000 pounds (25,000 kilograms) of depleted uranium chips in 125 drums were buried under two feet of dirt between 1952 and 1962.[27]

Another east-side burial ground was located just off Central Avenue, which separated the plutonium production area to the north from the rest of the plant. Beginning in April 1954, Dow hauled 1,045 drums of liquid and solid waste contaminated with uranium and plutonium to this area and covered them with dirt. This site became known as the "Mound." A little farther north was a hastily dug pit where barrels filled with highly toxic nickel carbonyl cylinders were temporarily buried after the 1957 fire. Those cylinders were unearthed and destroyed by explosion in June 1963.[28]

Although the plant continued burying nuclear waste into the 1970s, Rocky Flats managers always contended burial was a necessary but temporary solution required to maintain weapons production. The exhumation and destruction of the nickel carbonyl cylinders and the decisions about how to handle the new liquid wastes produced by the plutonium component machining in Building 776 lend support to their argument that burials were viewed as temporary. But this last case also shows how Dow and AEC officials blithely ignored the environmental consequences of their short-term decisions.

The "Jelly Factory"

The original designers of Rocky Flats gave little consideration to liquid wastes contaminated with radioactive materials. The bomb-making processes in 1951 created a small amount of such liquid waste, and the plant designers assumed it could be either burned or packaged in some form and shipped along with solid wastes for off-site burial. Building 774, constructed in 1952, was designed to reduce the volume of liquid wastes from Building 771 by filtering out and packaging the radioactive solids for shipment. Sludge from this treatment process was loaded into fifty-five-gallon steel barrels. The remaining, less contaminated liquid was pumped to solar evaporation ponds or holding ponds east of Building 771.

When Building 776 was designed in the mid-1950s, plant officials recognized that its plutonium foundry and fabrication operations would produce large quantities of liquid waste, so planners included a high-speed centrifuge to process plutonium-contaminated fluids. When the centrifuge failed to operate properly, engineers tried to develop a substitute process. Production waste kept accumulating, and waste from the cleanup of the 1957 fire added to the volume. Officials ordered eighty-nine contaminated oil drums from Building 776 to be buried at the Mound in September 1958, the last burial at this site.[29]

In the meantime, plant officials in July 1958 designated a storage area for plutonium-contaminated drums in a field across the road from the Mound. Near Building 903, this area, known as the "903 pad," was intended as a temporary holding area until an adequate waste disposal technique could be developed. The pad, initially just bare ground, became the plant's most notorious waste site. Drums, both fifty-five and thirty gallon, were also deposited there from uranium and beryllium production buildings.

The drums stored at the 903 pad were made of steel but not stainless steel, and they weren't built to withstand the often fierce Colorado winters. In addition, carbon tetrachloride and other chemicals corroded the drums' insides. In July 1959, just a year after the outside storage began, workers discovered that some drums were leaking plutonium-contaminated liquid into the soil. Instead of removing the drums, plant managers let them sit and simply ordered that ethanolamine, a rust inhibitor, be added to new drums before they were placed in the storage area.[30]

Plant engineers sought a way to separate the oil and carbon tet for reuse. They built a still in Building 771 and in May 1960 began testing barrels of liquid waste from the 903 pad. But the chemical change of carbon tet into hydrochloric acid severely corroded the distilling equipment, and tests were halted in September. Managers continued to have drums trucked to the 903 pad area.

Liquid wastes were also being deposited in a series of holding ponds. Nine ponds were eventually dug along the north and south tributaries of Walnut Creek, which drained from the northeast side of the plant site, and two were dug near Woman Creek to the southeast. Some radioactive and nonradioactive toxic wastes were discharged directly into Walnut Creek. In addition to plant wastes, Rocky Flats also accepted radioactive and other contaminated wastes from outside facilities, including Coors Porcelain Company of Golden. The AEC contracted with Coors in 1960 to make beryllium and beryllium-uranium fuel elements for Project Pluto, an experimental supersonic missile system that never panned out. Beginning in 1961, Coors shipped hundreds of thousands of gallons of liquid waste to the plant, most of which went into the ponds until Rocky Flats stopped accepting off-site waste in 1971. Some waste drums from Coors apparently were also stored in the 903 pad area.[31]

Workers reported large-scale deterioration of the 903 pad drums in January 1964. By then, thousands of the drums were sitting in the field. At about the same time, plant engineers, who had abandoned their attempt to separate the carbon tetrachloride from the lubricating oil for reuse, found a way to filter the contaminated liquid wastes. The "solidified" waste then was stored or shipped to an AEC site in Idaho as transuranic (TRU) mixed waste, the designation for waste containing high levels of plutonium and other radioactive elements with atomic numbers larger than uranium's.

Equipment in Building 774 filtered the spent liquids to remove particles larger than one micron (about one-hundredth the thickness of a human hair) and mixed them with calcium silicate to form a gel. Workers started referring to Building 774 as the "Jelly Factory." This building's mixer-extruder system, with various modifications, was used in the following decades to produce "pondcrete," which was supposed to harden like concrete but never did. It became a subject of environmental concern. Until 1973 the liquid wastes went either to the solar evaporation ponds or, for those less contaminated, to the "B" series of holding ponds and then into Walnut Creek and the Great Western Reservoir — the water supply for the Denver suburb of Broomfield.[32]

Due to mechanical difficulties and other delays, the Jelly Factory didn't begin receiving regular shipments from the 903 storage area until January 23, 1967. By then, the 903 field contained 5,240 drums, holding approximately 262,000 gallons of waste organic liquids. Sixty-eight percent contained plutonium-contaminated liquid and most of the remainder held uranium waste. Plant officials estimated that 5,000 gallons of oil containing about three ounces (eighty-six grams) of plutonium leaked from the drums into the soil.[33]

Other contamination was caused during the transfer process itself. One plant official described how the last contaminated oil drums were moved. "They were transferred on a forklift and the operator of the forklift was not aware that, as he was driving down the road on Central Avenue from the 903 area and made the turn at the warehouse corner toward Building 771, a good portion of the way he was sloshing oil out on the street."[34]

It took a year and a half, until June 1968, before all the drums were transferred to the Jelly Factory for processing. During that period, rain and wind spread some of the plutonium-contaminated soil beyond the 903 storage field. But the largest releases occurred after June 1968 and were caused both by high winds and by the plant's haphazard efforts to contain the contamination by paving over the area. Some dispersion occurred in November 1968 when the 903 field was graded. Then, reflecting the same nonchalant approach to nuclear waste that led plant managers to create this temporary storage area in the first place, the field sat uncovered and subject to wind dispersion until July 1969, when workers spread gravel fill over the area. The asphalt cover, which gave the 903 "pad" its name, wasn't completed until November 1969.[35] The 903 mess was covered up, literally. But by that time extraordinary events had occurred that would force Dow and the AEC to disclose the fiasco to the public.

EIGHT

Close Call — The Mother's Day Fire

◆

"Remarkable" Savings

Despite being well insulated against public scrutiny, the Atomic Energy Commission (AEC) and its contractors were forced to rev up their public relations machine in the mid-1960s. Although secrecy, plus thousands of jobs and hundreds of millions of dollars, had worked well for Rocky Flats to this point, the AEC wanted to ensure public support. The agency was feeling pressure nationally. Congressional hearings on radiation, the nuclear testing debate, and, most significantly, the 1962 Cuban missile crisis made nuclear weapons more conspicuous.

In May 1965 Dow Chemical Company held the third restricted media tour of Rocky Flats in the plant's fourteen-year history to show off its new $1.1 million "nuclear safety" building, known as Building 886. "Basic research into the qualities of plutonium will be performed here, providing data for its own sake and supplying information leading to better handling, use, production, and shipping of the highly sensitive and increasingly useful element," a *Boulder Daily Camera* reporter wrote. He called the tour an effort by Dow "to cement better relations with people of the Boulder-Denver area, which has little opportunity to learn of the plant."[1]

The following year, despite the touted "nuclear safety" building, worker radiation exposures at Rocky Flats shot through the roof. No media tours took place. The public wasn't told what was happening. Eighty-seven of the plant's 1,200 plutonium production workers received penetrating radiation doses exceeding the AEC's liberal 5 rem standard. That was a 2,000 percent jump over the four workers exposed in 1965. These 1966 exposures amounted to more than fifty percent of the exposures greater than 5 rem in all of the AEC's two dozen nuclear weapons facilities around the country. Dow traced most of the problems to production changes that enabled the plant to make more nuclear bombs. But little was done until after the plant reported eighty-eight excessively high worker exposures in 1967, constituting more than eighty percent of the AEC's national total.[2]

Dow managers at Rocky Flats had a higher priority than worker safety. They were under contract to meet the AEC's demands for more plutonium processing and weapons manufacture at the lowest-possible cost. And unless the demands were met, the AEC wouldn't pay the company a bonus on top of its cost-plus contract. The pressure for production intensified after the AEC consolidated its plutonium fabrication work at Rocky Flats in 1965 and shut down the pit operations at the Hanford plutonium-finishing plant. Rocky Flats became "the sole source of plutonium nuclear weapons parts." And the facility received highly enriched uranium components from Oak Ridge instead of manufacturing them in Building 881, which was converted to producing stainless steel parts for the pits.[3]

With a new plutonium production building still on the drawing boards, the Rocky Flats managers scrambled to make do. They transformed an administrative office area and cafeteria in Building 771 into a plutonium recovery area, adding five new dissolution glove box lines. They crammed new equipment into existing plutonium-manufacturing areas in Building 776–777. They altered the handling procedures for nuclear bomb cores, or pits, returned from the stockpile and containing high amounts of radioactive americium 241. Rather than removing the americium, workers were told to blend up to eighty percent of the returned plutonium pits directly into the foundry and subsequently into the manufacturing process. "This change was reflected by significant increases in exposures to all personnel in the foundry and fabrication areas," a contemporary Dow document observed.[4]

The plant's top managers knew exactly what they were doing. They traded worker safety for higher productivity. "Over the past several years there has been a strong emphasis on seeking more efficient production methods in an effort to reduce the cost of producing plutonium for weapons," an internal Dow report blandly observed in November 1967. "This emphasis has resulted in some remarkable savings in cost in the face of more stringent processing requirements, but some of the changes have contributed to exposure increases." Higher worker exposures didn't count in the AEC and Dow financial equation. The 1967 report stressed there was no turning back from the production changes. "It is not possible to revert to old processing techniques without causing large additional capital expenditures and gross increases in the operating costs associated with plutonium processing."[5]

A Union Dilemma

Dow's complacency toward worker safety infuriated Jim Kelly and the other leaders of the plant's new production workers' labor union, the District 50 arm of the United Mine Workers of America. Workers elected this union to be the plant's bargaining representative in October 1964 and chose Kelly, still a radiation monitor in Building 771, to be vice president of new Mine Workers Local 15440. "Safety was always a battleground with Dow Chemical," Kelly said. "They resisted every attempt by the union or its members to get involved in safety or safety decisions." In 1965 Dow refused the union's contract demand for a joint safety council.[6]

Jim's older brother, Pat, was on the union's negotiating committee. "For the company, money was always the determining factor when it came to installing safety equipment or new safety procedures or whatever," said Pat Kelly, who since the mid-1950s led the workers' push for greater protection against radiation. Dow Chemical's own documents confirm his point about money. "The periods required from the budgetary and construction standpoint have in some cases resulted in a considerable lag in reducing radiation fields," the company acknowledged in summarizing the 1965–1968 period.[7]

Given their past activities, the Kelly brothers might have been expected to lead the charge for Rocky Flats worker safety in 1967 and 1968. In a way they did, but out of the public eye. Engaged in an internal struggle over nuclear power with the United Mine Workers international union, Jim and Pat Kelly were beginning to discover that the public could be an adversary as well as an ally when it came to things nuclear.

The District 50 unit of the Mine Workers union, which represented Rocky Flats, also represented employees in a number of crafts and industries, including uranium miners. The international union's core membership, however, consisted of coal miners. Union leaders worried nuclear power would erode the coal industry and reduce jobs. So the Mine Workers leadership mounted an attack on nuclear power plants, coupled with an attack on radiation dangers. Union leaders came to Denver in November 1967 to testify at public hearings against the Fort Saint Vrain helium-cooled nuclear power plant north of Denver being proposed by the Public Service Company of Colorado. They warned radiation would endanger the people of Colorado.

After some Rocky Flats workers met one of the visiting union leaders at a motel to discuss deteriorating safety at their own plant, an article describing the meeting appeared in a Denver business weekly. District 50 officials and local president Jim Kelly refused, however, to discuss publicly details of the radiation safety problems at the plant. They didn't want to lend any support to the national union's broad assault on nuclear energy, fearing this could affect their own plant's existence and jobs. While the Kelly brothers worked with friendly members of Congress to pressure the AEC for better safety standards, they avoided the Denver-area media. Instead the union local released public statements supporting the nuclear power industry. "We were a very militant and strong union that believed in both nuclear power and having a strong nuclear deterrent," said Pat Kelly. A few months later the United Mine Workers expelled District 50. The Rocky Flats local union remained independent until it merged in 1972 with the United Steelworkers of America.[8]

Addressing Radiation, Ignoring Fire

Radiation had become even more politically visible by late 1967. On the local community level, Marcus Church discovered that radiation worries were affecting his attempts to sell land adjacent to Rocky Flats. A real estate consultant requested additional information from Church's realtor about contamination. "Do you know what the Atomic Energy – Dow Plant produces? Is there radiation or other polution [sic] hazards?" the consultant asked.[9]

And within the nuclear weapons complex the high worker radiation exposures at the plant finally caught the eye of AEC officials. "The Rocky Flats personnel exposure control program has not been effective in maintaining exposures within the prescribed limits," an operations manager from the AEC's Albuquerque office wrote in November 1967.[10] At the request of AEC headquarters in Washington, Dow Rocky Flats prepared a seventy-four-page report in January 1968. It stated that some worker exposures resulted from a special project that wasn't directly related to the plant's bomb-making mission. Namely, under contract to the government's Argonne National Laboratory, outside Chicago, in July 1967 the plant began making nuclear fuel elements for a "Zero Power Plutonium Reactor" by blending seventy percent depleted uranium with thirty percent plutonium. The process unexpectedly vaporized americium and increased worker exposures to radiation.[11]

Dow's radiation report explained that most exposures stemmed from changes in plutonium-processing and fabrication procedures. Exposures had escalated during 1966 after a new conveyor system began operating in Building 776–777, the cavernous foundry, manufacturing, and assembly facility that occupied an area the size of about two football fields. This windowless structure originally consisted of two units separated by a common concrete block wall, but the wall had been removed in the early 1960s to ease the movement of plutonium parts and scrap.[12]

The new conveyor system was called a "chainveyor." It consisted of long horizontal chains, like large bicycle chains running around sprockets. The system was mounted from the ceiling above the serpentine glove box lines and a few feet above the floor of the glove boxes. Chainveyors were also used to move material between the various glove box lines. Plutonium carriers known as "pendants" hung from small hooks welded at regular intervals along the chainveyor chains. A pendant was a flat, round tray about ten inches in diameter. A thin stainless steel rod ran from beneath the tray, curved around, and attached to the chain hook. A small steel fence welded around the outside of the tray kept material from sliding off. Many pendant trays carried specially designed containers known as "bird cages," which held cans of plutonium filings and other material. Workers also placed plutonium ingots about the size of thick school tablets on edge between the pendants' bars.

Workers moved plutonium from the overhead chainveyors to glove box floors by means of miniature "elevators," which were tall glove boxes with transparent plastic walls. Platforms inside these elevators lowered plutonium from the chainveyors to the glove box line floor, where workers manually passed the plutonium along the glove box line from one position to the other as they performed their different tasks. When the plutonium reached the other end of the glove box line, another "elevator" lifted it back to the chainveyor and it was transported to another glove box line. The chain links were designed to break if something got jammed so the plutonium couldn't pile up and cause a criticality. The whole chainveyor system was enclosed by plastic (Plexiglas) windows fitted into a stainless steel frame, with glove portholes cut into the windows for maintenance. The chainveyor system looked like a series of long tunnels running above the glove box lines throughout the factory.[13]

While the chainveyor system enabled workers to move plutonium more efficiently through the various foundry, manufacturing, or recycling steps in Building 776–777, it left a large amount of plutonium sitting in the conveyors and glove boxes while awaiting processing. "It is recognized that a high inventory of plutonium on conveyor systems adds significantly to exposure levels," Dow's January 1968 radiation report stated. The report also noted that plutonium waste in the glove boxes meant more plutonium 241 was decaying into dangerously radioactive americium 241. "Continuing emphasis has been given to the need for 'super' housekeeping in glove box lines to prevent the accumulation of aged material and the associated americium growth," the radiation report claimed. But in an amazing display of institutional forgetfulness, the report didn't mention that plutonium chips and other waste had spontaneously ignited and caused numerous blazes, including the 1957 fire.[14]

The report's sole focus was radiation. And Dow assured the AEC it was taking steps to decrease the radiation exposures in Building 776–777. "First, a greater effort is under way by Manufacturing to reduce the inventories to lowest practical levels," the report emphasized. "Second, funding and high priority have been established for conveyor line shielding."[15]

Dow reminded the AEC that $700,000 in radiation shielding construction was already under way and that the plant had requested $3.5 million for additional shielding, aimed mainly at reducing neutron exposures. The shielding consisted primarily of Plexiglas and a thick, brown plastic called Benelex, a laminated material like masonite that was glued together. It was used to build walls around the chainveyor system and to make casket-like containers called "jewel boxes," which temporarily stored plutonium along the glove box lines. During 1968 some 1.17 million pounds, or 585 tons, of Benelex and Plexiglas shielding was added to Building 776–777. Unfortunately, although the Benelex blocked neutrons, this material was flammable.[16]

"Routine" Fires

Fires flared frequently at Rocky Flats. The plant's fire department had been called out to hundreds of fires in the years since the 1957 blaze heavily damaged Building 771. The most serious was a 1965 plutonium fire ignited in Building 776–777 when workers tried to unplug a clogged drain. Although the fire was quickly extinguished, more than 400 employees were contaminated during this accident. Most of them inhaled radioactive particles and received internal exposures from alpha radiation, so their exposures didn't show up in the plant's figures for external penetrating radiation caused by beta particles, gamma rays, and neutrons. From 1966 to May 1969 alone, the department responded to 164 fires. Thirty-one were plutonium fires, twenty-two in Building 771 and nine in Building 776–777.[17]

Countless other plutonium fires had broken out but were extinguished by workers, and the fire department was not even called in. "There is no good estimate of the number of plutonium fires not reported to the fire department," a 1969 Rocky Flats document stated. When plutonium filings, or chips, ignited spontaneously, workers dropped the chips into machining oil to put them out. "This kind of fire is considered routine," the document noted.[18]

Instead of alerting plant managers to an ever-present danger, the "routine" small fires bolstered their attitude that burning plutonium could easily be controlled. In reality, however, managers and scientists in the late 1960s knew little more about plutonium's strange characteristics and behavior than they had known before the 1957 fire. "The unpredictable nature of plutonium metal is well recognized but not completely understood," a 1969 document stated. "Many physical variables affect the behavior of plutonium, but the complexity and interactions of those variables have not been determined." Still, everyone dealing with plutonium at Rocky Flats knew it was pyrophoric — some forms could ignite spontaneously in air at low temperatures. The document noted, "It is difficult to assign an ignition temperature to the many physical forms and crystalline phases of plutonium metal." For example, small plutonium filings ignited easily while plutonium metal, such as "buttons" or components weighing more than seven ounces (200 grams), did not.[19]

From 1965 on, workers handled increasingly large quantities of plutonium metal in Building 776–777. At any one time, more than 7,000 pounds (3,100 kilograms) were located there. Most arrived through an underground tunnel from Building 771 as the hockey-puck-sized buttons weighing more than a pound apiece. Other buttons were shipped by truck from the AEC's Hanford and Savannah River plants, which employed nuclear reactors to produce plutonium from uranium 238. Old warheads returned from the stockpile and manufacturing scrap recycled from Building 776–777's own machining operations accounted for the rest.[20] The workers in Building 776–777 went through an elaborate process to make plutonium metal into shells and assemble them and other parts into nuclear pits, used most often as H-bomb detonators.

Super Housekeeping Needed

The factory floor in Building 776–777 was surreal, resembling a cross between a huge laboratory and a cluttered laundromat. Hundreds of stainless steel glove boxes, raised off the floor like rabbit hutches, were welded together to form four major glove box lines, like assembly lines. The chain-veyor system ran above each glove box line. Individual glove boxes, with leaded plastic Plexiglas windows and portholes for arms or sets of glove boxes branched off the main lines at short intervals. Some boxes, often stacked two or three high, contained furnaces, about the size of household ovens, to melt the plutonium for casting. Others held machines to roll, cut, grind, and shape the bomb parts. When glove boxes were not in use, the long rubber gloves hung inside out from the portholes. Underpasses about six feet deep and four feet wide were located in a few places along the glove box lines so employees could go from one side of a line to the other by walking beneath it. These underpasses, dubbed "sheep dips" by workers, had no floor drains.[21]

Building 776–777 became even more crowded after the Benelex plastic anti-radiation walls were installed. The building also had no sprinkler system, due to fears that water would react with the plutonium and cause a localized criticality chain reaction that could deliver a lethal dose of radiation to anyone close by. Fire inspectors were worried. In March 1969 David Patterson, chief of the AEC's Industrial Safety and Fire Protection Branch in Washington, D.C., inspected the building. "This facility is one of the most important to the program, but had practically no built-in fire protection or suppression equipment," Patterson wrote. His report mentioned that a Dow official asked what could be done about the building's vulnerability. "I commented that the problem is apparently recognized by the [AEC] commissioners, since a recent report expressed concern about the fire and safety risks in Rocky Flats facilities, which concentrate 'all the eggs in one basket.' "[22]

Building 776–777 was a firetrap. Besides the flammable plastic walls, many of the pendants hanging from the chainveyor were made of magnesium. Although lightweight, this metal was flammable. Finally, the "super" housekeeping of glove boxes and equipment called for in Dow's January 1968 radiation report was occurring at a snail's pace even though workers discovered large amounts of waste. A waste pit beneath one machine cleaned in March 1969 "contained approximately 74 kg. [148 pounds] of sludge from which 13 kg. [28.6 pounds] of plutonium was recovered," the AEC's fire investigation report noted.[23]

Plant managers probably assumed that the cleanup problems would go away when Building 776–777 was replaced by a huge, modernized facility called Building 707, which was nearing completion in spring 1969. But some employees were worried about the state of Building 776–777. Worker

Larry Crehore complained to union president Jim Kelly about rags and other waste in the plutonium-filled glove box lines. Because the building usually operated three shifts (day, evening, and midnight) five or six days a week, the production lines occasionally were left unattended. Crehore and Kelly proposed that Dow assign roving radiation monitors to the building to do spot checks around the clock. The company declined. "Dow Chemical would have nothing to do with that because they hated that monitor classification. They always considered that classification to be overhead," Kelly said.[24]

Two of Building 776–777's four major glove box lines, the north and south foundry lines, originated in Room 134, the main manufacturing space on the structure's west side. These two foundry lines were nearly identical, each 100 feet long and containing eight furnaces inside glove boxes as well as the production and storage glove boxes. Foundry workers melted the plutonium, both buttons and scrap, and cast it into "feed" ingots weighing between fifteen and eighteen pounds (seven and eight kilograms) apiece. After assaying them to determine the content of plutonium isotopes, workers remelted and blended most of these ingots and cast them into flat, rectangular 24.2-pound (11-kilogram) ingots about the size of thick elementary school tablets. Ingots with a high americium content were sent to a special extraction unit.

The chainveyor carried the plutonium production ingots to the fabrication line, also enclosed within glove boxes. There workers rolled out the ingots like cookie dough and cut them into pieces for presses to shape into thin hemispheres, or half shells, weighing a couple of kilograms each. Workers machined the hemispheres to the correct specifications. Conveyors carried the parts to the 777 assembly side of the building, where workers eventually welded the plutonium metal hemispheres together and joined them with other components to form the nuclear bomb pits.

The plutonium-machining process created considerable waste. The lathes, milling machines, and other machine tools left fine metal chips as well as larger pieces, all of which were to be recycled. Workers put this plutonium scrap, still oily from the machining lubricant used with the cutting equipment, into steel cans within the glove boxes and returned them by conveyor to Room 134. To prepare these plutonium chips for remelting in the foundry furnaces, hydraulic presses squeezed them together to form one-inch-by-three-inch briquettes weighing about 3.3 pounds (1.5 kilograms) each and resembling big coconut macaroons because of their composition. The finished briquettes were placed in stainless steel "soup" cans 5.5 inches deep and four inches in diameter and kept in storage glove boxes. Although the cans had lids, they didn't fasten and frequently fell off when the cans were moved, so workers just left the lids off.[25]

Before being pressed into briquettes, the plutonium chips were supposed to be dipped in successive baths of carbon tetrachloride cleaning solvent in order to remove the machining oil still sticking to the surfaces. Such degreasing was dangerous, however, since the chips spontaneously ignited so easily—the cause of many "routine" fires. Workers had learned from bitter experience that burning chips that came into contact with carbon tetrachloride could cause small explosions. To avoid such accidents, production managers curtailed the degreasing. Consequently, when the hydraulic presses made briquettes, they also squeezed out oil and some tiny plutonium pieces onto the glove box floors. Workers wiped up the oil with rags, frequently leaving them in glove boxes until they were saturated.[26]

Mother's Day

Sometime late in the morning of Sunday, May 11, 1969, plutonium flecks in rags on the floor of a briquette press glove box on the north foundry line spontaneously ignited. The rags began burning. The glove box ventilation fans, which continually pulled air into filters on the building's second floor, sucked heat from the oily rag fire into a nearby storage glove box and eventually ignited a plutonium briquette sitting in a lidless can. It began burning like a charcoal briquette.[27]

When the Building 776–777 day shift had ended on Saturday, May 10, the facility held 7,641 pounds (3,473 kilograms) of plutonium at various stages of manufacture. Seven of the eight furnaces on the north foundry line contained ingots. Most of the magnesium parts carriers on this line, the north-south conveyor line, and the center glove box line were full. Everything was ready for production to resume with the midnight shift Sunday night.[28]

Although no operations were scheduled in the building's 776 wing on Mother's Day Sunday, two utility operators were on duty because the fans and ventilation equipment required continuous monitoring. A three-worker team reported to the building's 777 side about noon to prepare a special-order shipment for Los Alamos. They packaged finished bomb parts in the extreme northeast corner of 777. By that time the plutonium briquette in glove box number 134–24 on the building's northwest side had been burning for one or two hours, charring a hole in the fourteen-foot-by-two-foot Benelex plastic "jewel box" in which it was stored. While the

Benelex didn't flame up, it released combustible gases. The heated gases ignited other briquettes and initiated a slow burning of more plastic in the storage box. The fire should have immediately triggered heat detectors, but they had been removed from the storage glove boxes about two years earlier to make room for the new anti-radiation jewel boxes. The detectors sat useless on the floor under the glove box.[29]

The smoke in the north line's exhaust system gradually clogged the filters. More plutonium ignited. Heat spread to the combustible rubber gloves and plastic windows and flames erupted. "Up to this time, the fire was still undetected by the few people who were in the building that day because the smoke, flames, and heat were contained within the glove box system," according to the AEC's December 1969 accident report.[30]

The fire spread quickly once the glove box's plastic Plexiglas windows and glove portholes were breached. Because the glove box lines were maintained at low air pressure to keep plutonium particles from escaping, the inrushing air fanned the fire into the north foundry line and toward the building's 777 wing. Luck then intervened for the first time, but not the last. During the Saturday shift, workers doing measurements had left a metal plate blocking the north line. So the fire turned into the north-south chainveyor line instead of racing into 777, much of which had no second floor and, consequently, an extremely vulnerable roof.[31]

At 2:27 P.M. the building's heat detectors finally triggered an alarm at the Rocky Flats fire station. A minute later utility operator F. H. Coleman, who had been checking another building, returned to the second floor of 776. He smelled smoke and pulled a manual alarm. Already on their way, Fire Captain Wayne Jesser and three firemen arrived at the building's west end within minutes and entered the building. They found heavy smoke and fire, with flames shooting eighteen inches above the top of the north foundry line. Jesser ordered one fireman to attack the fire with a handheld carbon dioxide extinguisher while he moved to the east end of the line with a fifty-pound carbon dioxide carrier mounted to a cart. He inserted the nozzle into the conveyor line and discharged it. The carbon dioxide had no effect. The fire was out of control.[32]

Jesser faced a momentous decision. The Rocky Flats firefighters had been ordered repeatedly never to use water on a plutonium fire because of the dangers of a criticality, an explosion — or both. The fact that the 1957 fire had been successfully fought with water was regarded as a lucky fluke. Jesser, who had battled the '57 fire, realized water could put his firemen's lives at risk. And if the water caused a hydrogen explosion, the whole building might be destroyed and the Denver area contaminated. Against those risks, Jesser knew for sure that if the fire weren't controlled, the building would collapse and radiation would be released. Water was his only option. At 2:34, just five minutes after entering the building, Jesser ordered the men to bring in fire hoses.[33]

Dense black smoke filled the huge factory floor. An explosion sent two fireballs the size of basketballs hurtling toward the ceiling. The edges of the thick plastic safety walls, intended to protect workers from radiation exposures, were burning. The glue in the laminated plastic fueled the fire. Hanging fluorescent light fixtures clattered down as intense heat melted the fasteners attaching them to the ceiling. Glowing drops of lead fell like rain from the shielding around the overhead conveyors. The firefighters, finding their way through the smoke by following emergency evacuation arrows painted on the floor, wore hard hats along with their moon suits and air tanks. They used fine spray nozzles and sprayed into the ceiling, where the gases from the disintegrating plastic were burning. They tried to avoid spraying water directly onto the plutonium.

The blaze burned brighter than anything Bill Dennison, a plant guard and auxiliary firefighter, had ever seen. It reminded him of forest fire movies, "except that back in the smoke and flame we could see the distinctive brilliance of burning metal, which we assumed was plutonium, but was probably both plutonium and [the] magnesium carriers."[34] Even as firefighters battled the fire inside the two-story concrete building, the huge ventilation fans pulled flames into the filter system designed to prevent plutonium contamination from leaving the building. Two of the three banks of paper filters already had burned out and the third was beginning to burn when the second and most significant stroke of luck occurred. A fireman accidentally backed his truck into a power pole outside the building and cut off the power. The fans, which had been sucking the fire into the filter bank, stopped spinning, just as similar ones stopped during the 1957 blaze. But this fire was still out of control.[35]

Smoke and a Soft Roof

Jim Kelly's phone was ringing when he and his family walked in the door after a Mother's Day lunch at a local restaurant. "Jim, I need you to come out here right away — 776 is burning," his boss told him. "We've really got a mess this time." Kelly left immediately. He wouldn't return home for twenty hours.[36]

Dozens of other workers were arriving at the plant when Kelly got there at about 3:15 P.M. After passing through the checkpoint, he got to the building and put on coveralls, shoe booties, and a respirator. He was told to check Building 776–777's flat roof for radiation. "I was scared," he recalled. "When I got up there, I could see no flames coming up." The building's roof vents curved downward so that any exhaust would first hit the top of the roof. "I went to the exhaust areas, then did some quick checks by shuffling around with the booties and then checked the bottom of the booties to see if they were picking up any radiation count. There was nothing there." The filters were holding. He came down. Shortly afterward, around 3:45, gray and black smoke began pouring from the exhaust vents. It rolled off the building rather than rising high in the sky. Still, drivers on the Denver-Boulder turnpike ten miles away could see the smoke plume. Several firefighters were ordered onto the roof to keep it hosed down.[37]

The roof was a typical 1950s layered design. Fluted steel sheets were fastened to steel ceiling girders and covered by three-fourths-inch flame retardant Styrofoam. Plywood sheets, five-eighths inch thick, were glued to the Styrofoam and coated with thick butyl rubber. The roof was exposed directly to the first floor over the building's 777 east wing, which had no second floor, and over three two-story-high work bays in the 776 wing. The intense heat, later estimated at 400 degrees Fahrenheit on the metal roof's underside and 320 degrees on the upper side, particularly affected 776's bay areas. "The most severe damage in that area appears to be a nearly complete melting of the Styrofoam component of the roof," according to one July 1969 report. The decomposition of this material caused smoke, which traveled along the fluted roof to its edges and was emitted. Although the fire didn't break through the roof, one area got soft. The firefighters managed to keep the roof relatively cool by spraying thousands of gallons of water onto it.[38]

By about 4:00 P.M. the water was beginning to contain the fire inside the building. But it caused extreme danger for the firefighters. Moving along the glove box line, they saw the foundry area ablaze. The only way to get there was through the "sheep dip" passageways. But these underpasses, which had been built without drains because anything that went into them was considered contaminated and had to be cleaned up, were now filled with water. Bill Dennison, fully aware of a possible criticality from the plutonium and water combination, took a deep breath and waded through. The fire in the foundry was so hot that it dried his wet coveralls. A falling light fixture hit him on the head, but only dazed him slightly thanks to his hard hat.[39]

At this point, plutonium's unknowns worked in favor of the firefighters. The plutonium oxide "ash" from the burned metal became sticky like dough when it was drenched with water. "One fireman told us how he tried to take a hose and push all the plutonium down into one corner so he could really squirt it. It wouldn't move; he was unsuccessful," said Rowland Felt, an AEC scientist sent to investigate the fire. Felt explained that if the fireman had been able to push the plutonium together, he probably would have triggered a chain reaction criticality.[40]

Although no criticality occurred, forty-one firefighters, guards, and other employees who fought the fire sustained radiation doses. The firefighters inside the building had to work in short shifts due to the fire's intense heat. Radiation monitors checked them each time they came out of the building. Those contaminated were sent to Building 559 to shower with water and a sodium hypochlorite solution. Fifteen employees sent to be decontaminated had received significant doses. A fireman whose respirator mask had been torn off momentarily received the highest dose.[41]

The firemen contained the fire by 6:40 P.M. and by 8:00 had extinguished it "for all practical purposes," according to the fire investigation report. Still, as in 1957, plutonium continued to smolder and fires reignited. Lending credence to the conclusion that heat and moisture would ignite plutonium, workers discovered a fire Monday morning in a plutonium storage glove box on the south foundry line far away from the big fire.[42]

Hundreds of Square Miles

The Denver and Boulder newspapers all carried stories about the fire on Monday, May 12. The *Denver Post* story was typical. The afternoon paper's page-three headline read, "Radioactivity: AEC Weapons Building Burns." Readers were told that the production building hit by fire Sunday was still too "radioactively hot" for fire investigators to enter, the fire caused "no injuries," no radioactivity had been released into the atmosphere, and the contamination was confined to the building itself. The last claim would be challenged a few months later by a local group of independent scientists who discovered plutonium in soil near the plant.

An AEC investigation team arrived at the plant on Tuesday, May 13, to determine the fire's cause and assess damage. The plant's managers and workers began the task of cleaning up Building 776–777 and shifting production to Building 707, the nearly completed replacement facility. "We had a meeting with the whole plant and said, Hey, everybody's going to have to be involved," Jim Kelly recalled. "We got the message across that this was survival, that if the plant didn't get cleaned up, all the jobs were going to be gone." The plant then employed 3,216 people, of whom 1,761 were rank-and-file workers.

The AEC completed its initial investigation in August. Its report, classified secret, concluded that two tons of the Plexiglas windows on two glove box lines and one conveyor line were consumed by fire and tons of the plastic walls were also damaged. Investigators estimated that less than ten percent of the 7,641 pounds (3,473 kilograms) of plutonium in Building 776–777 was damaged or burned to oxide and that ninety-nine percent of the plutonium had been retrieved. Unlike a wood fire, where the ash can't be turned back into wood, the oxide left from burning plutonium can be reprocessed into metal without a significant loss of material. The AEC estimated the plutonium recovery costs and the value of the lost plutonium as $22.3 million. Added to the $48.4 million in damage to the production building, the fire's total $70.7 million price tag broke all previous records for U.S. industrial accidents.[43]

The AEC investigation report estimated the fire would cause a six-to-nine-months delay in Rocky Flats nuclear bomb production, but concluded that the AEC's commitments to the Department of Defense for warheads could be met with one minor exception. The report also noted that the fire didn't breach the building, although contaminated smoke had escaped the damaged filters and plutonium had been deposited on the roof and nearby ground. Firemen leaving the building also had tracked some plutonium outside. Investigators concluded that no contamination had gone off-site. Later studies found that little or no contamination was dispersed.[44]

The long-secret AEC fire investigation report of August 1969 sharply criticized both AEC and Dow management for neglecting fire safety in the Building 776–777 complex. Among the problems, the report said managers made decisions to add equipment and structures on an ad hoc basis. "This 'Topsy-like' growth led to overcrowded conditions that made compliance with fire safety regulations even more difficult, if not impossible." It faulted the managers for the series of decisions leading to the installation of combustible radiation shielding materials in the building. It blamed Dow for lacking "a competent and centralized safety organization" at the plant. Finally, the report concluded, "A major loss to a vital weapons production facility occurred because of the failure of the AEC management system to assure compliance with AEC fire safety policy."[45]

The AEC investigation report equivocated about the fire's origin, as did the Serious Accident report the agency issued in December. "The exact cause of ignition is unknown; however, plutonium in the form of chips or lathe turnings is a pyrophoric material," according to the December accident report. The fire investigators' conclusion that the fire originally started in oily rags laced with plutonium did not appear in the investigation report. Atomic Energy Commission officials "were afraid it was going to implicate certain individuals, so the lawyer didn't allow us to put that into the report," investigator Felt revealed in 1996. The agency preferred to imply that the fire's origin was a mystery. Moreover, AEC officials didn't want to remind anyone that they had completely ignored the findings of the investigation report prepared after the 1957 fire at Rocky Flats. "If they had read that, digested it, and thoroughly implemented it, we wouldn't have had a fire in '69," Felt said.[46]

After the 1969 fire, Dow managers shrugged off the plant's near miss with disaster, according to the AEC investigation report. "The Dow official in charge of nuclear safety emergency planning advised the [investigation] board that there was no need to have plans for possible off-site damage or personal injuries, since it was not possible for serious off-site contamination to occur, and expressed the view that if such contamination were possible the plant should not be located where it is," the report observed. "He seemed singularly unswayed by the fire on May 11. The possibility that it might have resulted in a significant off-site release of plutonium was countered by the observation that it did not happen. The same general attitude and approach was reflected by Dow general manager's [Lloyd Joshel] comments when this subject was discussed with operating board members."[47]

In contrast, top AEC officials knew Denver had barely escaped a catastrophe. If the fire had burned through Building 776–777's already softening roof, thousands of pounds of deadly plutonium in the form of powdery ash would have exposed hundreds of thousands of women, men, and children living nearby to toxic radiation. Only the "heroic efforts of the firefighters" limited the blaze, the investigation report noted. Otherwise, "there would have been complete loss of Building 776–777 and its contents and a major release of plutonium to the environment."[48]

The AEC's director of Military Application, U.S. Air Force general Edward Giller, described the Rocky Flats fire in less bureaucratic language. Testifying before Congress in 1970, Giller admitted that if the fire hadn't been contained, "hundreds of square miles could be involved in radiation exposure and involve cleanup at an astronomical cost as well as creating a very intense reaction by the general public exposed to this." He continued, "In the fire we had last year we kept it in the building. If the fire had been a little bigger it is questionable whether it could have been contained."[49]

The 1969 fire had been contained physically, but it demonstrated that the plant posed a serious danger to the community. Even the little that was publicly known about the fire jolted local scientists, the Denver-area media, and some citizens. Had they known the full truth about the risks to which they and their families were being subjected, they would have been out-raged. The fire could have caused a Chernobyl-scale disaster seventeen years before that 1986 nuclear accident in the former Soviet Union became an everyday word. Secrecy's thick walls prevented full disclosure about the Rocky Flats fire. But a new phase was beginning on this mesa at the edge of Denver.

NINE

A Magnet for Scientists and Activists

Ed Martell

Ed Martell responded to news of the May 11, 1969, Mother's Day fire at Rocky Flats by contacting fellow members of the Colorado Committee for Environmental Information. This group of Boulder-area scientists firmly believed the public needed independent technical information about government programs, particularly military projects. The Colorado Committee had recently criticized the U.S. Army for storing dangerous chemical agents at the Rocky Mountain Arsenal, its former chemical weapons facility just northeast of Denver whose products included mustard gas and nerve gas. The group also opposed "Project Plowshares," the Atomic Energy Commission's (AEC's) plan to set off "peaceful" underground nuclear explosions in western Colorado and elsewhere. The Rocky Flats fire gave the group an opportunity to take on an issue literally in its own backyard.[1]

Martell offered to head a Colorado Committee subcommittee to look into the fire. He immediately requested details from Dow Chemical officials about the blaze so he could study possible off-site contamination. "They practically barred the door," recalled Martell, at the time a fifty-one-year-old experimental chemist based at the National Center for Atmospheric Research laboratory in Boulder. But Dow underestimated this tall, pudgy, blue-eyed man, who frequently punctuated his statements with laughter.[2]

After Dow's rebuff, Martell phoned General Edward Giller, an old Pentagon acquaintance. Giller's Military Applications division oversaw the nation's nuclear weapons production complex. "He knew me and knew that I wasn't talking nonsense," said Martell, a West Point graduate, retired lieu-tenant colonel, and University of Chicago Ph.D. who specialized in radia-tion fallout. In the mid-1950s he was assigned to the Armed Forces Special Weapons Project to study the radiation effects from nuclear bomb tests. During a series of H-bomb tests in the Pacific Ocean during 1954, Martell changed his opinion about nuclear weapons. "I became quite a pacifist. If you appreciate the effects of thermonuclear explosions, you aren't going to be disposed toward the military and wars as the means of settling national affairs." He resigned from the army but continued studying radiation and came to Boulder in 1962.[3]

Martell told Giller about Dow Chemical's response to his information request. "So he called up the director of Rocky Flats and read the riot act to him," Martell said. "They were supposed to be open and as completely honest as possible without a breach of security and classified information." A few weeks later, Giller flew to Denver to meet with Colorado governor John Love. He then drove to Boulder and met with Martell and other members of the Colorado Committee for Environmental Information. Giller assured the scientists, as he had the governor, that no public danger had resulted from the fire. Giller said a special AEC team was investigating the accident and agreed Dow would answer a number of technical ques-tions posed by Martell's group.[4]

Rocky Flats and Rulison

The Colorado Committee scientists appreciated Giller's promises. Still, they wanted an independent investigation by Martell, whose laboratory research group possessed the necessary equipment. In August 1969 Martell and his radiochemical assistant Stuart Poet began measuring surface soils around Rocky Flats. They dug up shallow, one-half-inch-depth samples in undisturbed soil along fence lines and other unplowed places and calculated the plutonium 239 and strontium 90 in each sample. To account for the fall-out from atmospheric nuclear weapons tests, they also took samples from other sites along Colorado's Front Range and estimated the background concentration of radionuclides in surface soil. By comparing the samples, they could determine if excess plutonium existed around Rocky Flats.[5]

At about the time Martell and Poet began their scientific work, a handful of citizens demonstrated outside Rocky Flats' west gate in August to com-memorate the Hiroshima and Nagasaki bombings. Similar to a few other small protests in the past, it drew few participants. The top priority for most citizens concerned with war and peace issues was stopping the daily death and destruction in Vietnam. Anti-war protests had stepped up across the country, following the Tet offensive in January 1968. In late summer 1969 thousands of Coloradans were preparing to travel to Washington, D.C., to join other peace activists from around the nation in the biggest anti-war demonstration yet.[6]

The AEC responded to the fire by adding more safety features, such as sprinklers, to Building 707 as well as improving the commission's fire regulations. Although small plutonium fires continued to break out, workers deemed only a handful serious enough to formally report during the plant's next twenty years of plutonium processing.[7] In August 1969 the AEC felt no serious public pressure to change its activities and plans, either at Rocky Flats or in western Colorado. There the agency was about to explode the underground nuclear test called "Rulison" near the small town of Rifle. Its purpose was to test the hypothesis that nuclear explosions could release natural gas without irradiating it. On September 10, after the American Civil Liberties Union and the Colorado Open Space Coordinating Council in Denver failed to get a court injunction to stop it, the AEC set off a forty-kiloton device 8,440 feet underground. The explosion amounted to twice the power of the Nagasaki bomb. Although the AEC reported no significant radioactive release from the shot, its industrial partner wasn't able to market the Rulison gas. The AEC continued planning a second nuclear natural gas test in Colorado, called Project Rio Blanco.[8]

Yet as the AEC went about its usual business, a gradual change in public knowledge was occurring. Media coverage of the 1969 Rocky Flats fire didn't evaporate as it had after the 1957 blaze. The local and even the national media continued to do stories about the accident and the plant's operations. In September the *Los Angeles Times West* magazine carried a lengthy article by reporter Roger Rapaport titled "Secrecy and Safety at Rocky Flats." Its subtitle asked, "Where Does Security End and Obfuscation Begin in the Handling of Plutonium?" This basic question would be posed frequently in the coming decades.

The AEC Denies, Reveals

After concluding its internal investigation of the Mother's Day fire, the AEC issued a press release in December 1969. It asserted, "There is no evidence that plutonium was carried beyond plant boundaries." Martell and Poet disagreed. They had found plutonium in the soil along Indiana

Avenue, the public road just east of Rocky Flats, in the form of plutonium oxide dust particles about .00001 inch in diameter. Anyone inhaling such a minute particle would be subjected to radiation "millions of times more intense than that from an average, naturally occurring radioactive dust particle of the same size," they observed. The Colorado Committee concluded the 1969 fire was "the most likely source of the contamination." In January 1970 the group passed along the findings to the AEC, Colorado's governor, and the news media.[9]

Atomic Energy Commission and Dow officials vigorously disputed the committee's claims, but their denials took a strange twist. At a February 10, 1970, meeting in Denver with Colorado Committee members and state health department staffers, the Rocky Flats officials admitted radioactive contamination had gone off the plant site. They then declared it hadn't come from the 1969 fire, but from the 1957 fire and from leaking nuclear waste drums previously stored on what had been renamed the 903 pad. The officials stressed "such trace amounts [of radionuclides] present no risks to the health of employees in the plant or to citizens in the surrounding area."[10]

The disclosures backfired on the AEC and Dow. The news media criticized the government and its contractor. Their concealment of the earlier incidents made the new safety assurances suspect. And rightly so, because unbeknownst to the media and public at the time, the AEC and Dow were continuing their deception. The problems at the plant leading up to the 1969 fire were well concealed in secret documents, for example. Lying was secrecy's natural companion.

Three weeks after the February 1970 meeting, Roy L. Cleere, executive director of the Colorado Department of Health, wrote Dow, complaining that the company should have informed the department about the 1957 and 903 pad radiation releases immediately after they occurred. "It does not seem reasonable that the Department of Health should be required to learn of incidents such as these in this manner [the February meeting] or indirectly through the news media some ten years after the incident occurred," Cleere wrote. "This is especially true if it involves potential or suspected general population exposures."[11]

It turned out that when Martell and the Colorado Committee scientists did further studies of the off-site plutonium, they confirmed the AEC and Dow claim that the contamination hadn't come from the 1969 fire. Simultaneously, however, the independent scientists questioned new AEC claims that the plant had released just thirty-eight millicuries (.0038 curie) of plutonium to the environment during normal plant operations since 1953. The Colorado Committee's preliminary tests indicated more than one curie in the tested areas. The committee conceded, "The most difficult and uncertain part of this whole problem is the assessment of the risk to the people in the Denver metropolitan area." They argued that the government should err on the side of caution and relocate the plant.[12]

But the tremendous risks from the Rocky Flats plant demonstrated by the 1969 fire hadn't penetrated the local or national consciousness. After all, the fire hadn't caused a catastrophe. Unlike the Chernobyl nuclear reactor accident in the Soviet Union seventeen years later, there were no deaths or abandoned Colorado towns littered with irradiated toys and other poisoned artifacts of life. The federal government, including Congress, considered nuclear weapons production at Rocky Flats both necessary and a risk worth taking. And most members of Congress, who knew how the federal facility siting game was played, weren't sympathetic to the belated safety complaints from Coloradans. This became clear during an April 1970 congressional hearing, where General Giller testified about the 1969 fire. Senator Allen J. Ellender, a Louisiana Democrat and the subcommittee chair, asked Giller if some members of the scientists' Colorado Committee for Environmental Information wanted Rocky Flats relocated.

"One or two members of the committee felt that 'we don't care where you go, but leave Colorado,'" Giller responded. Ellender then suggested, "I suppose the same people may have been instrumental in having you come there in the first place." Colorado's senator Gordon Allott, a Republican, interjected that his state's citizens had legitimate concerns. Yet he acknowledged, "It is understandably difficult to provide all the information that some segments of the public might desire."[13]

Segments of the Public

The "public" actually consisted of several different publics with various interests and perspectives about Rocky Flats. Some, such as the plant's neighbors and workers, had been involved with the facility since the beginning. But the 1969 fire had opened the door to a much larger cast of characters, including independent scientists and citizen activists. From a relatively small, intense Eugene O'Neill play, the Rocky Flats drama would become like *Aida*, with a cast of hundreds.

After the fire, rancher and developer Marcus Church was among those who wanted reassurance that everything was fine at Rocky Flats. He couldn't make money developing his adjacent land if the plant were dangerous, or perceived to be dangerous. And he had all kinds of development ideas, from trailer parks to office buildings. When many local news stories appeared about the discovery of off-site contamination, Church wrote his sister, Ruth McKay, in April 1970 that a plutonium "scare is being aired." Church's attorney Charles Beise called the media stories "flagrant, abusive journalism." A picture of seventy-two-year-old Church, standing with hands in pockets in front of his Church Ranch billboard, appeared along with a full-page article in the March 1972 issue of the *Dow Corral*, the Rocky Flats employee newspaper. The article was headlined, "Since We're Neighbors Lets [*sic*] Be Friends."[14]

Jean Woodis, divorced from Rudy Zehnder and remarried, still lived just east of the plant and raised dairy cattle. The 1969 fire didn't worry her at first, she said, for the same reason that living next to Rocky Flats had never bothered her. "I guess I had trust that there'd be no problem. I never gave it a thought. I didn't mistrust the government at that time," said Woodis, a friendly woman who moved to this farm in 1947 and watched the area undergo changes. She had first gotten running water in the farmhouse in 1958 and could finally install an indoor bathroom. Woodis, who had raised seven children, was forty-three years old at the time of the 1969 fire and ran the dairy operation on sixty-seven acres. Her cattle and land would soon come under close scrutiny.[15]

Other Rocky Flats neighbors had been jarred by the fire into realizing the plant might pose a real, although unclear, danger to the surrounding area. Eugenia Abbott, a petite dynamo known to everyone by her nickname "Bini," and her husband, Meade, had lived since 1960 on their eighty-five-acre ranch. It sat just a mile and a half southeast and downwind of the plant and less than a mile south of Jean Woodis's farm. Meade worked at an accounting firm in Denver, and Bini, who had designed and supervised construction of their ranch house, raised a few horses and looked after the place. She was a dedicated environmentalist. She had been mildly curious about the government facility on the mesa before the fire, but now she was worried.

"We'd had malformed baby horses. A couple had misplaced bladders," Bini Abbott said. After reading about Martell's soil contamination results, she wondered if radiation caused the horses' problems. She began keeping parts of deformed dead animals in a storage freezer so they could be studied, as they later were. Abbott also went to hear Martell and others talk at public meetings and began a long process of education and involvement with Rocky Flats issues.[16]

The plant's production workers union was a "segment of the public" with considerable clout among Democrat politicians. Within months of the May 1969 fire, the union's chronically poor relations with Dow soured even further. "I think some of the people that Dow put into the positions that dealt with labor got cocky," said local union president Jim Kelly. "They felt they were far enough along in the cleanup that they didn't have to be reasonable with us anymore." Union officials again turned to their allies in Congress.[17]

Kelly and others let members of the Joint Committee on Atomic Energy (JCAE), particularly its Democratic chairman, Chet Holifield of California, know about Dow's slipshod safety and nuclear waste practices. They disclosed the existence of the "Mound," where barrels of nuclear waste had been stacked and covered with dirt. Dow, on the other hand, claimed workers were sabotaging plant operations by slitting glove box gloves. Such incidents did occur during the cleanup of Building 776–777 after the fire, putting workers at risk. Employees "would go in there to go to work and put their hands in the gloves and would get contaminated with plutonium," said Jack Weaver, who had moved up the ranks and was working as a production crew leader. In investigating the incidents, the FBI conducted lie detector examinations on thirty-five employees in November 1969, and AEC investigators interviewed another 280 employees but never identified the culprit or culprits.[18]

Labor-management antagonism at the plant simmered during the winter and early spring 1970. Union leaders felt they had a good chance to wring concessions from Dow in upcoming contract negotiations. Both local and national trends seemed to favor them. Locally, Dow was barraged with negative publicity due to the Colorado Committee's and union's charges of environmental contamination. Dow countered with public relations efforts that included inviting local and county officials to a March 1970 meeting to hear Dr. Chester B. Richmond, from the AEC's division of biology and medicine, lecture about the overblown fear of radiation. In order to respond to congressional inquiries, the AEC pulled together information about the burial of contaminated material at Rocky Flats but still hoped to keep it secret from the public. "There will be no public announcement made regarding this buried material," the AEC's Giller wrote in an April 1970 letter. "However, we will respond to direct questions if asked."[19]

Nationally, even as anti–Vietnam War protests dominated the domestic scene, the environment had become a major issue. In the aftermath of Rachel Carson's book *Silent Spring*, published in 1962, an environmental movement had grown to the point that its influence was being felt in Washington. Environmentalists around the country held the first Earth Day demonstrations in April 1970. Dirty air and water and dangerous chemicals aroused the general public. Congress passed the landmark National Environmental Policy Act, which went into effect on January 1, 1970. Among other things, it established the Environmental Protection Agency (EPA), which soon would be a significant player at Rocky Flats.

Private industry's poor environmental practices weren't much different from those taking place behind the fences at Rocky Flats and other AEC nuclear weapons production facilities. Citizens were concerned about local contamination. And some citizens opposed nuclear weapons production due to the risk of global nuclear war. They saw such a war as the greatest environmental threat of all. Carson herself wrote that the advent of nuclear weapons made her realize humans could "change drastically — or even destroy — the physical world." Still, deeply entrenched Cold War attitudes among policymakers and the public insulated the AEC's nuclear weapons complex, which included eight major production plants, four research and development facilities, and the Nevada test site and employed more than 40,000 employees. The AEC, on grounds of national security and the Atomic Energy acts of 1946 and 1954, declared its nuclear activities exempt from environmental regulation. The agency would be able to maintain that legal stance until the mid-1980s. This didn't mean, however, that AEC contractors such as Dow Chemical were exempt from other disputes.[20]

In May 1970, the same month Building 707 went into full production at Rocky Flats to replace fire-damaged 776–777, negotiators for Dow and the union began wrestling over a new contract. After they failed to reach agreement on salary and working conditions, the union went on strike at the end of June. Charges and countercharges flew for seventy-one days before a compromise contract was signed on September 9, 1970.[21]

Rocky Flats didn't become a major public issue that fall. In the gubernatorial race, for example, the Democrat challenger tried, but failed, to make the plant a campaign issue by criticizing incumbent Republican governor John Love as being too passive toward the AEC. Love easily won reelection. But the complaints about Dow, particularly from the union, did have one receptive local audience — peace and environmental activists. Unlike the union, however, these activists didn't simply want Dow to be replaced as the AEC's contractor. They wanted the plant shut down, which would cost the workers their jobs.

Peace and Environmental Activists

Over the years, a few small demonstrations and protests by individuals had taken place sporadically outside the west entrance to the Rocky Flats plant. The demonstrations were organized by groups such as the Boulder Workshop in Nonviolence and attended by a handful of people who mainly saw the plant as embodying the danger of global nuclear war. But Ed Martell's study of plutonium in the soil localized the threat.

"Nobody knew anything about Rocky Flats until his study," said Judy Danielson, who used Martell's scientific work as a tool to organize citizens against the plant. During the months leading up to the 1972 elections, twenty-eight-year-old Danielson and some two dozen other members of the newly formed Citizens Concerned About Radiation Pollution rang the doorbells of homes just east of Rocky Flats. They asked residents if they could take a scoop of dirt from each of their yards to test for radioactive contamination. "Most people were really open to having you come into their yard," Danielson recalled. "People were concerned about their health." Members of the group put spoonfuls of the dirt in plastic bags, each labeled with the resident's name and address, and carried them in suitcases to public meetings where candidates for congressional seats were appearing. The activists asked the candidates to send the dirt in for analysis. "We said, 'This is in our backyard. What are you going to do about it?'" Danielson said. "We wanted to get a little [media] coverage and make the plant an issue. And it was fun."[22]

It was also serious business, as Danielson knew well. A physical therapist by training, she had worked from 1968 to 1970 in a Saigon rehabilitation center with a nonprofit humanitarian organization called Vietnam Christian Service. She had been deeply affected by her war experiences. After returning to the United States, she and other former volunteers traveled in several states to speak about their experiences and show a documentary about the war. After moving to Denver from Connecticut in the summer of 1971, Danielson practiced physical therapy at a local hospital and continued to be active in anti-war and other peace activities. Through these activities she became friends with Pam Solo, a young woman who would soon play a leading role in the national anti–nuclear weapons movement.

Born and raised in Denver in a staunch Roman Catholic family, Solo was a nun in the politically liberal Sisters of Loretto order. The sisters typically didn't wear nuns' habits and worked with many peace and social justice organizations. Their activities ranged from anti-consumerism actions such as giving away money in downtown Denver at Christmastime to joining with Clergy and Laity Concerned About Vietnam to protest the Vietnam War at the U.S. Air Force Academy chapel near Colorado Springs. Some sisters, including Solo, also participated in the soil-sampling campaign near Rocky Flats.

Solo, in her midtwenties, was well known in the Denver activist community. Completely unassuming, this intelligent, attractive woman made her presence felt at meetings by her respectful approach to others as well as her articulate arguments and creative ideas. She saw a strong connection between the U.S. war in Vietnam and the nuclear arms race. Both, Solo believed, stemmed from the militarism running through the fabric of American society. "In particular, the preparation for nuclear war was an integral part of Colorado's economic, transportation, and social systems," she observed. As the Vietnam War wound down, with U.S. ground forces withdrawn from that battered country in 1973, Solo devoted more and more energy to stopping the nuclear arms race.[23]

Solo and Danielson were hired in early 1974 to share a staff position at the Denver office of the American Friends Service Committee (AFSC), a longtime Quaker-based organization headquartered in Philadelphia. Nationally, the AFSC was conducting a public campaign to expose the nation's militarized economy by focusing on the B-1 nuclear weapons bomber and its local industry contractors. "But not every community was home to a major B-1 contractor," Solo noted, adding that Denver was, however, home to Rocky Flats. Through the AFSC she and Danielson organized a coalition called the Rocky Flats Action Group. It consisted of peace and environmental groups, including Environmental Action of Colorado. The coalition's goal was to "build a campaign with a broad base of citizen support for the closing of Rocky Flats, putting disarmament and peace conversion on the public agenda," according to Solo.[24]

A New Political World

The Rocky Flats Action Group uniquely combined the peace activists' grassroots organizing skills with the growing popular appeal of environmentalism. Colorado environmentalists already had won a major political victory in 1972 when voters passed a referendum by a three-to-two margin to bar the state from spending money to attract the 1976 Olympics to Colorado. Bringing the Olympics to the state would spawn greater population growth and adversely affect the environment, the activists successfully argued. In addition, many environmentalists began collecting signatures for a 1974 ballot initiative, which voters would approve, to halt "peaceful" nuclear blasts in the state. (The AEC conducted its second nuclear test, called Rio Blanco, in western Colorado in May 1973.) The leader of the anti-Olympic effort, Democratic state legislator Richard Lamm, ran for governor in 1974. Another liberal Democrat, Timothy Wirth, was in a race for Congress in the congressional district including Rocky Flats. Solo, Danielson, and other Action Group leaders felt they could influence Lamm and Wirth.

Other constituents also had their eyes on the Democratic candidates, especially Wirth. A tall, handsome, energetic John F. Kennedy–style Democrat, Wirth was running against longtime Republican representative Donald Brotzman. Brotzman had never supported the Rocky Flats production workers union in its disputes with Dow Chemical. Leaders of the union, which merged with the United Steelworkers of America in October 1972 and became Steelworkers Local 8031, were sure Wirth would be different. And Wirth needed union support to win the tough race against Brotzman.[25]

Pat Kelly, whose brother, Jim, had been reelected president of Steelworkers Local 8031, became an active worker in Wirth's 1974 campaign and developed a close relationship with the candidate. "My brother took to Tim Wirth far more than I did," Jim Kelly said. "I didn't have the confidence that he could win." Jim had come to prefer a different venue — using the media to promote union interests. During the 1970 strike, he had been especially impressed with the way a few local television reporters covered the story. "There were three guys who believed that one side was telling the truth and one side was in the beginning of one of the biggest cover-ups of all time," Kelly recalled. "They followed our strike, put us on TV, presented our facts, took our documentation, tried to convince the public that what we were saying was right because they had the documents in their hands. I'll never forget them."[26]

Kelly's next major involvement with the media came in 1973, when Rocky Flats accidentally released tritium, a radioactive form of hydrogen, into the reservoir supplying water to the town of Broomfield east of the plant. The Colorado Department of Health, which began sampling air, water, and soil around the plant following the 1969 fire, detected elevated levels of tritium in Walnut Creek on April 24, 1973. Since the creek flows from the plant's north side production area into Great Western Reservoir a mile to the east, the facility was immediately suspect. Without analyzing any water samples, Dow and AEC officials assured the health department that the plant possessed no tritium source that could account for the contamination. These denials, and the failure by the AEC and Dow to analyze water samples, continued for several months. Finally in September 1973 the health department turned to the EPA, and its laboratory confirmed the tritium findings.[27]

Health department officials detailed the situation in a September 14 letter to Colorado governor John Vanderhoof, who took over as governor after John Love resigned to become the Nixon administration's "Energy Czar." The officials explained that the tritium contamination, while 3,000 times background levels, had reached but not exceeded the state's standard for radiation exposure of the general population. "However," the letter stated, "whether or not the standard has been exceeded, we consider any such exposure totally unnecessary and unwarranted."[28]

Vanderhoof disclosed the tritium incident at a September 18 press conference. The AEC reacted by ordering an investigation, which quickly discovered that the Lawrence Livermore laboratory had trucked plutonium scrap metal contaminated with tritium to Rocky Flats. The plant hadn't monitored the scrap, so when the metal was processed, the tritium entered the waste stream and some ended up in Broomfield's drinking water reservoir. Although the Colorado Department of Health collected urine samples in Broomfield and determined the tritium posed no health threat, the episode further damaged the plant's reputation. And it caused a scare in the Broomfield real estate industry.[29]

In the weeks following Governor Vanderhoof's press conference, the local media carried dozens of stories. People were quoted criticizing the health department for failing to notify local government officials when it discovered the tritium, the AEC for its poor supervision of the plant, and Dow for its flat denials and inaction in trying to identify the tritium source. Dow was the main target for many, including Jim Kelly, who gave interviews to several reporters. "I spoke out because I knew what was wrong. I knew that Dow was lying," Kelly recalled, saying that the company lost all credibility. His opinion was echoed by an internal Rocky Flats report several years later that summarized the tritium accident. "Perhaps the greatest loss was to plant credibility as evidenced by more than 100 articles unfavorable to Rocky Flats' handling of the incident," the report concluded.[30]

Those hundred-some articles came on top of thousands of others written and broadcast about Rocky Flats since the 1969 fire. The political climate had changed, and Dow Chemical, as plant operator, was being forced by elected politicians to answer questions. The days when Colorado's U.S. senators Big Ed Johnson and Eugene Millikin received praise for bringing home any kind of federal facility from Washington were slipping away. Economic largesse, subsidized by federal operations such as Rocky Flats, was no longer the sole measure of political success among the people who had been immigrating to Colorado in growing numbers. The state's population had reached about 2.5 million in the early 1970s. Environmental risk now counted, as the public demonstrated with its 1972 anti-Olympics vote.

But the importance of Rocky Flats to the Denver economy hadn't lessened. *The Denver Post* reported in January 1972 that the plant would soon begin a $130 million remodeling job aimed at preventing a repeat of the 1969 fire. The plant employed 3,700 people, often in three shifts, seven days a week. And over the years, hundreds of millions of federal dollars had poured into the community in worker salaries and commercial contracts.[31]

Nationally, however, public and political pressure had been mounting against the AEC and its handling of nuclear power and nuclear weapons. The December 1970 issue of *Look* magazine blasted the AEC in an article titled "The Nuclear Threat *Inside* America." It began, "For twenty-four years the Atomic Energy Commission has grown up fat, powerful, unquestioned. . . . Now it is under attack." The article then laid out the broad-based criticism of the AEC, from its dual role as promoter and regulator of atomic energy to its lack of oversight at Rocky Flats to its nuclear waste disposal practices. Such criticism continued to grow over the years.

Thus when the tritium controversy erupted at Rocky Flats in fall 1973, the AEC was in too much trouble itself to bail Dow out. In fact, the agency had appointed a new AEC Rocky Flats manager named William Colston who got tough with Dow, much to the chagrin of the company and the delight of the union. "Colston was a thirty-six-year-old guy who had more brains than all the rest of Dow Chemical put together and enough guts and integrity to use them," Jim Kelly said. "He told the whole world that tritium is out here. It isn't supposed to be here, but it is."[32]

Marcus Church's Trout Club

Marcus Church watched the unfolding public drama around Rocky Flats with increasing frustration. The nuclear weapons plant had continued to disrupt his development plans. His Rocky Flats Industrial District had gone nowhere, despite careful planning. He wanted to take advantage of the Denver area's population growth, which was making many landowners and developers rich. "Ten years, two plants on ten acres," he complained in a 1970 letter to his sister. Aside from a few sales of fieldstone, Church's other successful undertaking near the plant was the Rocky Flats Fishing Club. The club, little more than a modest fishing lodge, was located on his small lake less than a mile south of the nuclear weapons facility. Church had acquired the entire lake, known as Rocky Flats Lake or Smart Reservoir, in the mid-1950s. He and his friend and attorney Charles Beise agreed that it would be fun to stock the lake with trout and set up a fishing club. The club drew more than two dozen Denver area business executives as members. For Church and Beise, the lake and fishing club came to symbolize their belief that the Rocky Flats area was completely safe, even after the 1969 fire. Amid conflicting information about Rocky Flats, these men chose to believe the government's version.

After the December 1970 *Look* magazine article appeared, Beise wrote the Rocky Flats Fishing Club members to report that the head of the Colorado Water Pollution Control Commission said, "We should continue to fish free from any doubt or fear whatsoever." Beise told the members this state official called the *Look* article "irresponsible journalism."[33]

Church was reassured and decided to redouble his efforts to sell his land, perhaps even to the federal government. The real estate company he hired proposed that very thing to the AEC's Washington-based general manager, Robert Hollingsworth, in an August 25, 1970, letter. "The logical purchaser in our opinion for the lands [*sic*] highest and best use is the Atomic Energy Commission . . . ," the company wrote. Although this proposal initially seemed to go nowhere and Church picked another company to try to sell his land, the AEC liked the idea of a buffer zone.[34]

Church wasn't aware of the AEC's buffer zone leanings when he invited his two nephews, Charlie and Perry McKay, to come to Colorado in March 1971 to join him and other area landowners in a restricted plant tour arranged by Dow officials. The tour's purpose, according to a Dow memo, was to establish "a feeling of confidence in these property owners that the Rocky Flats plant does not pose a threat to their welfare." After the March 26 tour, Beise wrote a Dow official, thanking him for the tour and adding that "it is unfortunate that irresponsible journalism, such as Look Magazine, is allowed to go unpunished because to the misinformed Rocky Flats is a dangerous area."[35]

For the defenders of Rocky Flats, the media had become an enemy. In a December 15, 1971, talk to a civic group, Dow's health physics manager, Edward A. Putzier, said the amount of plutonium released from the 1957 and 1969 fires was no greater than "a pinch of salt or pepper" and complained that the media was exaggerating the radiation dangers. A story about the meeting was headlined, "Putzier: Press Plagues Rocky Flats."[36]

Despite switching real estate companies, by the end of 1971 Marcus Church still had no buyers for the approximately 3,100 Rocky Flats acres he wanted to sell. Still, he remained mildly optimistic. He wrote his sister on November 16, "We might get a break one of these days and find somebody that does not believe *all* the hog-wash that the press dreams up." Indeed, in early January 1972 Church was approached by a prospective buyer. So he wasn't thrilled when an AEC official informed him later that month that about 1,400 acres of his land was included in a proposed buffer zone. "This of course might be a blessing in sheeps-clothing," he wrote his sister, "but I cannot forget the problems in 1951 in dealing with the Gov't."[37]

But the AEC decided a buffer zone for Rocky Flats was the way to go. General Giller explained at a congressional hearing on April 20, 1972, "It is the kind of plant and the kind of public relations interface that we have out there so we feel it is prudent to have a bigger area." Six days later, Giller elaborated, "To move that whole Rocky Flats plant would probably cost us half a billion dollars and this is a prudent investment protection against public pressure to move."[38]

As in 1951, Church and the other landowners couldn't stop the AEC's "taking" under the Fifth Amendment's condemnation procedures forcing landowners to sell their property if the government needed it. After getting funding from Congress for the acquisition, the AEC announced in February 1974 that it was buying 4,550 acres to form a buffer zone around the plant's industrial area. A third of the land belonged to the Church family.

Meanwhile, Marcus Church managed to sell a bit of his other land even though the controversy about Rocky Flats continued to grow as peace and environmental activists focused on the plant. In fall 1972, for example, a new state law required developers to submit an evaluation of potential radiation hazards in land they proposed to subdivide. The battle over "safe" radiation levels escalated, with all but the experts baffled about the exact significance of the tiny numbers associated with radiation. The Colorado Department of Health adopted a provisional standard of "0.2 disintegrations per minute per gram of dry soil." In light of the contamination spread from the 903 pad, that standard "amounts to a virtual moratorium on development" of the area east of Rocky Flats, the *Rocky Mountain News* reported.[39]

Developers, along with Dow and AEC officials, complained that the proposed standard was unnecessarily stringent. The state Board of Health was responsible for setting the final standard and held two public hearings in February and March 1973. Attorney Charles Beise, representing Marcus Church, was among those testifying at the February hearing and claimed that the stringent standard was being promoted by people like Ed Martell, whom Beise referred to as "some kook from Boulder" without naming him.

Martell, the nuclear chemist, appeared at the March 21 hearing. He urged the health board to stick by the health department's original standard, arguing that less strict standards "are so questionable that there could be serious exposures from levels several magnitudes below the standards." Nonetheless, the health board voted to make the standard ten times more lenient, setting it at "2.0 disintegrations per minute of plutonium per gram or per square centimeter of surface area," which translated to .01 microcurie (millionths of a curie) per square meter (1.2 square yards).[40]

A few months after the debate over levels of plutonium in the soil, the tritium story broke in fall 1973. Suddenly the public had to worry about irradiated water, too. The tritium fiasco was the last straw for Dow Chemical at Rocky Flats. After twenty-two years as the AEC's contractor, Dow was on its way out by the end of the year. In late November the congressional JCAE summoned AEC and union officials to a secret hearing in Washington, D.C., in its private rooms in the Capitol building. In December the AEC announced it was taking bids from companies interested in operating Rocky Flats. Four months later, Dow said it would not compete for a contract renewal. In November 1974, after evaluating bids from seven firms, the AEC announced its selection of a Rockwell International Corporation subsidiary to run the plant. The typical cost-plus contract gave Rockwell immunity from certain lawsuits. The company also had the opportunity to move managers in and out of the plant and train them at taxpayers' expense. The selection of Rockwell was the AEC's last major action at Rocky Flats. The agency was split into two parts, and in January 1975 the Energy Research and Development Administration (ERDA—which two years later was renamed the U.S. Department of Energy) took over the AEC's nuclear weapons production activities and some energy work. The Nuclear Regulatory Commission took over the AEC's nuclear power role. Nothing changed in the nuclear weapons complex with the ERDA's creation. But Dow's departure from Rocky Flats looked to some like an opportunity for positive change. Marcus Church didn't see it that way, however. He was fed up.

TEN

Local Hazard, Global Threat

"Tiger in a Papier-Mâché Cage"

Voters didn't choose a new president during the November 1974 elections. But the nation and the Republican Party were still reeling from Richard Nixon's resignation in disgrace the previous August, followed by Gerald Ford's succession. In November, Coloradans elected Democrats Richard Lamm as governor and Timothy Wirth as U.S. representative in the Second Congressional District, which included Rocky Flats. Both men received strong support both from union members and from environmental and peace activists.

In December, Lamm and Wirth made good on their joint campaign promise to these two constituencies by appointing an eleven-member task force. This "Lamm-Wirth Task Force on Rocky Flats" was to study the plant's operations and make recommendations about its future. Pat Kelly of the United Steelworkers Union (and brother of Jim, the president) and Dr. John "Jock" Cobb of the University of Colorado Medical Center (and a member of the American Friends Service Committee and the Rocky Flats Action Group) joined an influential group made up primarily of state and local politicians and health officials.[1]

When the task force began meeting, Rocky Flats was again making news. "Cattle Near Rocky Flats Show High Plutonium Level," read a *Rocky Mountain News* headline on December 5. The story cited an Environmental Protection Agency (EPA) report indicating that cattle around Rocky Flats contained higher levels of plutonium than cattle near the nuclear weapons test site in Nevada. A few weeks later the EPA reversed itself, saying the first conclusion was based on too little data.[2]

Nobody followed these developments more closely than Marcus Church. The government's buffer zone "taking," expanding the plant area to more than ten square miles, was concluded in November 1974. For his part, Church had grudgingly signed over 1,450 acres for $4.16 million, or $2,869 an acre, but retained the mineral and water rights and kept his irrigation ditches and storage ponds on the property. This time Church didn't contest the sale price in court, as he had done successfully when the U.S. government "took" 1,200 acres of the family's land in 1951 for the original plant site. Church had bigger fish to fry. If the government needed a buffer zone for the plant, it clearly was hazardous. He concluded the government had been "bamboozling" him all along.[3]

On April 2, 1975, Church quietly submitted a formal claim against the U.S. Energy Research and Development Adminstration (ERDA), which had succeeded the AEC three months earlier. He charged the federal government with negligently contaminating the family's land and water near the Rocky Flats plant. For himself and on behalf of the land he held in trust for his sister, Church demanded $19.9 million in damages. By law, the ERDA had six months to settle the claim. Then Church would be free to file a lawsuit against the government and its contractors.

The forty-page brief supporting Church's claims cataloged the incidents made public about the plant since the 1969 fire. Although stating that "all of the facts" about the contamination caused by the plant were not yet known, the brief contended that the adverse publicity alone had made the remaining Church land worthless. "It is as if the government had moved a tiger in a papier-mâché cage onto land adjoining plaintiffs' lands. Maybe the paper cage will hold, but no man in his right mind is going to move next door and find out," stated the April brief. "No market exists. Zoning changes and development are prohibited. The sole and only cause of this damage is the establishment of the Rocky Flats plant and gross negligence in its operation."[4]

Anticipating the ERDA wouldn't settle the claim, during the next six months Church's attorneys, Charles Beise and Howard Holme, continued building a case. Holme took the lead in lining up expert witnesses on radiation contamination, began filing extensive requests for government documents under the federal Freedom of Information Act, and started preparing briefs that later would serve as basic historical resource material for both activists and journalists. After the six-month time period expired, at the end of October 1975 Church turned his claim into a $19.9 million lawsuit against the government, Dow Chemical, and Rockwell International, which had taken over as the new plant operator.[5]

Earlier in October the Lamm-Wirth Task Force issued its final report on Rocky Flats. The 121-page report, based on public hearings and other research, was a masterpiece of compromise. "Our Documentary Report is intended as an educational statement prepared to place the Rocky Flats Plant (RFP) into an objective and proper perspective," the introduction stated. "Although we believe that such a plant can under ideal conditions be operated safely, we have become aware of a number of specific occurrences which cause deviations from the ideal." The report ignored the larger issue raised by activists, who argued the United States shouldn't be making weapons of mass destruction at all.

The report cited several specific events that threatened public health and safety, including the plutonium contamination from the 903 pad and the 1973 tritium release. "We believe it an inescapable conclusion that there is risk associated with the RFP," the report noted. "Since the Task Force is unable to authoritatively assess many of these risks, we have asked in our recommendations that independent agencies investigate into many areas where we felt lacking." Those areas, such as the danger associated with low-level ionizing radiation, would be the subject of study and debate for decades to come.

Among its many recommendations, the task force did suggest that Congress and the president consider phasing out the Rocky Flats plant's nuclear-weapons-manufacturing operations and converting the facility to a "less hazardous" energy industry, such as solar research and development. It also recommended that the federal government fund a permanent public monitoring committee appointed by the governor and the Second Congressional District representative. And acknowledging the plant's importance to the Denver economy, the report stressed, "In evaluating these alternatives, strong consideration should be given to maintaining the economic integrity of the Plant, its employees, and the surrounding communities."[6]

Both the task force report and the Church lawsuit received extensive media coverage. Church's friend and attorney Beise again felt compelled to reassure the members of the Rocky Flats Fishing Club. "If plutonium exists at the lake and in the fish, the ingestion of this meat is far less harmful than the breathing of plutonium," he wrote the members on December 2, 1975. "Living in Denver may be hazardous. I have been as fully informed as a layman can be. I continue to fish and eat the fish at the lake and, hopefully, will do so for many years to come."

Rockwell's Bomb Making

Rockwell International formally began managing Rocky Flats on July 1, 1975. "It didn't mean anything other than the title on our paycheck changed," said Jack Weaver, who had accepted a management position two years earlier in Building 771, the plutonium-processing facility. "For me, being a foreman, I was a little bit apprehensive because it's typical for a company to keep the workforce, but they typically bring management with them. Fortunately I was far enough down the food chain, and what they really brought was the upper level of management."[7]

The Rockwell executives, headed by plant manager Robert O. Williams, were familiar with government contracts. The company, with annual sales of $4 billion, was among the top ten Pentagon contractors. But Williams and his associates had never run anything like Rocky Flats, the nation's only large plant processing plutonium and making it into nuclear bomb cores. The top management needed the expertise of production managers such as Weaver.

Weaver, unlike most managers, intimately knew Building 771's production process since he had started on the ground level as a chemical operator thirteen years earlier and moved up the promotion ladder. Smart and hardworking, Weaver was supervising the midnight shift from 12 A.M. to 8 A.M. when Rockwell entered the picture. "I liked working the midnight shift. It afforded me a lot of time with my family," said Weaver, whose son was ten and daughter six at the time. "It didn't afford me a lot of time to sleep." Weaver's first encounter with his new boss came as Rockwell began a six-month transition period before officially taking over from Dow Chemical in July.

"This guy named Bob Williams shows up in January 1975 on the midnight shift and gets introduced as the new plant manager, and I thought, 'Wow, this is pretty neat.' The existing Dow plant manager didn't want anything to do with the midnight shift," Weaver recalled. Later, Williams occasionally would come back and walk through the building, "which was kind of unusual for a plant manager," Weaver said.

The Rockwell executives also got off to a good start with the unionized production workers. Among the company's first tasks was to work out a new contract with Steelworkers Local 8031. Negotiators for the two sides reached agreement on economic as well as safety and working conditions. "It wasn't that all went well at every turn" during the negotiations, a union history noted. "It was, however, a time of building a bond of respect between Union and Rockwell." Several years later that bond unraveled.[8]

The Rockwell executives also made a favorable impression on some anti–nuclear weapons activists. "They were very personable, especially Bob Williams. He was definitely a PR person," recalled Judy Danielson of the American Friends Service Committee. "He was a communicator. We had interesting discussions. Pam [Solo] would give him books and he'd read them."[9]

Rockwell was trying to change the plant's image. The company began giving limited public tours of the facility in July 1975. Williams was more accessible to the media as well as to the activists. But, said Danielson, "I think it was mostly PR. I didn't see anything change." For despite the administrative changeover from Dow to Rockwell, the structure and mission of Rocky Flats remained the same. The U.S. government owned the plant and paid a contractor to process plutonium and manufacture nuclear weapons.

Activists and Scientists

The contest for public opinion continued with peace and environmental activists in the Rocky Flats Action Group on one side and the government and Rockwell on the other. Both sides used fear. The government employed the Cold War specter of communism in contending Rocky Flats was vital to national security and claiming everything about its nuclear weapons operations had to be kept secret. The Action Group argued the plant was dangerous to both the world and the Denver area. Group members came up with the catchy slogan "Local Hazard Global Threat" to describe the plant.

The big threat, the threat of global nuclear war, resulted from the reality that the United States and Soviet Union had each built enormous arsenals of nuclear weapons. In 1975 the United States possessed 28,100 nuclear weapons compared to the Soviet Union's 17,900, although the explosive force of the Soviet arsenal was much greater than its U.S. counterpart.[10] This Cold War standoff was aptly described as a "balance of terror." Ever since the fragile nature of this "balance" had been exposed during the 1962 Cuban missile crisis, negotiations on an international level and between the two superpowers had achieved some arms control successes. Among them were the Partial Test Ban Treaty of 1963, which banned atmospheric tests of nuclear weapons while allowing them to continue underground, and the Strategic Arms Limitation and Anti-Ballistic Missile treaties of 1972, which sought to prevent the nuclear arms race from escalating further.

In the United States, nongovernmental advocates of arms control included longtime groups such as the Federation of American Scientists and newer organizations such as the Council for a Livable World. The *Bulletin of the Atomic Scientists* continued to be the voice of concerned scientists. But anti-nuclear activists, in U.S. groups such as SANE and international organizations such as the United Kingdom–based Campaign for Nuclear Disarmament, felt the arms control approach was too timid, given the risk of global catastrophe. They wanted the arms race to stop and disarmament to commence. On a local level, Pam Solo, Judy Danielson, and other Denver organizers knew that the dangers posed by Rocky Flats had to be made tangible to convince the general public to react. The activists had to present local hazards in terms of the plant's risk to public health and safety and the environment.

The activists first used scientist Ed Martell's soil studies after the 1969 fire to raise the issue of plutonium dispersal from the plant. In the ensuing years, Martell spoke frequently at public meetings and testified before the Lamm-Wirth Task Force in April 1975. But Martell, a radiation expert, had become frustrated with the media and others whose claims exceeded the scientific evidence. "The issues are so complex that the news media often oversimplify problems," Martell complained. "And not just the news media." He learned, for example, that a Denver medical researcher exaggerated Martell's findings at a scientific meeting in Los Alamos. "I warned him that if he ever quoted me out of context again, I'd really raise hell," Martell said.[11]

By the mid-1970s, Martell wanted to devote his full energy to his own research and leave Rocky Flats to others. One of those others was Dr. Carl Johnson, a medical doctor and veterinarian who in 1974 became chief health officer for Jefferson County, where Rocky Flats is located. "The first thing he did was come up here and spend two hours with me," Martell recalled. He said Johnson's involvement "allowed me to get back to science." But he added, "I didn't always agree with him." Martell was most impressed with soil sampling Johnson conducted in 1974. Using a whisk broom and vacuum cleaner, he collected dust from homes east of Rocky Flats and discovered that plutonium concentrations were much higher in surface dust than in soil samples, which meant that the wind could readily disperse plutonium particles. Johnson also found that plutonium levels in soil where a large housing development was planned exceeded the Colorado Health Board's two disintegrations per minute per gram of soil standard by a factor of seven.[12]

But Martell, like many others, criticized the sloppy methods Johnson used over the next few years in trying to generate more concern over public health damage from Rocky Flats. Johnson gave talks and published studies suggesting that the plant had caused higher than expected cancer rates and infant mortality in nearby communities. Johnson was not a trained epidemiologist. His methodology and findings were roundly criticized, even by some physicians who shared his opposition to the nuclear weapons plant. Still, Johnson confirmed the worst fears of activists, some of whom viewed him as a hero.[13]

Activists also jumped on other claims of Rocky Flats damage in order to promote their two-pronged peace and environmental campaign against the plant. "One of our most creative actions was to take Lloyd Mixon's pig to a Task Force meeting. Mixon, a farmer who lived near Rocky Flats, had all these deformed animals," said Solo, describing a 1975 event. "One was a pig named 'Scooter' that had been born without any hind feet. We put the pig in a box and presented it at a Task Force hearing in front of the cameras. Made all the papers."[14]

Radiation scientists found no evidence that Rocky Flats had caused the deformities in animals from Mixon's farm, which actually sat about three miles east of the plant. Nor did they find high radiation levels in Jean Woodis's dairy cattle or in Bini Abbott's deformed horses, all of which were located just east of the plant. Abbott said independent scientists studied some of the horse body parts she had been saving in her freezer. "Nothing was found," she said, adding that she learned horse deformities were not uncommon. "At the time [the horses died] I wondered if their ovaries were irradiated. Now I think that was far-fetched."[15]

Activists and Workers

The Rocky Flats Action Group realized that the thousands of people employed at the nuclear weapons plant formed a strong pressure group to keep the facility running. While opposition to Dow Chemical's operation of the plant had created a short-term alliance of interests between activists and union leaders, any long-term collaboration required a plan to provide alternative jobs for workers. The activists believed the conversion of military industry into nonmilitary production, an idea being propounded by scholars such as Seymour Melman, offered a viable solution. Solo and Danielson introduced this idea into the dialogue they had developed with Jim Kelly, president of Steelworkers Local 8031.

"Judy Danielson and Pam Solo were the first [activists] that I met and had a lot of respect for," recalled Kelly. "I knew immediately they were honest. I knew immediately they believed in what they were doing. And more than anything I believed that their effort was not to hurt our people, that their effort was that things had to be done right if they were done at all."[16]

Kelly had worked at the plant for nineteen years by 1975. Union workers repeatedly elected him to represent them. Nobody was a more forceful spokesman for worker interests across the board: salary, benefits, safety, and health. But over the years he had begun to make distinctions between the workers' interests and the nuclear weapons they were producing. "I had my own views about the nuclear issue. I had to separate out what was needed and what was not," Kelly said. "I was a firm believer that there was a force in the country that wanted to go and just make bombs to make money." The peace activists' notion that military industries should be converted to peaceful products wasn't foreign to Kelly. "I always kept in the back of my mind that there would come a day when there would be talk about using the plant for something else. I was looking down the road at what would happen when nuclear weapons weren't needed anymore," he said.

Kelly's attitudes had led him to support formation of the Lamm-Wirth Task Force in 1974, and his brother's membership on it, and to engage in discussions with peace activists. And this put him at odds with some union members. "There was momentary talk of impeaching me for being involved in any sort of a task force to study Rocky Flats," Kelly recalled. "It was very tough being a union official and trying to balance yourself between the membership and what was really going on in the real world, because the membership tends to shut themselves off from the real world. The membership always wanted to look at a demonstration or group of demonstrators or task force as something that would only be around a few days and then they'd be gone."

Kelly knew that opposition to the plant wouldn't go away and that the activists did want to close it down. Even the organizers who genuinely cared about the fate of plant workers understood their expressed concerns were a hard sell. "We didn't want the plant there . . . but we also wanted some provision for the workers," Judy Danielson recalled. "I think they thought we were just saying that, although we really did care." The discussions about conversion didn't go very far. When activists brought in an English union leader to talk about the successful conversion at his plant, Jim Kelly was the only worker to show up, Danielson said.

"The workers and those wanting to close the plant have become polarized in the last year," Pam Solo wrote in 1977. "The workers feel personally attacked when the plant, both its mission and its safety, are called into question. Reasons for this polarization seem to stem from their own judgment that Rockwell is doing much better than Dow had done and also from fear of losing jobs." But a different kind of polarization was also occurring.[17]

Polarized Activists

By 1977 the Rocky Flats Action Group coalition had done much to raise public awareness about the plant. It sponsored meetings to educate activists and the general public about the facility's operations. It published two booklets, the second a twenty-page work titled "Local Hazard Global Threat" — the group's slogan. It held demonstrations, including a release of balloons near the plant site to illustrate how far the wind could transport the plant's contamination.

While opposition to nuclear weapons production held the coalition together, conflicting strategies began pulling it apart. "The environmentalist approach to Rocky Flats organizing was and continues to be somewhat different from the peace activist community," Solo observed at the time. "As we continue to build the campaign, ranging from exposing the local hazards to calls for disarmament, these dilemmas seem to get thornier." She noted that the American Friends Service Committee, for which she worked, wanted to make connections between high U.S. military spending and its economic and political effect on Third World countries. Environmentalists wanted to keep the issues more narrowly focused, pursuing a "not in my backyard" approach instead of the "not in anyone's backyard" disarmament tack favored by peace activists.[18]

Nationally, many environmental organizations were focusing their energy against commercial nuclear power plants. They worried their campaign for public support would be damaged if nuclear weapons were added to the equation and their pro-nuclear opponents could charge them with being communist dupes. In the aftermath of the Vietnam War, conservatives were playing on public frustration and laying the ideological foundation that would soon catapult Ronald Reagan into the White House. "Fearing that political issues would cloud their work, environmentalists were most anxious that the problem of the Soviet Union not be brought up," Solo wrote. She noted that "ferocious struggles broke out" among environmental groups and the peace organizations, which in 1977 formed the Mobilization for Survival (MOBE) with its slogans "Zero Nuclear Weapons," "No Nuclear Power," and "Fund Human Needs." This same year the federal government established the U.S. Department of Energy, which absorbed the ERDA entirely and pieces of other agencies. On October 1, 1977, the

Department of Energy became a cabinet-level executive branch department employing about 20,000 federal workers and enjoying an annual budget of more than $10 billion. Along with setting national energy policy, the department still was responsible for producing nuclear weapons.[19]

Recognizing the need to address both nuclear weapons and nuclear power, the national peace and environmental groups compromised. They agreed to sponsor two simultaneous national demonstrations at the end of April 1978, one at a commercial nuclear power plant in Barnwell, South Carolina, and the other at Rocky Flats. Solo and Danielson and the American Friends Service Committee's (AFSC's) allies in the Rocky Flats Action Group along with their friend Michael Jendrzejczyk from the national office of the Fellowship of Reconciliation began organizing the Rocky Flats demonstration.

"We put a slide show together and made a lot of contacts about Rocky Flats organizing," Danielson recalled. Solo and Jendrzejczyk took the slides, the "Local Hazard Global Threat" booklet, and other material and traveled around the country, talking to activists and the media. Interest began building. The organizers invited nationally known speakers to attend the rally, including Daniel Ellsberg, the former Rand Corporation employee who had leaked the secret Pentagon Papers history of the Vietnam War to the press — and thus the public — in 1971.

The organizers planned to follow the April 1978 rally with a "symbolic" civil disobedience demonstration on the railroad tracks leading into the plant. "We knew we were going to get an enormous amount of national attention," Solo said. "We were conducting this dialogue with the union and with state and local officials and neighborhood people. We said the CD [civil disobedience] would be symbolic — not a real blockade but a symbolic action to show that we had the power to do a real blockade."[20]

Five thousand people turned out for a rally that began on April 29 outside the west gate of the Rocky Flats plant. They listened to speaker after speaker decry the nuclear arms race. Ellsberg condemned nuclear weapons production. By the end of the second day dozens of people, led by Ellsberg, wanted to do more than symbolic civil disobedience. They sat on the railroad tracks and refused to leave. They called themselves the "Truth Force," the literal translation of "Satyagraha," Gandhi's term for nonviolence. Supporters brought tents, sleeping bags, food, and ponchos because the weather had turned rainy.[21]

"It kind of took us by surprise when people said, 'We're not going to leave,'" Danielson said. "And we felt responsible because we'd organized this rally." She and Solo were furious. The blockade undermined years of careful grassroots organizing, including the relationship they had built with some workers, and designed to create broad public opposition to Rocky Flats. "The dialogue that we had going really went to pot," Solo recalled.[22]

The public image of the Rocky Flats protest changed radically. Instead of a large peaceful rally, television cameras recorded police arresting demonstrators over the course of the next several months as the blockade continued. "This was a hippie band — they were students, or unconnected, and had no responsibilities and could defy the establishment and were really enjoying it," Danielson said. "They could live out there in their tepees for days on end and didn't care if they had a shower. We thought the average American would write us off."

Yet the two organizers noted that the protests had a positive side. Solo said, "A lot of people were recruited into the movement through that action. I don't know if we lost anybody in the long run. I also don't know whether we could have pursued our original plan if Dan Ellsberg hadn't been a speaker and we'd followed our path." Solo's own path widened after April 1978. She recognized that an end to the arms race required going from protest to policy, as she so appropriately titled her later book. "This new peace movement needed national coordination to maintain cohesion and exert the power it was developing by its local presence," she wrote. She would help coordinate this new peace movement.[23]

Solo, for AFSC, and Jendrzejczyk, for the Fellowship of Reconciliation, began building a nationwide network of groups campaigning against nuclear weapons production. This network became the foundation for the nationwide Nuclear Weapons Freeze campaign that Solo, along with Boston researcher Randall Forsberg and others, successfully organized in the early 1980s. Solo also became active in the international movement against nuclear weapons, which became particularly strong in Western Europe. The presence of this movement, coupled with other factors, contributed to the atmosphere that later enabled Soviet leader Mikhail Gorbachev to take initiatives toward ending the Cold War.

At Rocky Flats, despite the growing protest movement, the plant kept adding to the global nuclear threat. Even as demonstrators were being arrested on the plant's railroad tracks the plant continued processing plutonium and churning out nuclear weapons. Nine thousand demonstrators attended an April 29, 1979, peace rally, and nearly 300 people, including Daniel Ellsberg, were arrested for criminal trespass. Two months later Ellsberg and 253 others were convicted, and he and many others had to pay the maximum fine of $1,000.[24] Dangerous in the eyes of activists, the plant and its mission also had plenty of supporters. And they had learned a thing or two from the anti–nuclear weapons activists.

Steelworkers Local 8031 members voted at a regular meeting in early 1979 to plan and sponsor a "pro-nuclear rally." They allocated $20,000 from union coffers for a rally fund and established an organizing committee. They soon launched the pro-nuclear Citizens for Energy and Freedom group, which described itself as "a grassroots organization dedicated to promoting the continued development of nuclear power." The group's first rally took place in June at the Fort Saint Vrain nuclear power plant, north of Denver. Then on August 26, 1979, an estimated 16,000 people attended a support rally outside Rocky Flats.[25]

For once, Marcus Church didn't follow newspaper accounts of the demonstrations. Just three months short of his eightieth birthday, Church was in the hospital. His health had been deteriorating for some time. He had gout. He needed hearing aids. His eyesight was going bad, and he wore a patch over his right eye, following a detached retina operation that hadn't worked. Saddest of all, his wife, Anne, was afflicted with what would later be known as Alzheimer's disease and was in the hospital room next to his.

In late August, Church's nephew Charlie McKay flew in from California, where he owned and operated a restaurant. He arrived at the hospital late in the afternoon. "They had him sitting up in bed with his hair brushed, face washed, glasses on," McKay recalled. They talked. When a nurse came in to give Church a shot, he refused. "I think he had made up his mind that, 'that's it, I'm going to die,'" said McKay. After sitting in the dark with his uncle Mark, he left the hospital at about 10 P.M., threw down three scotches at a local bar, and headed back to the Church home. In the middle of the night the doctor phoned to tell him Marcus Church had died.[26] The family legacy, including the Rocky Flats lawsuit, passed to Charlie McKay.

ELEVEN

Under Siege

Contradictions

For several years after his uncle Marcus Church died in 1979, Charlie McKay lived a commuter's life. He continued operating the restaurant he developed in Fallbrook, California, near San Diego while spending several days a month in Colorado taking care of Church Ranch business. And the future of this business rested partly on the outcome of the lawsuit that Church, on behalf of himself and the McKays, had filed in 1975 against the U.S. government and its contractors at Rocky Flats. After a flurry of depositions and motions in the late 1970s, Church's extended illness and subsequent death stopped the suit's momentum.

McKay met in early 1981 with the family's attorneys to discuss strategy. "At that time, the lawsuit was sort of in limbo. Nothing was happening," McKay recalled. He and the lawyers concluded that the U.S. Department of Energy (DOE) on one side and the state of Colorado and Jefferson County on the other were all part of the problem. The DOE contended the Church Ranch land around the plant was safe. But the county, backed by the state, was refusing to issue building permits or even discuss any development of the very same land. "If the plant's saying that it isn't contaminated and they're saying it is contaminated, then somebody's wrong here," said McKay. He told his attorneys to add the state and county to the lawsuit as defendants to "force everybody to come into one room and talk." This strategy would reap large dividends in a few years.[1]

The contradiction among levels of government that McKay and his lawyers spotted was just one of many stresses and strains afflicting Rocky Flats in the early 1980s. President Ronald Reagan's administration ordered the plant to produce more nuclear weapons even as the old facility continued to deteriorate. A brand-new, $215 million plutonium-processing building didn't work. More workers reported job-related diseases. Environmental Protection Agency (EPA) officials scrutinized the plant's waste operations. State and local politicians talked about public health and safety but didn't want jobs or income to the community to be lost. Peace and environmental activists kept protesting. The news media became more aggressive, within the constraints of "national security" secrecy. The siege of Rocky Flats was beginning.

The "Evil Empire"

Ronald Reagan's successful 1980 presidential campaign urged voters to forget the "malaise" preached by Democrat Jimmy Carter. We are still number one, the land of opportunity, defender of the Free World, Reagan declared. Our defeat in Vietnam was an aberration. Reagan, a Republican, said the United States had to stand up to the Russians, who invaded Afghanistan in 1979. He called for a larger military budget and more advanced nuclear weapons.

These weapons were to be produced at Rocky Flats and the other specialized plants in the DOE's nuclear production complex. Rocky Flats was a key and vital facility. It was the only weapons plant in the country capable of taking plutonium, processing it into metal, shaping it into the precious hollow cores for nuclear weapons, and adding other core components to make "pits" on a large-scale basis. The pits were the "bomb within the box," which detonated, or triggered, the H-bombs. This prompted the idea that Rocky Flats produced nuclear "triggers," a euphemism used regularly by the news media. As the nation's military budget, including the nuclear weapons portion, took off under President Reagan, so did the rhetoric. He dubbed the Soviet Union the "Evil Empire." He joked about bombing Russia. The general public at first seemed unfazed by such comments and apparently approved his hard-line stance. But the Reagan administration's vociferous saber rattling worried some people that a global nuclear war could really happen, with an utterly devastating impact. Writer Jonathan Schell articulated this concern in his powerful 1982 book titled *The Fate of the Earth*. National groups such as Physicians for Social Responsibility (PSR) published compelling data on the medical consequences of nuclear war and organized public symposia around the country. Australian physician Helen Caldicott captivated audiences by her vivid scenarios of nuclear destruction in speeches that became known as her "bombing run" talks.[2]

The nation's anti–nuclear war movement grew larger and more active, with the Nuclear Weapons Freeze campaign as its major political vehicle. The basic idea was that the United States and Soviet Union should halt, or freeze, the production of nuclear weapons as a first step toward disarmament. Activist Pam Solo was instrumental in these efforts. "I went on to head the disarmament efforts nationally for AFSC and the freeze because the progress on Rocky Flats was totally dependent on changing the political relationship between the U.S. and U.S.S.R.," Solo explained. "I continued to stay very much involved in Colorado and started Freeze Voter to send a message to Democrats and Republicans alike that people wanted them to enact a freeze and not just pay lip service to it."[3] Voters in western Massachusetts passed the first Freeze referendum in 1980, marking the first time American citizens had the opportunity to vote on nuclear weapons. By the time hundreds of delegates from around the country met for the second annual National Nuclear Weapons Freeze Conference in Denver in 1982, Freeze initiatives had appeared on ballots in many communities, including Boulder. Several congressional representatives spoke at the conference, including Democratic representative Patricia Schroeder of Denver, whose reelection campaign was being managed by activist Pam Solo. Schroeder criticized the presence of Rocky Flats next to a major metropolitan area.

Other Colorado politicians had been maneuvering carefully through the debate over Rocky Flats. Local congressman Tim Wirth, representing the state's Second Congressional District, appeased his conflicting labor and activist constituencies by persuading the U.S. Department of Energy to commence the "Long-Range Utilization Study" of the plant in 1980. In agreeing, the DOE set two important conditions. First, the study assumed a "nuclear weapons facility such as Rocky Flats was essential to national defense policy, and thus the alternative of simply closing the facility was not considered." Second, the study only looked at the costs of various options, such as relocating the plant versus keeping it where it was, and didn't examine worker safety or other issues that would exist regardless of the plant's location. Wirth and Governor Lamm appointed a new eleven-member Blue Ribbon Citizen's Committee to monitor the DOE study. Jim Kelly, now an international representative of the United Steelworkers Union, was one of the committee's members. Another was state representative Federico Peña from Denver, elected the city's mayor in 1983 and much later, in 1997, appointed U.S. Secretary of Energy.[4]

While this constrained long-range Rocky Flats study was in process, the

DOE released two other reports that underlined the facility's value to the local community. Each report pointedly noted that the plant's relocation would result in an annual revenue loss of more than $110 million to the Denver area. And federal dollars would be needed to pay more than $2 billion to relocate the plant and restore the site. The DOE then released its own long-range utilization study in February 1983. This study stayed in the $110 million ballpark for local losses and concluded the plant's relocation would cost about $3 billion and take twenty-four years to complete.[5]

When the utilization study was completed, any decision to relocate Rocky Flats "was still beyond reach," recalled David Skaggs, a Boulder attorney and former marine elected to the state legislature in 1980. "But the study legitimized discussion of the future of the plant in a way that hadn't been mainstream in the discussion before." Anti–Rocky Flats activists, however, saw the studies and relocation discussions as little more than a federal government effort to pacify the public while continuing to produce nuclear weapons. The DOE had recently awarded a $470,000 contract for the construction of four new concrete block air-conditioned guard towers around the plant's plutonium production area. This wasn't seen as a step toward decreasing production.[6]

By 1983 some local activists were frustrated that their efforts hadn't halted nuclear weapons production at Rocky Flats. Some of the earliest organizers, Pam Solo and Judy Danielson, for instance, moved away from local anti-nuclear organizing and new people took up the cause. The activists had experienced some minor successes, such as persuading the U.S. Department of Housing and Urban Development to require developers to disclose potential health risks to home buyers near Rocky Flats. But the Reagan administration had lifted this requirement in 1982. The Freeze Campaign had raised public awareness of the danger of nuclear weapons. But then President Reagan threw the anti-nuclear movement a curveball in March 1983 by announcing his own opposition to nuclear weapons.

In what became known as the "Star Wars" speech, Reagan called on the nation's scientists to develop new technologies that would make nuclear weapons "impotent and obsolete." He had been persuaded that a high-tech defensive shield could be erected against nuclear-armed ballistic missiles. He established, and Congress funded, the Strategic Defense Initiative to develop new anti-missile weapons systems. But defenses against nuclear weapons were more science fiction than science. In addition, Star Wars threatened the viability of the 1972 Anti-Ballistic Missile Treaty, a cornerstone of arms control that had effectively prevented a new arms race in "defensive" weapons.

Massachusetts Institute of Technology physicist and former *Bulletin of the Atomic Scientists* editor in chief Bernard Feld talked about Star Wars as being "spherically absurd — absurd no matter which way you look at it." Physicists at major research universities such as the University of Chicago signed pledges not to take any Star Wars money. Still, the idea had influential backers, including physicist Edward Teller, the so-called father of the H-bomb. With the president's backing the country spent tens of billions of dollars before the scheme was eventually abandoned. The Star Wars notion, promoted by elaborate television cartoon depictions of the way such a system might work, did capture the public's imagination, however. This, along with the reality of congressional politics in Washington, D.C., drained some energy from the Freeze Campaign and the national anti–nuclear weapons movement.[7]

The Encirclement

"In the spring of 1983 we began talking about doing something else at Rocky Flats," recalled Tom Rauch, a Denver activist who had been organizing against the plant since 1972. He and other anti-nuclear activists decided to promote an "encirclement" of the plant, an action inspired by English women protesting nuclear missiles at their country's military base called Greenham Common. The goal at Rocky Flats was to have citizens join hands and encircle the plant's perimeter in a peaceful protest.

October 15, 1983, was a beautiful, sunny fall day. Grass in the open space surrounding the Rocky Flats plant had already turned a golden brown. Splashes of yellow and red from changing leaves were visible in the foothills just west of the plant. Many protestors brought picnic lunches. But they had been warned not to bring their children due to potential health risks. "The encirclement was a marvelous experience. Fifteen thousand people showed up, and we covered all but two or three miles of the seventeen-mile perimeter," explained Rauch, a congenial former Catholic priest who joined the staff of the American Friends Service Committee in summer 1983. "The focus was on the arms race, not health and safety. There was not so much focus on the plant's local threat as earlier. There wasn't any solid evidence of health and safety issues that would convince the public."[8]

"The encirclement was a way for people to express their feelings about the way the nation was going," Rauch said. But he added, "Looking back, I don't think it had a political effect." Indeed, the encirclement was more poetry than politics. It happened in the spirit of Allen Ginsberg, the Beat

Generation poet and New Age precursor who resided part-time in Boulder and participated in demonstrations at the plant site. In his poem "Plutonian Ode," Ginsberg wrote of the need to "destroy this mountain of Plutonium with ordinary mind and body speech."[9]

The news media paid fleeting attention to the encirclement, as did the plant employees. The employees' attitude was, " 'Well, the peaceniks are back, and they're going to ring the plant site,' " recalled Jack Weaver, a Rocky Flats plutonium production manager. "It was kind of like — 'Don't you have something better to do in life than to just stand out here and hold hands and chant around the plant site?' I never paid a whole lot of attention to it one way or another." As he drove by the protesters on his way to work, Weaver said he thought, "I'm doing something that I think is valuable to the country. And oh, by the way, the reason you're out here able to protest is because I'm doing what I'm doing."[10]

A Plutonium White Elephant

As the demonstrators held hands, Weaver had his own hands full, trying to get the plant's newest plutonium-processing facility, Building 371, up and running. This building was intended to replace Building 771, the plant's very first plutonium production and fabrication structure, which had opened for business thirty years earlier. With a projected life span of twenty-five years, Building 771 should have been replaced in 1978.

The impending obsolescence of Building 771 had been noted earlier, shortly before construction began on its replacement. The Atomic Energy Commission's (AEC's) General Edward Giller told a congressional hearing in 1970 that this plutonium-processing building was an "old, outmoded, and increasingly hazardous operation" that had to be replaced. At a House hearing on April 20, 1972, Giller elaborated on the problems in Building 771. "The present facility is deteriorating due to the severely corrosive atmosphere inside the glove box lines. The corrosive atmospheres, composed primarily of nitric acid fumes and hydrogen fluoride, attack the chemical process equipment and the glove boxes that contain the process equipment," Giller told the representatives. "The corrosion causes equipment and glove boxes to fail, resulting in spills or leaks of contaminated materials into the working areas. These spills or leaks potentially subject personnel to radiation and to the hazard of inhaling airborne contamination."[11]

Six days later, Giller appeared before the Senate to explain why Congress should appropriate funds for the AEC to construct a facility to replace

Building 771, which "was built in the 1950s based on old building codes." He said 771 was built for a small amount of material but "has grown internally like Topsy. We try to keep it safe, but it has come to a point where it is time to replace that facility, and this [Building 371] is the one we are referring to."[12]

When construction started in 1972, Building 371's underground multistory design incorporated the latest contemporary technology along with safety features the AEC deemed necessary after the 1969 fire. For example, "inert" air—primarily nitrogen with an oxygen content of less than ten percent—was used in glove boxes instead of room air in order to minimize the risk of plutonium fires. Such features, however, added to construction costs. Combined with the high inflation rates of the mid-1970s, these costs drove Building 371's price tag from the original estimate of $77 million to more than $215 million by the early 1980s. Trying to keep prices from climbing even higher, engineers changed some processes and equipment midstream. Plastic and carbon steel parts were substituted for stainless steel wherever possible. Construction fell way behind schedule.

In what ended up as monumental wishful thinking, the Rockwell managers held dedication ceremonies for Building 371 in spring 1980. An open house tour for workers and their families took place in March, followed by a more limited tour for dignitaries and the news media on April 10. Managers announced the building would undergo "cold" (nonradioactive) testing for more than a year and become fully operational in August 1981. Already three years behind schedule, further problems began emerging.[13]

In April 1981, as Rockwell prepared to begin "hot" testing of plutonium processes in Building 371, the company assigned Jack Weaver to work directly under the building manager. "My job was to figure out the building, teach the people how to run it, and start the puppy up," Weaver said. "So I'm walking down the building every day, tracing pipes, and the building's 'cold' at this point so I can get into every room. Construction is still heavily going on." In addition to becoming familiar with the building, Weaver and his crew found many problems, such as cracks in concrete walls that had been poured years earlier. "We found twenty-three cracks, stripped the paint off, force-grouted the cracks, epoxy sealed them, and painted them over."

Building 371 was built to perform two different kinds of plutonium-processing operations, called aqueous and pyrochemical. The aqueous process was the traditional chemical-based plutonium purification operation that had always taken place in Building 771. It required eight to ten weeks to transform plutonium into metal "buttons." The pyrochemical process had limitations but was faster and used mainly for reprocessing nuclear bomb cores that had over time become dangerously radioactive to airplane crews or others required to handle them. Such bombs were removed from the weapons stockpile, sent to the Pantex plant outside Amarillo, Texas, for dismantling, and the plutonium components sent back to Rocky Flats for reprocessing and refabrication into new bombs. Components also were returned simply so the plant could refashion them into new models.[14]

After several delays, plutonium was first brought into Building 371 in June 1981, and Weaver's crew began testing the pyrochemical process. After it operated correctly for several months, the workers began testing the more extensive aqueous process, mirroring the one in Building 771. But there was a big difference in the way the various plutonium solutions were moved around in the two buildings, Weaver pointed out. "771 is a basic, single-plane facility where everything's on one floor. In 371 you start out on the ground floor and go to the basement and go to the subbasement and then pump back up to the ground floor again. So you'd have all that in-between stuff holding material up," said Weaver. Building 371 contained seventy-seven miles of processing piping, and a lot of plutonium could get stuck there. Indeed, when Weaver supervised the first inventory in April 1983, he discovered about twenty-five percent of the plutonium put into the system had been held up in the piping or ducts. "And that was not acceptable," he said. By contrast, he said, about 2 or 3 percent of the plutonium introduced into Building 771 couldn't be accounted for in its twice-a-year inventories.

Department of Energy officials told Rockwell to find and account for Building 371's missing plutonium. "So we spent until April 1984 flushing and cleaning and trying to find this stuff," Weaver said. "We got down to where we were only missing about twelve percent of the plutonium we initially put in the system." That still wasn't good enough. He told the DOE's head of plutonium accountability that the building's design was flawed. "I told him that this building wasn't designed to do what it's supposed to do, so I'll have to D&D [decontaminate and decommission] this building to find everything." Department of Energy officials ordered Rockwell to cease all aqueous processing in Building 371, but they left the costly structure standing. It could be used for storage. An adjacent waste facility, called Building 374, could still be operated.

Despite Building 371 being out of commission in 1984, the DOE still expected Rockwell Rocky Flats to meet its plutonium production goals. The military wanted new nuclear warheads. Rockwell, under DOE's supervision, had no alternative but to keep Building 771 running, even though it should have been retired six years earlier after twenty-five years of operation. "Now you're into thirty, thirty-five years and the building is inadequate because you're running old equipment, you're having to replace equipment, you're having breakdowns and you're having more contamination and spills and stuff like that," said Weaver, who had been transferred back from Building 371 and appointed Building 771's manager in August 1985.

The problems at Rocky Flats weren't limited to the plutonium production and waste buildings, located inside the 138-acre maximum security portion of the plant known as the "protected area." This plutonium area lay within the fenced, 384-acre industrial area, which by the mid-1980s consisted of more than 100 buildings, compared with just twenty in the early 1950s. Many of the structures were obsolete. Decades of nuclear weapons production, accompanied by poor environmental and waste practices, had left much of the site contaminated. Moreover, more workers were coming down with job-related illnesses — at least one of which was not caused by radiation exposure.

Beryllium Disease

Marvin Thielsen suffered from a hacking cough by the early 1980s. It couldn't repress this stout, good-natured man, who always had a joke to share with his fellow Rocky Flats employees, but it did worry him. Having worked at the plant for more than twenty-five years, Thielsen, in his sixties, was looking forward to retirement and relaxation. Yet the cough was getting worse. He suspected beryllium dust was the cause.[15]

Like many Rocky Flats employees, Thielsen worked in several different production buildings over the years. After his 1958 glove box accident in Building 771, when a piece of glass sliced his finger and contaminated him with plutonium, he worked in two other plutonium buildings for the next ten years. During this period, medical tests showed Thielsen had a plutonium "body burden" of .54 (fifty-four percent), or more than half the allowed amount. In 1967, when Dow Chemical was forced to address the increased radiation poisoning among plant workers, the company decided Thielsen should no longer work with plutonium. "As has been our practice concerning these individuals with body burdens greater than fifty percent, we recommend that M. C. Thielsen be removed from further exposure to plutonium," a company report concluded on February 2, 1967.[16]

Dow officials moved Thielsen away from radiation exposures and assigned him to beryllium metal production in Building 883. "If I'd have known what beryllium is, they'd have never got my ass in there to work on it," Thielsen said later. Plant supervisors knew beryllium dust was dangerous because they issued respirators to Thielsen and other workers. But they didn't inform workers about the extent of the beryllium risks.

Beryllium is a light metal whose toxic properties had been known since the 1930s, when it was commonly used in fluorescent lightbulbs. The federal government set tough workplace standards in 1949. Because beryllium's atomic structure makes it a rich source of neutrons, early nuclear scientists also employed it in experiments. But oxygen in the air causes beryllium to oxidize, similar to the way oxygen can cause iron to rust. Researchers ofteɪ inhaled the beryllium dust, which like asbestos fibers or coal dust attacks the lungs and can cause disease similar to the coal miners' dreaded "black lung" disease. A small percentage of the population is particularly vulnerable to beryllium. Some nuclear scientists, including Enrico Fermi's assistant Herbert Anderson at the University of Chicago, died of berylliosis.[17]

In the mid-1950s beryllium became a component in the weapons scientists' newly designed nuclear bombs. Lighter than aluminum and six times stiffer than steel, beryllium was used in the tamper, or reflector, which lay next to the bomb's hollow plutonium core. When the fission bomb exploded, the beryllium slowed down the neutrons reflected off the tamper. These slower neutrons fissioned more efficiently and enhanced the plutonium chain reaction and thus the explosive power of the bomb. In 1958 Rocky Flats began producing beryllium components in a section of Building 444, a facility mainly fabricating depleted uranium. A casting and machining operation was installed for the beryllium blanks, which arrived from an outside vendor in the shape of bowls of pressed-powder beryllium.[18]

Beryllium parts production was expanded in 1966 into Building 883, another uranium building that contained excess space because the AEC sent the plant's enriched uranium operations to Oak Ridge. So while Building 883's "A" side still rolled out and machined depleted uranium, the "B" half of the building, which had previously rolled enriched uranium, was converted to beryllium work. "That's where you heat the beryllium out and hot-roll it, right in the open and shear it," said Thielsen in his husky voice. "And you're in there with those asbestos coats and asbestos mittens that catch fire when you're working with them. And you've got a respirator — and that's your protection." The fabric in the mittens burned despite the asbestos covering. When workers pounded out the fires in the gloves by hitting them together, they spread dust. Beryllium dust also was created when the metal was cut.

Unlike the "hot" (radioactive) plutonium side of the plant site, where glove box systems encased the radiation and protected workers, the "cold" beryllium production areas were wide open. In Building 883, a line was painted down the floor to divide the beryllium and depleted uranium sides of the factory. Beryllium dust traveled throughout the building, even into nearby offices. A designated smoking area was nothing more than a bench at one end of the factory floor even though workers might inhale beryllium dust while smoking. But a big part of the risk came at the machines.[19]

"You work in there with all that dust. It gets all over your respirator. How are you supposed to get your respirator off without getting dust all over everything?" Thielsen asked. "A guy would come around and swab our noses with a Q-Tip at the end of the day — but we never did see any results." In March 1976, when Thielsen still worked in beryllium building 444, a Rockwell report tersely concluded, "This work does not constitute additional exposure risk for this employee."[20]

Thielsen soon began feeling the results of beryllium poisoning. He complained to a company doctor of a cough in 1977, a persistent cough a year later, and then the hacking cough hit him in 1980. Although the plant's first reported case of berylliosis came in 1984, Rockwell didn't have Thielsen tested for berylliosis for four more years. He tested positive, as did many other employees. In 1990 the DOE began to study the effects of beryllium at all its nuclear plants. By 1996 the agency had identified more than fifty cases of chronic berylliosis, including three dozen at Rocky Flats.[21] By then some workers had already died, Thielsen among them.

In the course of his medical examinations, Thielsen admitted he had smoked up to half a pack of cigarettes a day for twenty-five years. But cigarette smoking didn't keep physicians at National Jewish Hospital in Denver from diagnosing berylliosis. Cigarette smoking did, however, affect the claims made by workers with cancer who charged that radiation exposure at Rocky Flats had caused their sickness.

The first publicized workers' compensation case charging radiation poisoning was filed with the State of Colorado in 1970. About a dozen other cases were filed by the early 1980s, and more would follow. Workers, or their surviving families, had a difficult time convincing judges that the cancer had been caused by Rocky Flats if they had a history of smoking cigarettes. Lawyers for the DOE and its contractors vigorously fought the workers' compensation claims at Rocky Flats and the nation's other nuclear weapons production facilities. But this wasn't the DOE's only fight. The atomic agency increasingly found itself doing battle against a sister federal agency along with outside environmental groups.[22]

Church Suit and the EPA

The American public's genuine and active concern about the environment took a long time to penetrate the U.S. Department of Energy's weapons production division. "At [DOE] headquarters, the Office of Defense Programs, preoccupied with the Reagan arms buildup of the early 1980s, devoted little time and energy to environmental issues," an agency history observed.[23] The nuclear bomb makers, first in the AEC and then in the DOE, were used to operating autonomously, without real oversight. But the Joint Committee on Atomic Energy (JCAE), which had always shielded the AEC, was abolished in 1977, so the bomb makers had to develop a different strategy.

DOE officials took a two-tiered approach to the numerous environmental laws being enacted. On one level, they sought to demonstrate that the agency was capable of regulating itself and would voluntarily comply with the law. Thus, paralleling the requirements of the National Environmental Policy Act, the DOE and its predecessors prepared environmental assessments and environmental impact statements for the atomic agency's sites. This resulted in reports such as a 1980 environmental impact statement that basically supported the status quo at Rocky Flats.[24]

On another level, however, DOE officials steadfastly contended the Atomic Energy Act exempted the nuclear weapons complex from laws such as the 1976 Resource Conservation and Recovery Act (RCRA — pronounced "Rickra") or the 1980 law popularly known as "Superfund." The federal Environmental Protection Agency initially accepted this interpretation. But in 1984 the Natural Resources Defense Council, a national environmental group that included nuclear weapons researchers, won a lawsuit to force the DOE in Oak Ridge, Tennessee, to conform to RCRA's hazardous waste regulation. The DOE didn't appeal but claimed that "mixed" hazardous and radioactive waste still was exempt from EPA jurisdiction. At Rocky Flats, the question of RCRA violations would soon blossom into an FBI investigation.[25]

The Department of Energy and its co-defendants chose 1984 as the year to settle the Rocky Flats lawsuit the late Marcus Church had filed nine years earlier. In December the DOE and its contractors agreed to pay the plaintiffs and intervenors more than $9 million in an out-of-court settlement. Because other plaintiffs had joined the case and a sizable sum was paid to the lawyers, Charlie McKay, his brother, Perry, and their mother, Ruth, received about $6.8 million in July 1985, most of which went to pay off debts on the Church Ranch property.[26]

Under the settlement agreement, the state of Colorado agreed to provide the McKays "a duly executed certificate that the retained McKay lands have been tested for levels of plutonium and americium and that such tests show the concentrations of such materials are at or below the State Standard." The state's Department of Health issued the certificate in July 1985.[27] This pleased Charlie McKay, who two years earlier had stopped commuting and moved to Colorado to work full-time at Church Ranch. Recently divorced from his second wife, McKay was ready for a new start, which included developing the land just like his uncle Marcus Church would have wanted.

By settling the Church lawsuit, the DOE and its contractors regained control of some information they preferred to keep from the public. Under the settlement, announced in summer 1985, the plaintiffs agreed to return to Rockwell "all copies of documents and materials" obtained from the government defendants during the lawsuit's discovery process or through Freedom of Information Act requests. Such documents and materials could have been useful to journalists or to other potential plaintiffs in other lawsuits that would be filed.

Pressure against Rocky Flats was mounting. Inside the federal government, the EPA had proposed in 1984 that Rocky Flats be included on its National Priorities List — part of the Superfund law listing the nation's most contaminated sites. But the law didn't yet allow federal sites to be listed. The DOE and EPA continued sparring over jurisdiction, with the DOE especially recalcitrant about accepting RCRA regulation of mixed waste. This angered some members of Congress. At a March 1986 hearing of the Senate Environment Committee, Ohio Democratic senator John Glenn characterized DOE's environmental problems as a "national scandal."[28]

On top of this criticism came the Chernobyl accident in April 1986. This accident at a dual nuclear power and nuclear weapons reactor in the Soviet republic of Ukraine caused reverberations around the world due to its widespread dispersal of radioactive material. The DOE's nuclear weapons plants came under increased scrutiny, and the agency promised to intensify its safety reviews of these facilities.[29]

Just three months after Chernobyl, the DOE announced in July 1986 that it had reached an "agreement in principle" with the State of Colorado and the EPA and would sign a federal facility compliance agreement covering Rocky Flats. The parties agreed to resolve issues involving hazardous waste, including radioactive mixed waste. And the DOE recognized the EPA's authority to regulate such waste under RCRA, although details remained to be worked out.[30]

The local and national media did positive stories about the new Rocky

Flats agreement and underplayed the continuing disagreements and problems at the plant. And this is exactly what the DOE wanted, according to an
internal agency memo dated July 14, 1986. This unsigned memo, written to
brief a top DOE official, noted, "Rocky Flats, an NPL [National Priorities
List] candidate, is in poor condition generally in terms of environmental
compliance. We have basically no RCRA groundwater monitoring wells,
our permit applications are grossly deficient (some of the waste facilities
there are patently 'illegal'). We have serious contamination, and we have
extremely limited environmental and waste characterization data for a site
of this complexity." Thus, the memo continued, "Much of the good press
we have gotten from the Agreement in Principle has taken attention away
from just how really bad the site is."[31] DOE officials didn't anticipate that
this candid assessment of Rocky Flats would soon be passed to the FBI as
well as to members of Congress critical of DOE operations. In less than a
year the memo would surface in newspaper articles.

TWELVE

Whistleblowers and the Feds

Jim Stone

The Energy Department's conclusion in July 1986 that Rocky Flats was in "really bad" shape was a secret kept from the public. But the plant's environmental, safety, and health troubles were well known to some Environmental Protection Agency (EPA) and state health officials, union leaders, and employees, including Jim Stone. In his job as a utility and ventilation engineer, Stone worked in various weapons production buildings at the site. And the more he saw, the more appalled he became. Building air ducts were contaminated with plutonium, equipment was outmoded, and plant managers were wasting money on inadequate renovations.

"Their concept was 'like for like' and they took it literally—making replacements to duplicate exactly what was done thirty years earlier," said Stone, a short, bald, outspoken man. He knew what had been done earlier because he helped design the ventilation systems for the plant's original production buildings back in the 1950s. In those days he had never set foot on the plant site. He then spent the next three decades doing engineering work in the Denver area before taking a full-time job at Rocky Flats in the early 1980s. Stone began urging the managers to "update and introduce efficiencies." Instead the facility deteriorated further. "I thought somebody would come in and shut them down," he said later.[1]

Rockwell building manager Jack Weaver shared Stone's view about problems at the plant. "I've got no quarrel with what he said about things not being up to snuff, 'cause they weren't," said Weaver, who was struggling in the mid-1980s to keep plutonium-processing building 771 operating.

"We've got a building now that's outlived its usefulness and its life span and we're trying to Band-Aid this sucker to keep it together." But Weaver was caught in the middle. Regardless of his building's condition, his task was to keep safely producing plutonium for nuclear weapons. And he expected Stone to come up with solutions. "He wasn't providing me with what I needed to make the building work," Weaver complained. "I requested that he not come back. If you can't help me, I don't need you."[2]

Rockwell fired Stone. "When I left in 1986, I took my reports with me and gave them to the FBI," said Stone, whose whistleblowing would become public three years later. "They told me they had never gotten data like this." To Stone's chagrin the agency sat on the information. "Nobody wanted to say, 'This is a dangerous place here.'"

Actually, some people had been saying this very thing for a long time. Plant workers, led by Jim and Pat Kelly, had been pointing out safety and health hazards since the 1950s. Concerned scientists, anti–nuclear war activists, and environmentalists had been challenging the plant's operations since the 1969 fire. Yet for the nation's leaders—both in Congress and the executive branch—whatever dangers existed at Rocky Flats and other government-owned weapons plants were always overshadowed by their conviction that nuclear weapons were vital for the nation's defense. And within this shared belief system, Colorado politicians and the general public focused on the plant's economic benefits while simultaneously expressing concern about safety. Rocky Flats employed more than 6,000 persons in the mid-1980s and paid them $280 million yearly in wages and fringe benefits. The plant also purchased $140 million in goods and services each year.[3] But international events were beginning to cast a new light on the nation's entire nuclear weapons complex. As this happened, environmental regulators and journalists began playing more active roles at Rocky Flats.

A "National Disgrace"

Arms control initiatives, pushed by nongovernmental groups in Washington, D.C., such as the Arms Control Association and the Council for a Livable World and backed by many members of Congress, were gaining momentum in the summer of 1986. In August the U.S. House of Representatives voted to place a one-year limit on nuclear testing, to have the United States abide by nuclear weapons limitations in the unratified SALT II treaty with the Soviet Union, and to freeze Star Wars spending. A month later, President Reagan preempted the arms controllers by announcing that he and Soviet general secretary Gorbachev would hold a summit meeting in Reykjavík, Iceland, in October. Although the meeting produced no tangible results, it benefited both leaders. Gorbachev faced a disastrous economic situation at home. He had begun pursuing "glasnost" (openness) to rectify his country's unadulterated lies following the Chernobyl accident and was trying to build a peace-loving image. Reagan also sought to portray himself as a conciliator. At Reykjavík he startled his aides by departing from his script and calling for sweeping weapons reductions.[4]

"There was a momentary flirtation with major nuclear disarmaments," recalled David Skaggs, who after six years in the Colorado legislature successfully ran for Colorado's Second Congressional District seat in the November 1986 elections. "We were all entertaining grander thoughts about changes in arsenals than had happened in a long time," said Skaggs, who would represent the district for the next twelve years. Such grand thoughts were in stark contrast to the down-to-earth nuclear and hazardous waste difficulties facing Rocky Flats and other Department of Energy (DOE) weapons facilities.[5]

After Congress reauthorized and amended the Superfund law in October 1986, the EPA was finally able to add Rocky Flats to its National Priorities List of most contaminated sites, an action formalized in September 1989. The act also strengthened the EPA's authority and expanded the states' responsibility for selecting appropriate cleanup remedies at these sites. But the DOE and Rockwell had their own ideas about disposing of some Rocky Flats waste. They developed plans in late 1986 to burn waste in an incinerator located in Building 776, the same building where the 1969 fire occurred.

"The first showdown over the plant was the incinerator issue," Skaggs recalled. "It was not at all clear to me that the incineration approach to dealing with this waste was a bad thing, but this presented a classic instance in which the difficulty of getting the public informed about a highly complex, obscure subject gets in the way of civil discussion in a democracy." Skaggs appointed an independent scientific panel to study incineration. But the panel's work was drowned out by a strong activists' campaign arguing that burning the waste would release plutonium into the air blowing over Denver.[6]

Local journalists followed the dispute closely during the first half of 1987, recounting the debate as well as informing the public about the plant's past activities. "Rockwell Admits 1981 Test Burn of Radioactive Waste," stated the headline of a *Denver Post* story in March. At the request of Skaggs and Colorado governor Roy Romer, a month later the DOE and Rockwell tabled their plans until further health studies could be conducted.[7]

The incinerator flap at Rocky Flats contributed to the broad attack on the DOE's nationwide nuclear weapons complex. On April 24, 1987, ABC News ran a documentary titled "The Bomb Factories," which described the entire complex as a "national disgrace." Problems at the DOE complex "constitute a threat to national security and a threat to public safety," according to ABC correspondent Richard Threlkeld. A few days later, a congressional hearing in Washington, D.C., released the DOE's July 1986 memo conceding that its compliance agreement at Rocky Flats was deceitful. A *Rocky Mountain News* story was headlined, "Government OK'd Flats Cleanup to Deflect Scrutiny, Memo Says."[8] The news story about the DOE's incriminating memo caught the eye of FBI agent Jon Lipsky in Denver. "There was [*sic*] a lot of allegations in there, very interesting, and I saw the excerpts, but I didn't have any way of getting a copy of that memo," he later told a congressional committee. Just a couple of weeks after Lipsky read the story, however, an EPA investigator brought him a copy of the memo. The investigator suggested the FBI and EPA team up on an investigation because of the high political stakes involved. "I mean, we knew the gravity of it," Lipsky explained at the congressional hearing. "We were talking about going after the United States government and a large contractor." Although the FBI opened a case file on Rocky Flats, the agency didn't begin a concerted investigation until more than a year later. The FBI had, however, just concluded a separate eighteen-month investigation that would soon make the newspapers.[9]

Warhead Models and Foot Massagers

An aerial photo under the large headline "Rocky Flats Fraud: Seventeen-Year Secret" dominated the *Boulder Daily Camera*'s front page on Sunday, August 23, 1987. The accompanying article documented how a top secret specialized unit at the plant "diverted taxpayers' dollars for seventeen years to make a staggering array of personal goods and gifts that might belong in a classy Fifth Avenue department store — not in one of the nation's biggest bomb factories."

Camera reporter Martin Connolly wrote, "The largesse included such products as gold-plated jewelry, silver minted medallions, finely engraved plaques, a $65,000 wine still, a $10,000 grandfather clock, and a suspended oak-and-birch spiral staircase that was smuggled out of the plant step-by-step in a false-bottom carrying case." Other items included hardwood foot massagers at a cost of $200 apiece. Workers made these items in the plant's

Future Systems Department, informally known as the "model shop," whose real mission was to design and build replicas of nuclear weapons for demonstration and training purposes. More than a dozen skilled craftsmen worked in this shop, which included fully outfitted machine, woodworking, and design equipment and a large variety of woods and precious metals.

As revealed in Connolly's article and in subsequent stories, a lawsuit, and a congressional hearing, the model shop had a long and sordid history. It operated from 1968 until 1985, when one of the workers, J. David Navarette, blew the whistle. Referring to the model shop's director, Navarette later explained that "after being ordered to produce the third set of house plans for Mr. Warren Rooker's use, which was to be his retirement home, I finally had had enough. I decided I wasn't going to take any more and it was time something had to be done." So in early 1985 Navarette told an official in Rockwell's employee relations office what was happening and this official notified the FBI.[10]

The FBI then conducted a joint investigation with the DOE's Office of Inspector General, an independent unit similar to those within other federal agencies. The investigators discovered that along with producing top secret weapons replicas, model shop workers had over the years spent an estimated thirty percent of their time making more than 4,000 personal items. These items served as gifts and awards for officials at the DOE, Rockwell, and other contractors or as mementos to employees for long service. For example, to fill an order from Lawrence Livermore National Laboratory, the model shop spent more than $11,000 for an elaborate walnut, medallion-studded plaque presented to physicist Edward Teller upon his retirement as the lab's director.

After concluding its investigation, the FBI turned the findings over to the U.S. Attorney's office in Denver. In May 1987 the U.S. Attorney declined to prosecute "based on lack of sufficient evidence of criminal intent upon which to prosecute [Warren] Rooker," the model shop director, according to an FBI official. In the meantime, however, reporter Connolly had been tipped off about the scandal and pursued his own investigation, which included lengthy interviews with Navarette and other employees. Shortly after the first *Camera* story ran in August, Navarette filed a lawsuit under the federal False Claims Act, a law that encouraged whistleblowers to expose fraud involving taxpayer funds. Rockwell and Lawrence Livermore eventually settled the suit in 1993 by agreeing to pay the government $450,000, of which $112,500 was designated for Navarette.[11]

Talking later about his Rocky Flats story, reporter Connolly noted, "This was one of the first media attempts to get behind the wall of secrecy out there. Ironically, it was about the model shop." The "irony," he explained, was that the model shop shenanigans were trivial compared to the dangers posed by the nuclear weapons and by-products from Rocky Flats. "My investigation was difficult, but it didn't involve plutonium theft or waste," he said. "It was the right kind of investigation, but the topic was a little off."[12]

Nevertheless, the model shop's garden-variety corruption incensed the public and Congress in a way that larger nuclear dangers usually hadn't. The estimated $1 million in frivolous items was minuscule compared with the hundreds of millions of dollars spent by the plant annually, but it was seen as a theft of taxpayer money. Moreover, the model shop symbolized deeper problems within the DOE's nuclear weapons complex. "Unfortunately, what occurred at Rocky Flats was not a breakdown in the system," Representative Mike Synar (D-Oklahoma) said during a December 1987 congressional hearing. "Rather, it was a dramatic exposé of how the system really works: Inadequate controls, limited accountability, and an attitude of indifference on the part of the government and contractor officials. Quite simply, the Department of Energy is not in control of its weapons complex."

Synar concluded the hearing with a warning to the DOE officials in attendance. "I think the *Denver Post*, in an editorial, put you on notice of what the American public thinks about this: If the Department of Energy cannot run these facilities honestly, what assurance can we give the American public that you can run them safely?"[13]

Federal Family Feud

As the news media regaled the public with the model shop scandal, far-reaching international events were occurring in fall 1987. In September, President Reagan and Soviet general secretary Gorbachev agreed to sign the Intermediate Nuclear Forces (INF) treaty eliminating intermediate- and shorter-range nuclear missiles. This was the first time ever the two nuclear superpowers agreed to dismantle and ban a whole category of weapons. It was the beginning of the end of the U.S.-Soviet nuclear arms race.[14]

At Rocky Flats, EPA inspectors and their Colorado Department of Health counterparts had become more aggressive in challenging the way the DOE and Rockwell continued to mishandle waste, particularly the more than thirty-one million pounds (fourteen million kilograms) of mixed nuclear and hazardous waste that the plant generated each year. The professional scientists and engineers employed by the environmental agencies recognized the dangers posed by mixed waste. First, as radioactive materials decayed, they could react with the hydrogen present in other wastes and produce hydrochloric acid, which corroded the waste containers. Second, unless the drums containing mixed waste were properly vented, hydrogen gas could build up and cause a small explosion that could disperse dangerous quantities of plutonium. In September 1987 the health department sent the DOE a "notice of deficiency" regarding the plant's waste treatment, storage, and disposal facilities.[15]

The previous May the DOE's headquarters had finally conceded the EPA's and states' jurisdiction over mixed waste. But some DOE officials weren't ready to change their ways. Raymond Romatowski, manager of the DOE's Albuquerque Operations Office, which oversaw Rocky Flats, exemplified the holdouts. In November 1987 Romatowski wrote a strongly worded memo to DOE headquarters, urging the agency to send "a message to EPA that DOE and its management contractors are willing to 'go to the mat'" to oppose the cleanup of Rocky Flats and other nuclear weapons facilities.[16]

A month later, Romatowski was called to testify at a congressional hearing on the Rocky Flats model shop. He claimed the fraud was insignificant and was the only problem he knew about at the plant. He also defiantly defended his decisions over the years to award tens of millions of dollars in bonuses to Rockwell International for its "very good" management of Rocky Flats. Romatowski's behavior clearly pleased some top DOE officials. In January 1988 the DOE gave him the secretary of energy's gold medal award for "unceasing efforts toward achieving excellence."[17]

But a strong crosscurrent had started flowing at the DOE. Even as Romatowski received his award, Secretary of Energy John Herrington was creating an "independent oversight panel" called the Advisory Committee on Nuclear Facility Safety. The DOE would soon use this committee to try to convince the public that the agency was taking a more responsible approach to its weapons plants and contractors. Romatowski wouldn't be around then, however. He left the DOE in March 1988 to work in Albuquerque for a company conducting technical tests for the DOE and the Department of Defense.[18]

DOE Rips Rockwell

During a U.S. Senate hearing at the end of March 1988, a top Energy Department official said the agency planned to consolidate its nuclear operations and Rocky Flats could be phased out in ten or fifteen years. This statement surprised plant workers, community leaders, and activists alike. "That's the first I heard of it," said Jim Kelly of the Steelworkers union. "But if it's coming from the top [of the DOE], we better start acting like a responsible union, making preparations for severance pay, relocation, retraining."[19]

In the wake of the DOE's new position, Congressman Skaggs fashioned a two-pronged policy aimed at satisfying both workers and activists. He argued that Rocky Flats had an important role in disassembling nuclear weapons and the best way to get the plant cleaned up was to keep it running for the time being. "The linkage of those two approaches was the core of my policy and what I said to both groups at the time," Skaggs recalled. The cleanup of Rocky Flats was estimated to cost $1 billion, while overall estimates for the nationwide cleanup and construction of new DOE facilities were in the $200 billion range.[20]

In addition to hinting it might abandon Rocky Flats, the DOE was also starting to take a tougher stance with plant contractor Rockwell International. *Rocky Mountain News* environment reporter Janet Day, who had been covering the plant for several years, got wind that a recent DOE safety and environmental audit had been highly critical of Rockwell. After filing a Freedom of Information Act request, she obtained the audit report and on May 21, 1988, wrote an article headlined, "DOE Rips Rocky Flats Management." In the audit's words, Rockwell exhibited "a breakdown in the classic management responsibilities to organize, direct, plan, and assess the safety of activities" at Rocky Flats. The audit demonstrated that after more than a decade of approving Rockwell's management of Rocky Flats and awarding the company tens of millions of dollars in bonuses, the DOE now was trying to distance itself from its contractor. The agency wanted to leave Rockwell to address environmental and safety problems all by itself. And those problems were growing like weeds after a spring rain.

Among the first safety issues to come to the regulators' attention was the "pondcrete" mess, which illustrated the extent of the plant's waste difficulties. On May 23, 1988, a foreman reported that containers of mixed nuclear and hazardous waste stored outside were deteriorating and the contents spilling out. The waste itself came from open pits, or ponds, which Rocky Flats began using in the 1950s to store and evaporate liquid waste. The DOE started phasing out the five solar evaporation ponds in the early 1980s and then in 1985 began removing the pond sediment, or sludge waste. Workers mixed the sediment with cement and poured it into large plastic-lined cardboard boxes, each about the size of a small refrigerator.

Realizing that this cement and sludge mix often didn't harden properly, the workers tested its consistency by sticking their thumbs into it.[21]

The DOE shipped these pondcrete blocks to the Nevada Test Site for burial as low-level radioactive waste. In late 1986, after about 2,000 blocks had been shipped and buried, inspectors in Nevada discovered that the pondcrete contained hazardous chemicals along with radioactive material and should be classified as mixed waste. Shipments stopped because the State of Nevada, in conjunction with the EPA, had not given the test site a permit to dispose of mixed waste, which was regulated under the Resource Conservation and Recovery Act (RCRA). Rocky Flats continued making pondcrete, however, and by May 1988 had produced another 16,500 blocks, which it stored outside on asphalt pads similar to parking lots. Battered by snow, rain, and wind, the cardboard deteriorated. That is when the foreman reported crumbling pondcrete was spilling from the boxes. The DOE and Rockwell suspended pondcrete operations and inspected the blocks. They eventually found that the pondcrete had not solidified in more than half, or some 8,000, blocks. Reprocessing the waste and repackaging it would take years.[22]

Shortly after the pondcrete spill was noticed, EPA engineers Nathaniel Miullo and Martin Hestmark, joined by two Colorado health department officials, inspected Rocky Flats for violations of RCRA rules. Miullo had been dealing with the DOE at Rocky Flats since 1986, after finishing his work as the lead EPA regulator at another Superfund site — the Rocky Mountain Arsenal, the U.S. Army's former chemical weapons facility northeast of Denver. Hestmark, an energetic young man with a master's degree in engineering ecology from the Colorado School of Mines and a background in chemical engineering, had worked on Rocky Flats for about a year.[23]

"We didn't have terribly friendly relations at the plant," Hestmark later said about the Rockwell managers. "Their feeling was that EPA was involved in territory where we had no right to be and that this jeopardized national security." During their June 1988 inspection, Hestmark and his colleagues were barred from viewing a number of areas on "national security" grounds. Still, the inspectors saw numerous RCRA violations involving the handling and storage of mixed radioactive and hazardous waste.[24] While the reports from the EPA inspectors became part of the FBI file on Rocky Flats, the public began hearing even more about the DOE's new approach toward the plant and Rockwell. A September 2, 1988, *Denver Post* editorial was titled "DOE Watchdog Finally Barks." The editorial was based on a news story reporting that the DOE's Advisory Committee on

Nuclear Facility Safety had nearly closed down the plant the previous February after an inspection team "discovered that nine safety violations first uncovered in 1986 still had not been corrected." The editorial concluded, "The advisory committee's more vigorous approach and commendable willingness to openly discuss problems at the facility are important steps toward restoring public confidence in Denver's nuclear neighbor."[25]

A month later, on October 7, 1988, the DOE did in fact order Rockwell to shut down Building 771 after a DOE inspector and two workers were contaminated when they inadvertently walked into an unmarked, unsafe room in the plutonium-processing structure. When word of the shutdown leaked out, it made local and national news. It was the lead story in the *New York Times*, which noted in a subheadline, "Problems at Colorado Weapon Plant Termed Similar to Those in Other Places." Bad publicity had become commonplace for the DOE weapons complex and especially Rocky Flats.[26]

Game Plan

Publicity had countervailing effects on the FBI's investigation at Rocky Flats. FBI agent Jon Lipsky cited news stories to explain the "low key" nature of the bureau's investigation from June 1987 until October 1988. "We were very discreet in contacting people, reviewing documentation, because there was a lot of publicity over this whole facility and . . . investigative nosing around could potentially damage something that we might contemplate later on, meaning an investigative technique," Lipsky explained at a congressional hearing in 1992.[27]

Yet all the publicity indicated a growing awareness among citizens and the politicians they elected that Rocky Flats had troubles. This atmosphere gave the federal agencies an incentive to push forward with their investigation. On October 21, 1988, the FBI and EPA investigators presented their preliminary conclusions about Rocky Flats at a meeting in Denver with acting U.S. Attorney Mike Norton and three of his assistants. Norton was receptive. "Having lost my oldest son to leukemia in 1983, I was more than ready to believe these public health threats were real," he said later. The investigators decided at the meeting that a search warrant would be the best way to obtain evidence, but no date was set to execute the search. "Potential targets are Rockwell International, employees of Rockwell International, the Department of Energy employees involved with Rockwell International at Rocky Flats, and other DOE employees," according to a meeting memo. The investigative plan included aerial surveillance and the sampling of creeks running off the site. Soon the investigative task force expanded its membership to include the Energy Department's Office of Inspector General.[28]

While the investigators moved into full gear, more negative publicity hit Rocky Flats. In October 1988 Idaho governor Cecil Andrus barred further shipments of transuranic waste to his state's "temporary" storage facility at the DOE's Idaho National Engineering Laboratory near Idaho Falls. Much of this waste came from Rocky Flats, which had been shipping it by train to the Idaho site for decades. With nowhere to go, barrels and boxcars full of the nuclear waste began stacking up at Rocky Flats, threatening to exceed within a few months the storage limit previously agreed upon by the state and the DOE. The DOE's quandary was that the designated site for permanent storage, the Waste Isolation Pilot Plant (WIPP) near Carlsbad, New Mexico, was significantly behind schedule. At a tension-filled meeting in November, Colorado governor Roy Romer told DOE officials, "If you can't dispose of the waste, you can't produce the material. If the limit is reached, Rocky Flats should not operate." A typical newspaper headline about the dispute read, "Ship Out Waste or Shut, Romer Orders Flats."[29]

Then in December 1988 the DOE released a study of 160 contaminated sites at sixteen of its nuclear weapons facilities around the nation. "Flats' Pollution Worst of Arms Sites," a December 7 *Denver Post* headline informed the public. The DOE had ranked the potential hazards at each site on a scale of zero to 10. Rocky Flats received a nine because of hazardous waste in the groundwater and the large population living nearby.

Shortly after this bad publicity appeared, an FBI plane with an infrared, or heat-sensing, camera flew over the plant on the nights of December 9, 10, and 15 to determine whether the incinerator was being operated in Building 771, which was supposed to be shut down. Investigators hadn't been tipped off that the incinerator was running; they simply had the technology to discreetly determine whether or not it was being illegally operated, according to FBI agent Lipsky. An EPA photo interpreter concluded that the Building 771 smokestack was hot. The photos also indicated the sewage treatment plant was illegally discharging liquid waste into Woman Creek.[30] During the first five months of 1989, the FBI and EPA investigators gathered more evidence. In the meantime newly elected President George Bush appointed retired admiral James D. Watkins as secretary of energy. Watkins was a nuclear engineer and veteran of Admiral Hyman Rickover's nuclear navy. In announcing the appointment Bush sent a message that the DOE's widespread environmental and safety problems needed immediate attention. He said he and Watkins both believed "protecting the environment . . . is not at all inconsistent with advancing both energy security and national security needs."[31]

After the U.S. Senate confirmed Watkins's appointment in March, he announced that the DOE would implement an action plan placing "higher priority" on the agency's environmental and waste management programs. He also directed the DOE's Advisory Committee on Nuclear Facility Safety to cooperate with the Defense Nuclear Facilities Safety Board, which Congress had established the previous September to review safety and environmental conditions in the nuclear weapons complex. Despite this apparent change in emphasis by Watkins, environmental groups and politicians criticized the DOE for continuing to emphasize weapons production over environmental cleanup. The Natural Resources Defense Council, for example, argued that the DOE's proposed budget "fails to direct adequate funding for this long overdue cleanup." In early April western governors sent Watkins a letter demanding "decisive federal action to establish a comprehensive national program for the cleanup of all DOE defense and research programs." They blasted the DOE for its history of challenging EPA and state regulatory powers.[32]

Secretary Watkins soon had a chance to demonstrate his willingness to change the Energy Department's operations. By June 1989 the joint investigative task force at Rocky Flats was ready to move. Investigators had prepared a 116-page application and affidavit for a search warrant arguing "probable cause" existed that environmental crimes had been committed at the plant. The alleged crimes involved violations of RCRA, the Clean Water Act, and other federal environmental laws. "In sum," the application stated, "the investigation to date shows a substantial history of RCRA issues and alleged violations at Rocky Flats, and establishes DOE's and Rockwell's clear knowledge of federal environmental law and regulation."[33]

The unprecedented search of a U.S. government nuclear weapons plant required approval from top federal officials. Energy Secretary Watkins signed a memorandum of understanding with the U.S. Attorney General, the EPA director, the FBI director, and the U.S. Attorney in Denver, giving the search a green light. Department of Energy officials at Rocky Flats were not informed, according to government documents.[34] At 8:00 a.m. on June 6, 1989, U.S. magistrate Hilbert Schauer in Denver issued a search warrant. The drama was about to unfold.

THIRTEEN

Shutdown

The Raid

On the warm Tuesday morning of June 6, 1989, more than a dozen FBI and Environmental Protection Agency (EPA) investigators gathered in a parking lot on the arid expanse outside the west security gate of the Rocky Flats nuclear weapons plant. At ten o'clock they entered the plant to confer with Energy Department officials. Around noon they returned to the lot and led a convoy of thirty vehicles, including two EPA mobile environmental crime labs, into the plant. The vehicles carried seventy-five investigators, some in suits and others in coveralls with "FBI" stamped on the back. The unprecedented "raid" on Rocky Flats had begun.[1]

Rocky Mountain News reporter Janet Day and photographer George Kochaniec, Jr., watched these activities from a car parked near the plant's entrance. "We were trying to be inconspicuous," Day recalled. "Once in a while George would hold up a map so it might look like we were lost. Afterward the FBI said, 'We knew you were there.' "[2]

While a source had tipped off the *News* reporter about the raid, federal officials hadn't bothered to give advance notice to Colorado governor Roy Romer. "I am outraged by the possibility that some possible criminal act has occurred at Rocky Flats that may have endangered the population of this area," an angry Romer said at a hastily called news conference Tuesday afternoon. "It jars me to the bone to realize that judgments we have made in Colorado about Rocky Flats may have been made on bad information."[3]

Coloradans had, of course, been making judgments about Rocky Flats for decades. And they had always judged the economic benefits to outweigh whatever health and environmental costs they knew about. Most people ignored the biggest potential cost — that the plutonium bombs produced at the plant would contribute to the holocaust of a global nuclear war. Fortunately, the United States and Soviet Union had avoided such a war.

Even before June 1989, political changes in the Soviet Union and nuclear arms control agreements demonstrated the Cold War was winding down, causing the national security rationale for Rocky Flats to dissipate. Governor Romer and other local officials had begun paying more attention to the plant's impact on public safety and health. Although Romer had sharply criticized the Department of Energy (DOE) and its contractor Rockwell International for their nuclear waste handling and disposal practices at the plant, the governor didn't possess documentation about the extent of the problems. The Rocky Flats Environmental Monitoring Council, which he and Representative David Skaggs set up in January 1987, had begun prying some information out of the DOE and Rockwell but hadn't gotten very far.[4]

The EPA and FBI investigators also lacked solid evidence of wrongdoing, which is the reason they searched and seized records in thirty-one Rocky Flats buildings and photographed and sampled twenty outside waste disposal areas. For a week and a half after they executed the search warrant on June 6, 120 investigators, including some from the DOE's Office of Inspector General, hauled away thousands of documents. Much of this material was soon presented to a special federal grand jury convened in Denver in August 1989. In contrast to this actual evidence from the plant, journalists — and through them the public — had to rely on information leaked by insiders or made part of the public record. The FBI's 116-page affidavit and application for a search warrant, containing "probable cause" that crimes had been committed, was the first major document released. It was made public three days after the raid.[5]

The FBI affidavit contained dramatic accusations, reported in the June 10 *Denver Post* under the banner headline, "Rocky Flats Conspiracy Alleged." One of two front-page stories highlighted the FBI's use of a "spy plane" in its probe. An infrared, or heat-sensitive, camera took nighttime photos revealing that "an incinerator in Rocky Flats Building 771 was used to illegally burn hazardous wastes at a time the plant manager said the building was closed." Lies, illegal midnight burning, high-technology cameras — it all made for fascinating, disturbing reading. But as can happen in search warrant affidavits, these stunning claims would prove to be wrong, although lesser charges would be supported. True or false, the widespread publicity attracted attention to Rocky Flats like never before. Even the

1987 "model shop" scandal paled beside this extraordinary U.S. government raid on one of its own nuclear weapons plants.

Reactions

Immediately after the raid, politicians, union leaders, and activists blasted the DOE's failure to properly supervise operations at its Rocky Flats plant. Congressman Skaggs, speaking to reporters in Washington, D.C., said, "The Department of Energy is simply not capable of doing an adequate job of policing itself." Representative Pat Schroeder of Denver said, "My entire career I've been questioning the things going on at Rocky Flats, and for too long they've just said everything's terrific." Steelworkers union leader Jim Kelly criticized the critics as well as the DOE. "I'm a little bit miffed at the Johnny-come-latelies. Where the hell were they twenty years ago, ten years ago, a year ago?" Kelly asked. "If we had independent oversight of DOE, we wouldn't have this type of thing over and over again."[6]

Energy Department secretary James Watkins had anticipated negative responses. On the day of the raid he went to Capitol Hill and briefed key members of Congress about the search warrant. He assured them he would keep a close watch on the criminal probe. A week and a half later the DOE reached agreement with the State of Colorado to spend $1.8 million a year to monitor the environment and promised to finance a study of the plant's health effects on area residents. Although weapons production continued at Rocky Flats during and after the raid, DOE deputy secretary Henson Moore announced that environmental safety was "top priority, even ahead of production."[7]

The DOE also granted EPA inspectors the top security Q clearances required for nuclear weapons facilities so they could enter restricted areas at the plant. In explaining his agency's new approach, Watkins conceded some past mistakes. "At Rocky Flats we nearly shut down the nation's nuclear deterrent because we refused to make even the slightest concession to environmental protection," he said. "We straight-armed EPA every time." To demonstrate the DOE's changed consciousness, agency officials announced in mid-June that they were suspending millions of dollars in performance bonuses designated for Rockwell. Watkins also sent a twenty-five-person "tiger team" of inspectors to Rocky Flats, initiating a practice that he would employ throughout the nuclear weapons complex.[8]

Many citizens didn't buy the DOE's proclaimed conversion to an advocate of safety and environmental integrity. The Denver and Colorado medical societies recommended the plant's operations be halted until the risk to workers and residents could be assessed. But these medical groups backed off after their leaders met with Governor Romer, who convinced them the plant should be strictly monitored but allowed to continue operations. Sixteen peace and environmental groups also demanded that Governor Romer use his moral authority to call for Rocky Flats be closed by July 4, since he had no legal authority to shut it. A number of other activists, with a wide range of agendas, called for the plant to be shut down.[9]

Some activists saw the raid on the plant as an opportunity to raise fundamental issues, such as the violence and militarism underlying the nuclear arms race. When Romer failed to act on the activists' appeal, LeRoy Moore began a water-only "fast of sorrow and solidarity with all victims of Rocky Flats." The fifty-seven-year-old Moore was a Nashville native and former Southern Baptist minister with a Ph.D. in religion and U.S. history from Claremont Graduate School in California. He believed firmly in nonviolence. After teaching religion at the University of Denver in the mid-1970s, Moore first practiced civil disobedience at Rocky Flats by getting arrested on the plant's railroad tracks during the April 1979 demonstration. Four years later he cofounded the Rocky Mountain Peace Center in Boulder and spent much of his time organizing against nuclear weapons production. His July 1989 fast lasted twenty-four days. In subsequent years, Moore would become a knowledgeable citizen watchdog over decisions involving Rocky Flats. A slim man with a gray-white beard matching the color of his shaggy head of hair, he and his probing questions became a regular feature over the years at the many public meetings concerning the plant.[10]

Other citizens hadn't made up their minds about the plant's dangers when the June 6 raid occurred. Bini Abbott, who continued to raise horses just east of Rocky Flats, still wanted to understand the precise environmental and health effects caused by the facility's operations. Her initial fear that radiation from the plant had caused deformations in her horses had been independently tested and shown to be groundless. Thus Abbott had been putting her time and energy into other causes such as saving wetlands areas threatened by residential and commercial development, although she always kept up with news stories about the plant. Soon she would be named to a state public health panel examining Rocky Flats.

When Abbott's neighbor Charlie McKay of Church Ranch heard about the FBI raid, he had a very personal reaction. "I thought, 'Oh, God, this is more bullshit, it's going to slow down my working with those guys,'" he recalled. "Those guys" were the DOE officials with whom McKay had been haggling for several years over his ability to mine gravel in part of the plant's "buffer zone" just west of the industrial area. McKay's family had retained mineral rights to the land when the DOE expanded the plant's boundaries in 1974 by forcing his uncle Marcus Church to sell the property.[11]

As part of his industrial development plans, McKay obtained gravel-mining permits from Jefferson County in the mid-1980s and informed the DOE of his plans. Just as he was about to begin mining in 1987, the DOE and Rockwell officials suddenly revealed that from 1982 through 1985 the plant periodically sprayed excess liquids from the "solar ponds" waste-holding area onto the land and there might be a contamination problem. The officials promised to give McKay details about the spraying so he could proceed with mining the uncontaminated part of the land, but this hadn't happened by the time the raid occurred.

For McKay, who had been involved with the plant in one way or another since he was a child and spent summers with his aunt Anne and uncle Marcus Church, the raid was just another example of the strange way the federal government behaved. "Rocky Flats, if you've ever worked with them at all, is a true bureaucratic quagmire of government bullshit," McKay said. After the raid, nothing changed in his dealings with plant officials except everything took longer. "There were more people in charge of something they didn't know anything about," he said. "There were more suits walking around, drawing a paycheck."

Exit Rockwell

The stream of bad publicity about Rocky Flats kept flowing throughout the summer of 1989. News stories reported previous spills, contamination, and accidents. The plant's difficulties were added to the lengthening list of problems at DOE facilities across the nation. In August workers from several nuclear weapons production plants testified before a U.S. Senate committee about the DOE's dismal health and safety practices. The same month Energy Secretary Watkins announced the DOE's first five-year plan, which committed the agency to cleaning up all of its two dozen production, testing, and waste sites within thirty years.[12]

Despite the June raid, the DOE and Rockwell continued operating the nuclear weapons production buildings at Rocky Flats. This meant that managers were continuing the plant's long-standing, and in some cases illegal, hazardous waste practices since no alternatives were readily available. Edward Goldberg, the DOE's acting plant manager, became worried as investigators documented the plant's violations. He and other DOE officials were all too aware that three high-ranking civilian officials at the army's Aberdeen, Maryland, test facility had been convicted earlier in the year for illegal hazardous waste disposal.

In late July, Goldberg threatened to halt operations at Rocky Flats unless he was given a guarantee against prosecution. The EPA agreed to temporarily allow "ongoing violations" until mid-September to allow the DOE to develop a waste plan that complied with the law. The plan went into effect on September 18, 1989, when the DOE signed a federal facilities compliance agreement with the EPA and Colorado health department. Secretary Watkins called the agreement the first in a "series of steps to refocus our priorities on environmental compliance."[13]

Meanwhile, Rockwell International executives had been preparing for a split at Rocky Flats with the DOE, an agency with whom they had experience. The California-based defense and aerospace company had operated the DOE's Hanford nuclear weapons production facility in Washington State from 1977 to 1987. Rockwell's record at that 570-square-mile complex was marred by sloppy practices, and the DOE didn't renew the company's contract in 1987, awarding it instead to Westinghouse Electric Corporation. At Rocky Flats, Rockwell executives threatened on September 15, 1989, to close the plant unless the government granted them immunity from criminal and civil prosecution for violating environmental laws.[14]

Six days later Rockwell filed a civil lawsuit against the federal government in Washington, D.C., claiming the company was trapped between the conflicting demands of the DOE, which wanted nuclear weapons production, and the EPA, which sought compliance with environmental laws. The next day, on September 22, the DOE announced an agreement with the company to terminate Rockwell's management contract at Rocky Flats "in the best interests of both parties." As new plant manager, the DOE named EG&G, Inc., a Wellesley, Massachusetts, engineering firm that was the principal operator of the DOE's Idaho National Engineering Laboratory, a nuclear research and development and waste site. EG&G announced it would receive a fixed annual fee of $15 million to run Rocky Flats, which had a $500 million annual budget. Although the Rockwell fee had been kept private, experts estimated the company received annual fees in the range of $10 million, excluding bonuses.[15]

Information about the plant's poor condition continued to leak out after EG&G took over. On October 7, the same day local media reported EG&G's four-year contract to manage Rocky Flats, a news story disclosed an inspection team's discovery of several pounds of plutonium in a Building

771 ventilation duct. Based on the team's report, the story said "significant quantities" of plutonium might have accumulated in other ducts in amounts sufficient to cause localized chain reactions, or "criticality accidents."[16]

Amid repeated charges of safety violations, Energy Secretary James Watkins "temporarily" and quietly suspended plutonium operations at Rocky Flats on November 13, 1989. The DOE acknowledged the shutdown only after Representative David Skaggs publicly called on November 29 for just such an action. He said the plant was too dangerous to operate. The fact that DOE officials hadn't bothered to tell the local congressman about the suspension of operations illustrated how little had changed at the DOE despite all the public controversy.[17]

Ironically, word of the temporary shutdown came the same day Skaggs and Governor Romer said the illegal contaminated waste burning alleged in the FBI's affidavit for the search warrant hadn't taken place. "I have concluded that it didn't occur," Romer said, based on his discussions with federal investigators and plant officials. He said the accusation had created unnecessary public concern about the plant's dangers. Skaggs made a similar comment to reporters. "I am reasonably confident that no midnight burning occurred at the Building 771 incinerator," Skaggs said. "I mention this because some of these allegations can easily distract us from the real safety issues at the plant."[18]

Safety had been an issue at the plant for decades, as union members could attest. Still, the first publicly acknowledged shutdown for safety reasons had occurred a year earlier in October 1988, after the DOE inspector and two workers were exposed to radiation. The shutdown lasted five months. This time Watkins traveled to Rocky Flats to explain the new suspension. He said during a December 1, 1989, news conference that the shutdown would last as long as necessary for EG&G to establish new management systems and install new equipment. "I won't start it up until it is safe," he said of the plant. Watkins meant it. For Rocky Flats was just one of several facilities in the nation's nuclear weapons complex the former admiral had ordered partially or completely shut down in previous months. The nuclear weapons facility at Savannah River in South Carolina was undergoing a $1.6 billion overhaul. The DOE's uranium foundry in Fernald, Ohio, was closed along with processing buildings at the DOE's Hanford and Idaho facilities.[19]

In December 1989 Watkins and other top DOE officials had no way of knowing Rocky Flats would never restart its plutonium operations. Thus the "temporary shutdown" was treated like one of the plant's typical twice-a-year inventories. The labyrinthine glove box system was left filled with containers of plutonium in process. This would come back to haunt the plant. Almost everybody, from workers to activists to state officials to Watkins, thought Rocky Flats would return to bomb making. But global events and local pressures would intervene.

The Nuclear Priest

In early 1990, after just a year in command of the Department of Energy, Watkins found himself caught between two dilemmas. One involved the contradiction between environmental cleanup and the DOE's mission to produce nuclear weapons deemed essential for national security by the president and Congress. The other involved the challenge of changing DOE's values, its intransigent "culture" of secrecy, unaccountability, and arrogance.

"There is an urgent need to effect a significant change in its deeply embedded thirty-five-year culture," Watkins observed about the DOE during his confirmation hearing. He said the DOE's values had "evolved from such heavy emphasis on achieving production goals, made within an atmosphere of collegial secrecy; that problems relating to safety, health, and the environment have not only been backlogged to intolerable levels but, in effect, hidden from public view until recently. So now we are paying the price for this long-term cultural misdirection."[20]

Watkins, a distinguished former admiral and submarine commander, found the DOE bureaucracy intractable. Although similar to the navy in its military orientation — $9.7 billion of DOE's $15.7 billion annual budget went to produce and maintain nuclear weapons — the nuclear agency lacked a strict chain of command. Watkins's orders might or might not be followed by DOE managers. In December 1989 he told a reporter that turning around the "management malaise and ineptness" at the DOE was a hundred times more difficult than anything he had previously attempted.[21]

With plutonium operations at Rocky Flats temporarily suspended, Watkins needed someone special to put in charge of the agency's complicated dealings with federal investigators, regulators, citizens' groups, activists, neighbors, a new contractor, and plant workers. In January 1990 he named Robert Nelson, the deputy manager of the DOE's nuclear weapons test site in Nevada, as the new Rocky Flats manager. Nelson, an articulate, friendly man in his late forties, possessed unusual attributes. He was an electrical engineer, a former navy submariner, and an ordained Episcopal priest. Nelson enjoyed saying he had "actually fired nuclear explosives" as a test controller in Nevada.

"As I tell people here," Nelson commented during an interview in his sparse, government-issue Rocky Flats office, "I'm one of the very few people on earth who uses the Rocky Flats products in the manner that they were designed to be used." Nelson didn't fret that the nuclear bombs produced at Rocky Flats, hundreds of which were exploded in Nevada, could also be used in war. A twenty-nine-year government employee, he accepted nuclear deterrence and the plant's role in it. He noted that the president of the United States annually determines the size of the U.S. nuclear weapons arsenal in a document called the Stockpile Memorandum. "In the most basic sense the president decides through that Stockpile Memorandum — with the National Security Council, the DOD [Department of Defense], the DOE involved — here's what ought to be built," Nelson said. "The Congress funds it and that becomes the marching orders for Rocky Flats."[22]

Those marching orders couldn't be fulfilled when Nelson arrived at Rocky Flats in January 1990. His main job was to get the plant ready to resume production as soon as possible. Throughout 1990 and 1991 DOE officials pushed for a rapid restart. For example, Secretary Watkins argued in April 1990 that plutonium pits from Rocky Flats were urgently needed for the Trident II missiles on nuclear submarines. He lost the argument when top navy officials testified in a closed congressional hearing a month later that the profound changes occurring in the Soviet Union meant a delay in Trident II warheads would not compromise national security. This pattern of announcements about restarting Rocky Flats followed by delays continued.[23]

In the meantime, EPA and state regulators won commitments from the DOE and EG&G, the plant's new contractor, to improve safety practices and begin cleaning up the facility's hazardous waste dumps and other environmental messes. To meet the new environmental tasks, EG&G began hiring additional employees, saying they were needed for environmental cleanup. Simultaneously, production workers were retained since plutonium production had only been "suspended." Some were continuing to produce nonnuclear weapons components, such as the stainless steel tritium containers. Others spent a lot of time in "training" sessions that emphasized safety. By mid-1991 the workforce topped more than 8,000 employees, an increase of 2,000 since the 1989 shutdown. "Every time I met with Governor Romer, he asked, 'What the hell are all those people doing out there?' " recalled Ginger Swartz, former executive director of the Rocky Flats Environmental Monitoring Council. He wasn't the only one wondering.[24]

The new hires worried the leaders of Steelworkers Local 8031, which represented the 2,500 production workers who were part of the total workforce. Union leaders feared that if the plant didn't begin producing nuclear weapons again and tasks shifted entirely to cleanup, the production workers would lose their jobs. In lobbying for a production restart, union leaders found a strong ally in DOE plant manager Bob Nelson.

The Cold War's Last Stand

The fall of the Berlin Wall in November 1989 symbolized the end of the Cold War. But the attitudes and behavior promoted during four decades of U.S.-Soviet tension didn't change overnight, especially on the front lines such as Rocky Flats and other nuclear weapons and military sites. Energy Secretary Watkins could pronounce the DOE's new concern for health and environment and the need for public participation, but the agency's field managers were still oriented toward making bombs, without oversight. Given the continuing multi-agency federal investigation at Rocky Flats, local DOE officials were forced to open many of their records. But the nuclear agency still employed "national security" arguments to resist information requests.[25]

"EG&G and DOE together were a real pain in the ass on records," recalled David Albright, a physicist working with the Colorado health department. The department asked him and several other scientists to plan the community health study that the DOE promised to fund following the June 1989 raid. Whenever his committee sought Rocky Flats plant data from the DOE and EG&G, "they insisted that almost everything was classified."[26] Such claims were not new to Albright, who had been contesting the DOE's weapons policies and practices for years as a staff scientist for the Federation of American Scientists and other organizations in Washington, D.C. He was familiar with the DOE culture. But at Rocky Flats he encountered something different, something deeper. "Everything was adversarial, hostile. The Cold War culture permeated Rocky Flats," Albright said. "You had this Cold War culture of paranoia and suspicion tied in with this culture of not caring about safety infractions."

The planning committee on which Albright served advised the Colorado health department to establish a special panel made up of scientists and citizens to oversee the long-term community health study. In September 1990 the department announced that Albright would be one of twelve members on its Health Advisory Panel. "The plant people were really mad that someone like me was put on the panel," recalled Albright, who is president of the Institute for Science and International Security. Among other things, he had recently coauthored an article in the *Bulletin of the Atomic Scientists* arguing that Rocky Flats should remain shut down. "Continuing the arms race by operating decrepit facilities such as Rocky Flats can no longer be justified as prudent, cautious behavior," Albright's June 1990 article concluded. "It is a reckless activity that weakens national security."[27]

Over the next few years, the Health Advisory Panel pushed the DOE to disclose pertinent records to the researchers that the health department hired to study the possible public health effects of Rocky Flats' operations. The panel then held numerous hearings to gather input and share the findings with the public. Information about community exposures was of particular interest to plant neighbor Bini Abbott, who had been appointed to the health panel as a community representative. In her persistent search for solid information about Rocky Flats, Abbott also continued to attend meetings sponsored by other groups and the DOE itself. "I wasn't taking sides; I just wanted to get educated," she recalled.[28]

In March 1991, on the heels of the Gulf War, the DOE asked Congress for an immediate supplemental appropriation of $283 million to correct remaining problems at Rocky Flats so it could resume plutonium production. Secretary Watkins warned that without the funds, the plant would have to lay off 2,000 workers. Congressman Skaggs accused Watkins of using scare tactics. And the prospect that the plant might restart drew local opponents to a DOE-sponsored public meeting on April 3 in the town of Golden, south of Rocky Flats. "The biggest surprise of the hearing was the absence of any significant show of support from 6,500 Rocky Flats workers whose jobs are at stake," *The Denver Post* reported.[29]

Plant workers responded by showing up in force a month later at a public hearing in suburban Thornton sponsored by several activist groups, including Greenpeace, the Rocky Mountain Peace Center, and Physicians for Social Responsibility. About 400 people jammed into the town's city hall. "The tie-dyed-pants-and-sandals crowd traded insults and facts with the more vocal group characterized by baseball caps and 'Operation Desert Storm' sweatshirts," according to a *Denver Post* story. When invited DOE and EG&G officials didn't show up, activists sat huge puppet caricatures in the chairs reserved for them. A speaker with Physicians for Social Responsibility was heckled as a "communist." Tensions ran high.[30]

The following month more than 300 people, including some fifty Rocky Flats workers, showed up for a public meeting at the United Methodist Church in downtown Boulder. Before the meeting began, a slender, mustached young plant employee wearing a black cowboy hat and boots strode up and unfurled a large banner at the church entrance: "Rocky Flats—

Working to Keep America Free." Several workers wore black T-shirts with the same slogan printed in green letters.[31]

During the next two hours, three dozen people presented three-minute statements for or against the plant's restart. Although the majority of the speakers questioned the need for Rocky Flats, given the Cold War's end, plant proponents had their say. Plant manager Bob Nelson, the only speaker who wore a coat and tie on this warm summer evening, said nuclear deterrence protects the country. "I would like to walk away, too," he said, adding he couldn't as long as nuclear weapons are needed.

Steelworkers union leader Jim Kelly, a taut man whose crew cut always looked fresh, asked the audience to recognize the plant workers as good citizens. "Think of all the good folks at Rocky Flats," he urged. "We will do the job and benefit the economy of this state and nation." Kelly, who attended almost every public meeting about the plant, repeated this economic theme during the following months. He expressed it most forcefully at a December 10, 1991, news conference called by Representative David Skaggs following the political disintegration of the Soviet Union.

For many years Skaggs, like his predecessor Tim Wirth, performed a tenuous political balancing act between his environmentalist and labor union supporters. But the Soviet breakup forced him to make a tough choice. "Given the current state of affairs in the world and the existing nuclear capabilities, I believe we do not need to restart Rocky Flats," Skaggs told the sixty people who attended the news conference in suburban Westminster's city hall. He went on to say that current plant workers should have the first shot at cleanup jobs. He added that he had introduced comprehensive legislation to guarantee health insurance, retraining, and other benefits to nuclear weapons workers.[32]

After reading his prepared speech, Skaggs fielded a few questions before Jim Kelly stood up. "David," he said with controlled intensity, "I don't have a question; I have a short statement. I'm not going to break tradition with myself—I'm going to say it like it is. This is a declaration of economic war on the United Steelworkers of America at that plant. We don't agree that the Cold War is totally over, and I think just this morning with what's going on in the Soviet Union, with Korea, with Iraq and with the rest of it—you and others are leading us down a path where we're not going to be ready when the country needs us again."

Yet Kelly, who had supported fellow Democrat Skaggs in every election, had expected this day to eventually come. That's why he had talked about economic conversion with activists back in the 1970s. So after making his hard-line introduction, Kelly urged Skaggs to fight hard for the workers.

"You've talked about taking care of the workforce, getting health insurance for those 'people who have been exposed.' Who's going to determine that? There isn't a company that has run that plant that will agree any of us has been exposed." Kelly correctly anticipated a major struggle over health care.

Six weeks later, President George Bush ended years of speculation about Rocky Flats. "We will cease production of new warheads for our sea-based ballistic missiles," Bush said during his State of the Union address.[33] The warheads in question, the W-88s for the Trident II missiles, were the sole rationale for restarting plutonium operations at Rocky Flats. Now, forty years after the first plutonium arrived at the facility, it was no longer in the nuclear weapons business. But Rocky Flats was far from out of business.

FOURTEEN

Infinity Rooms

Upheaval

The *Boulder Daily Camera*'s front-page photograph said it all. Row after row of Rocky Flats workers sat in metal folding chairs in the Steelworkers' union hall. Men and women of all ages, some holding children on their laps, stared glumly at a television monitor as President Bush delivered his January 28, 1992, State of the Union address. They looked more depressed than the headline on the accompanying story suggested — "Flats Workers Angrily Listen to Speech." Whatever emotions they felt, their working world was being turned upside down. They would never again be paid good salaries to produce nuclear weapons for their nation. A new era was beginning at Rocky Flats — the cleanup era.[1]

The day after the president's speech, Energy Secretary Watkins elaborated on the consequences for Rocky Flats at his press briefing in Washington. After the press conference, EG&G's Rocky Flats manager, Jim Zane, broadcast a statement to employees over the plant's public-address system. "I have just listened to the briefing Energy Secretary James Watkins gave to the media today and I wanted to share with you the gist of what he said," Zane began. "He confirmed that our present mission has been terminated and we are transferring immediately to a decontamination and decommissioning role."

Zane said that by 1996 the plant's employment would "be reduced to around 4,000 people." That number wasn't too much lower than the 5,000 to 6,000 people whom the plant had typically employed during its bomb production years. But in the two years since the "temporary" suspension of

plutonium operations in November 1989, EG&G had hired many employees, including managers, and boosted the plant's employment to 8,300.
With the cutbacks just announced, former union production workers worried they would not be among those retained for plant cleanup work and
would have to seek new jobs.[2]

"I'm getting up in years and don't have any marketable skills," a forty-
three-year-old radiation protection worker told a reporter. "I want my job."
The prospective loss of 4,000 jobs at the Denver area's largest industrial
plant concerned the community as well. The Rocky Flats employees earned
about $300 million annually. Economists estimated that their spending gen-
erated an additional 19,000 jobs in the region for support businesses such as
grocery stores and dry cleaners. "I think we'll see a ripple through those
businesses right away," said David Smith, president of suburban Broomfield's chamber of commerce. "They'll start pinching pennies more." In
addition, the production shutdown was expected to reduce the $200 million
that plant contractor EG&G, Inc., spent each year to purchase goods and
services in metropolitan Denver.[3]

While jobs were the top priority for Rocky Flats workers, both employees and retirees also worried about their health. Some workers had contracted cancer that they, or their surviving spouses, attributed to radiation
exposure. About two dozen had filed workers' compensation claims, with
mixed results. The plant contractors and Department of Energy (DOE)
usually contested the claims by arguing smoking had caused the cancer.
Other workers already had been diagnosed with the incurable lung disease
berylliosis. One of them was seventy-four-year-old Marvin Thielsen.

Retired since 1985, Thielsen liked to stop by the Steelworkers' union
hall, a nondescript two-story brick building in suburban Golden, a few
miles south of Rocky Flats. He would pour himself a cup of coffee and chat
with other retirees or with union officials working there. It reminded him
of his old coffee shop days in rural South Dakota before he came to Denver
in the 1950s. He still liked to tell jokes or describe the antics of his five
grandchildren. One day, dressed in his usual polo shirt and blue baseball
cap, Thielsen sat at a table in the hall and talked about the effects of berylliosis. "When I go up the twelve steps from my basement, I have to stop
twice," he said, his voice raspy as if from asthma. "It's like somebody cutting
off your air," he added. "Day by day you get worse." He had just three years
more to live.[4]

Thielsen's friend I. K. "Ike" Roberts said nobody knew the full extent of
diseases caused by the working conditions at Rocky Flats. "We'd like to get
government insurance for everyone," said Roberts, who was the union's

safety representative after working twenty-four years in the plant's beryllium facilities. "But if we can't get that, then we want the next-best thing, which is insurance for everyone with the diseases and for everyone who is later diagnosed with them."

Despite the efforts of local representative David Skaggs and Senator John Glenn of Ohio, Congress had repeatedly refused to provide comprehensive health coverage to nuclear weapons workers. Sixty-four-year-old Roberts was irate. "We're literally victims of the Cold War," he said angrily. "We've done their damn work, we took the chances, we got the radiation exposures, we got subjected to toxic hazardous materials, and now they want to throw our ass away."[5]

The workers' plight garnered some sympathy from activists after the DOE halted nuclear weapons production at Rocky Flats. Mainly, however, the activists celebrated the end of the dangerous U.S.-Soviet nuclear arms race. "This is a truly historic time," Tom Rauch of the American Friends Service Committee told an AP reporter. "I think it ranks right up there with the fall of the Berlin Wall and the dismantling of the Soviet Union," said Rauch, the former Catholic priest who had been organizing demonstrations at Rocky Flats since 1972. "After fifty years of developing and making nuclear weapons, we are saying that we are not going to do it anymore." LeRoy Moore of the Rocky Mountain Peace Center agreed. "But now we must insist that cleanup and environmental restoration get the highest priority," said Moore.[6]

Several groups had been insisting for years that the DOE work harder on cleanup. The Environmental Protection Agency (EPA) and the Colorado Department of Health pushed the DOE constantly to meet the terms of the agreements it signed. Among the more recent was the Interagency Agreement in January 1991, identifying 178 contaminated areas at Rocky Flats. The DOE promised to clean them up under a specific schedule. A year later the EPA and state health agency complained that the DOE violated the agreement by not asking Congress for enough money for cleanup activities.[7]

Pressure on the DOE to meet its commitments also came from public bodies such as the Rocky Flats Environmental Monitoring Council. Council member Melinda Kassen, an environmental attorney from Boulder, had become particularly well known for her informed and tough grilling of DOE and company officials. Frequent public meetings by the council and other groups as well as sustained media coverage continued to inform citizens about serious safety and environmental problems at Rocky Flats.[8] But who was to blame for the mess?

Rockwell's Crimes

In March 1992 Rockwell International Corporation pleaded guilty to committing ten environmental crimes — five felonies and five misdemeanors — at Rocky Flats. The company agreed to pay an $18.5 million fine under the plea bargain agreement reached with the U.S. Department of Justice over issues stemming from the June 1989 raid and subsequent federal grand jury investigation. The Justice Department did not charge individual company executives nor individual DOE officials with any crimes.[9]

Federal, state, and Rockwell officials applauded the settlement. But some peace and environmental activists complained that individuals, particularly DOE officials, would not be prosecuted. Referring to the crimes at Rocky Flats, environmental lawyer Kassen said, "The main individuals at DOE who allowed this to occur and who participated in the decisions not to comply with environmental statutes are going to walk."[10] A Denver judge approved the settlement agreement in June 1992. But in a move smelling of partisan politics, a congressional subcommittee chaired by Democrat Howard Wolpe of Michigan disclosed the following month that it was investigating charges that Rockwell had been treated too leniently by the Republican administration. The subcommittee began eleven days of hearings on September 10, two months before the November 1992 presidential and congressional elections. Meanwhile, some members of the special federal grand jury in Denver investigating Rocky Flats were angry about the settlement.[11]

The grand jury, impaneled in August 1989, consisted of twenty-three Colorado residents selected randomly from voter registration and driver's license records. The jurors included a schoolteacher, a hairstylist, a swimming coach, a rancher, and a lawyer. The lawyer had previously done some work against Rocky Flats, but most of the jurors initially knew little or nothing about the plant. "What's Rocky Flats?" rancher Wes McKinley, who was voted the jury's chairman, asked a fellow juror at their first meeting. He and the other jurors got a crash course during the next two and a half years as prosecutors from the federal U.S. Attorney's office in Denver guided their investigation. Meeting every month for a week at a time, the jurors examined 760 boxes of documents and heard 110 witnesses testify about Rocky Flats. The jurors were shocked when they learned about the plant's horrendous safety and environmental practices. They wanted Rockwell and DOE officials held responsible. Most of the jurors were furious about government prosecutors negotiating a settlement with Rockwell without indicting individuals. They prepared a report laying out their findings. The report, like all grand jury proceedings, was secret, due to the investigative nature of these juries.[12]

Someone leaked the grand jury report to *Westword*, an alternative Denver weekly newspaper. On September 30, 1992, the paper ran a lengthy story and excerpts from the report, which labeled Rocky Flats an "ongoing criminal enterprise." Reporter Bryan Abas quoted jurors criticizing U.S. Attorney Mike Norton's handling of the case. A few days after the story ran, Representative Pat Schroeder of Denver demanded a Justice Department investigation of Norton for possibly obstructing the grand jury probe. The congressional hearings already under way became more contentious. After considerable controversy and publicity, a federal judge released a censored version of the report in January 1993. The judge criticized the jurors for "rumor and conjecture" and refused to allow them to talk publicly about the case without being prosecuted.[13]

The grand jury's struggle to go public was a ready-made media drama that would last for years. Journalists labeled the group a "runaway" grand jury consisting of common citizens battling government bureaucrats to provide vital information to the public. Wes McKinley, the jury's foreman, couldn't have been better scripted for his part. He was a good-humored southwestern Colorado rancher with longish hair, muttonchop sideburns, and a thick mustache. Typically attired in blue jeans, a pearl-buttoned shirt, vest, boots, and white cowboy hat, McKinley's picture appeared in *Time* magazine and many other publications. The *Time* feature was titled "Sometimes It Takes a Cowboy."[14]

Can a "Culture" Be Indicted?

Lost in the media's coverage of the grand jury fight was the fact that rancher McKinley and his fellow citizens weren't the only outsiders who spent years learning about Rocky Flats. Federal investigators spent even longer, beginning with an examination of the "model shop" scandal in the mid-1980s. Then came the multi-agency investigation of environmental crimes, which resulted in the 1989 raid and the grand jury investigation. And the federal prosecutors, who included trained environmental lawyers, concluded for several reasons that the March 1992 settlement with Rockwell was the best they could do.

Investigators failed to prove the most spectacular crimes alleged in the June 1989 search warrant. The warrant claimed that Rockwell secretly burned contaminated waste at night and poured toxic chemicals into waterways. Upon closer inspection, investigators found that the infrared photographs taken by an FBI plane had been misread by a photo interpreter. And investigators could not prove the major illegal disposal charges. Instead of straightforward burning and dumping crimes, they discovered the complicated turf warfare occurring since the 1970s between two other big federal bureaucracies — the DOE and EPA.[15]

Investigators learned that jurisdictional disputes between the DOE and EPA over mixed hazardous and nuclear waste hadn't been resolved until 1987. "The more we got into it, the more we learned, the more evidence we gathered, the more research we did, we thought there were very serious problems with trying to charge mixed waste violations before June 1 of 1987," said Assistant U.S. Attorney Kenneth Fimberg, a Harvard-educated lawyer who directed the Rocky Flats investigation.[16]

Government prosecutors came to recognize the DOE's complex relationship with Rockwell and performed mental gymnastics to explain it. Rockwell had "captured" the DOE, according to the prosecutors' March 1992 memorandum accompanying the settlement. Yet they concluded, "DOE was both a contributing cause and also a victim of the crimes at Rocky Flats. While the investigation showed that DOE did not endorse the particular criminal conduct to which Rockwell has pled guilty, a prevailing DOE 'culture' allowed Rocky Flats' crimes to occur." This observation bolstered the argument by Rockwell's attorneys that the DOE was "completely in charge at Rocky Flats."[17]

Prosecutors apparently disagreed among themselves over whether or not individuals could be charged. Norton testified at the fall 1992 congressional hearing that indictments were not warranted. Fimberg said he thought "there was some evidence to support prosecution" of Rockwell officials. He added, "I think that they were marginal cases." Fimberg said he found no evidence of "prosecutable crimes" by DOE officials. "We found bad policy. We found bad management. We found poor oversight, the things that the legislative branch deals with frequently," he said. "Bad policy is generally not a criminal justice issue. I mean, if bad policy was a crime, a lot of policymakers might be committing crimes."[18]

In the end Rockwell's plea bargain and fine satisfied the diverse interests of the federal agencies and the company itself. The government, particularly the EPA, showed it was serious about punishing environmental violations. The FBI polished up its tarnished Cold War image by helping pursue environmental criminals. The DOE avoided prosecution of its managers while trying to distance itself from the mismanagement at Rocky Flats. And

Rockwell, for its part, paid a paltry sum — less than its recent bonuses from the DOE — and successfully prevented prosecution of its executives and employees. The dispute over the grand jury would remain a sideshow focused on punishing individuals.[19]

Yet Rockwell's acknowledged environmental crimes, the debate over the DOE's culpability, and the "gagged" grand jury fueled suspicions by the end of 1992 that the effects from Rocky Flats operations were even worse than suspected.[20] In addition, a number of civil lawsuits as well as studies of plant safety, health, and environmental impact were pending. The lawsuits included a $1 billion "whistleblower" suit filed by former plant engineer Jim Stone against Rockwell, a suit by two former workers claiming that they had been deliberately exposed to radiation, and a class action suit filed in 1990 against Rockwell and Dow Chemical on behalf of 40,000 people living within a few miles of the plant. The studies included the state health department's Health Advisory Panel effort to evaluate the impact Rocky Flats had on community health and safety.

Completion of the studies and resolution of the lawsuits depended on accurate and complete data. Some DOE officials were giving outsiders, including journalists, more access to information. A good example was Bob Nelson, who completed his first "temporary" assignment as Rocky Flats manager in April 1992 but was brought back later in the year when his successor was abruptly replaced amid complaints of sexual harassment. But many DOE officials continued to operate within the old national security and secrecy culture. This DOE culture came under sustained attack, however, after newly elected president Bill Clinton appointed a different kind of energy secretary.

"Not Your Father's DOE"

Hazel O'Leary, who took the Energy Department's reins in early 1993, was extraordinary in many ways. She not only was the first African-American and the first woman to head the DOE; she came out of the electric power industry. The fifty-five-year-old O'Leary had been executive vice president of Northern States Power Company in Minnesota. And she was an iconoclast. After becoming energy secretary she appointed as top aides some environmental experts well known to DOE bureaucrats as opponents. They included thirty-seven-year-old Dan Reicher, who as an attorney with the Natural Resources Defense Council (NRDC) in Washington, D.C., had battled the DOE for years over its environmental pollution. He became O'Leary's deputy chief of staff and chief environmental counsel.[21]

O'Leary believed strongly in the public's right to know about government decisions. In May 1993 she ordered DOE offices around the country to begin declassifying millions of Cold War documents. The following November, Reicher informed her about a forthcoming *Albuquerque Tribune* series of articles detailing how the U.S. government in 1945 began conducting radiation experiments on eighteen people by having doctors inject them with plutonium. O'Leary told him to add information about any such experiments to the material to be declassified. "It was another piece in our work to come clean," O'Leary explained to a reporter.[22]

And come clean she did. In an unprecedented December 7, 1993, news conference O'Leary released summaries of previously secret data about the nation's nuclear weapons complex. She disclosed the amount of plutonium produced and currently located at nuclear weapons factories, revealed that the government had concealed more than 200 nuclear weapons tests, and said the nation had conducted radiation experiments on at least 800 people. The United States had produced 98.1 tons of weapon-grade plutonium since the 1940s, 14.2 tons of which was still housed at Rocky Flats.[23]

O'Leary launched a new period of "openness" at Rocky Flats and throughout the DOE's nuclear weapons complex. Soon she incorporated her new approach in the tongue-in-cheek slogan, "This Is Not Your Father's DOE," which she used in public presentations. The characterization offended agency old-timers. And they didn't easily accede to information requests from public groups, other government agencies, or journalists. Struggles continued over where the line should be drawn between legitimate nuclear secrets and releasable information. But much material was declassified and included in studies published by the Colorado health department's advisory panel and other organizations. Arguments persisted over details and interpretations. Some citizens refused to believe studies that didn't confirm their own opinions. Yet the discussions and debates began taking place with significantly more DOE data and openness than before.[24]

Secretary O'Leary and her staff not only wanted a more informed public, they wanted to improve decision making at nuclear weapons sites across the nation by involving local citizens in the process. They decided to fund groups called Citizens Advisory Boards and looked to the Rocky Flats Environmental Monitoring Council, which had been renamed the Colorado Council on Rocky Flats, to serve as a model for these new groups. Governor Romer and Representative Skaggs helped set up an independent selection committee, which in turn chose the first Citizens Advisory Board in fall 1993. The new board consisted of twenty-three "stakeholders" — representatives of various groups with a stake in the decisions made about Rocky Flats. Members included plant workers, activists, academics, neighbors, and local elected officials. The board's main function was to learn about plant cleanup issues, hold public meetings, and provide the DOE and regulators with community-based recommendations about the plant's cleanup.[25]

New Name and Russians, Too

Shortly after plant manager Bob Nelson left Rocky Flats for good in fall 1993 and returned to the Nevada Test Site, DOE officials decided the plant needed a new name to reflect its cleanup mission. They asked the public for suggestions. More than 600 entries came in, ranging from "Plutonium Plateau" to "After Glow" to "Rocky Flats Environmental Technology Site." The DOE picked the latter in the summer of 1994. This optimistic name couldn't, however, hide the reality that the plant faced serious safety and security issues along with the challenge of the cleanup. Rocky Flats still held 14.2 tons of plutonium, more than half of which was metal and the rest in compounds and mixtures, and 7.3 tons of highly enriched uranium. Thousands of barrels of contaminated waste cluttered the rooms and hallways of former production buildings and were even stacked in parking lots.

"The high-concentration plutonium solutions and reactive plutonium scrap stored at Rocky Flats posed the most severe and immediate safety risk of any stored plutonium in the DOE Weapons Complex," the federal Defense Nuclear Facilities Safety Board warned in April 1994 after a nationwide examination. The DOE spelled out the risk the following August when a national team of experts completed a "plutonium vulnerability assessment" report. Among the dangers cited was metal plutonium stored in plastic bags and placed inside metal cans. Reactions between the plutonium and the plastic could create pyrophoric, or self-igniting, material. To reduce the risk of fire, the DOE resumed operations in one section of Building 707 to heat and stabilize less than two hundred pounds (ninety kilograms) of oxides.[26]

While plant officials addressed safety problems, they kept an eye on security against theft or terrorism. Plutonium was an invaluable commodity for any country contemplating a nuclear weapons program. Reports had been circulating about potential nuclear smuggling in the former Soviet

Union. Indeed, U.S. interest in ensuring that Russia maintain security while safely dismantling its nuclear arsenal had already led to an event that dismayed some Rocky Flats workers.

On July 21, 1994, seven Russian scientists passed by a phalanx of heavily armed guards, went through a metal detector, crossed a narrow open area flanked by high fences and rolled barbed wire, and entered the once top secret plutonium production and bomb assembly buildings at Rocky Flats. The Russians spent about an hour touring underground vaults that stored plutonium. Their extraordinary visit was made possible by a reciprocal inspection agreement signed earlier in the year by Energy Secretary O'Leary and her Russian counterpart, aimed at building trust into the process of reducing nuclear weapons.

"This is a very historic day for Rocky Flats, the United States, and for Russia and perhaps for all of mankind," said Mark Silverman, the DOE's manager at Rocky Flats. His enthusiasm wasn't shared by all the plant's workers. Four days later workers in Building 771, the former plutonium-processing facility, were still grumbling about the visit. "I have spent my life so that Russians would see the bottom side of bombs," said one man in his early forties. "And now they get brought here to see them from the top. I don't like it." The plant's public information officer later commented to a journalist touring the building that a lot of plant workers were disturbed by the Russians' visit. "They are out of touch with all the changes," she said.[27]

For DOE officials, Russians became much less threatening than possible terrorists. They wanted to ensure that no terrorist group could set off an explosion at the plant and release deadly radiation throughout the Denver area and beyond. They depended on plant guards to defend the facility. Starting with Dow Chemical, the plant's various contractors had supplied the guard force. But after security lapses were discovered in 1990, the DOE hired Wackenhut Services Inc., which commanded a unit of about 340 specially trained guards. Wackenhut, too, occasionally came under criticism but retained its contract.[28]

Along with the questions about security, critics raised concerns that plutonium had already been stolen from Rocky Flats. They pointed to 2,600 pounds (1,170 kilograms) of plutonium the DOE classified as material unaccounted for (MUF). But both DOE and outside experts concluded the figure reflected poor record keeping. They said most of the missing plutonium was contained in the thousands of tons of waste already shipped off the site and the rest was caught up in Rocky Flats building ducts and other places on the site.[29]

Rocky Flats Forever?

Cleaning plutonium out of ventilation ducts was just part of the plant's task, which was costing taxpayers more than seven hundred million dollars a year by the mid-1990s. But not all of the funds were being well used. In 1995 *Denver Post* environmental reporter Mark Obmascik received four years of the plant's internal financial records that he requested under the federal Freedom of Information Act. His July 2 story was headlined, "Flats Blunders Cost $32 Million." The occurrences at Rocky Flats "would be slapstick comedy — if the public didn't have to pay for it," Obmascik wrote. "When Rocky Flats janitors tried to change a fluorescent lightbulb, they made such a mess that taxpayers had to buy new clothes for everyone in the office," he recounted. "When contractors were caught padding overtime bills, they were paid to attend meetings denouncing their sins."

Coincidentally, the same month Obmascik's story was published Kaiser-Hill Company replaced EG&G as the DOE's contractor at Rocky Flats. The change belatedly reflected the plant's switch from bomb making to cleanup. Kaiser-Hill, a joint venture between two large environmental engineering firms, received a five-year contract with a cleanup budget estimated at $3.5 billion. Under a new DOE contract concept, eighty-five percent of Kaiser-Hill's fee was to be based on its performance in meeting cleanup goals. That gave the company a big incentive to record accomplishments. But Kaiser-Hill executives soon learned "cleanup" meant different things to different stakeholders.[30]

The question of cleanup standards loomed large. How clean was clean enough? The answer depended on the projected land use for the ten-square-mile Rocky Flats site. More than ninety-three percent of the site's 6,551 acres formed the plant's "buffer zone." The approximately four hundred remaining acres were occupied by landfills and former industrial facilities, including the highly contaminated and specially protected plutonium production area. Under EPA regulations, land intended for residential housing was held to much stricter radiation standards, for example, than land designated for commercial use or as open space. Thus EPA officials as well as activists worried when the DOE talked about Rocky Flats as a future "wildlife refuge." Although EPA officials didn't expect Rocky Flats ever to be used for housing, they wanted the site cleaned up to residential standards.[31]

Land use issues generally involve more politics than science, and Rocky Flats was no exception. The DOE and groups such as the DOE-funded Rocky Flats Local Impacts Initiative argued the community would benefit from converting the plant's nonradioactive buildings to commercial operations. In contrast, the Future Site Use Working Group, consisting of environmentalists, public officials, and citizens, recommended the site be a restricted access area open to scientists studying cleanup technology. And private developers such as Charlie McKay wanted as few restrictions as possible on land use. "There may be some buildings out there that are so contaminated that you do have to encapsulate them until you can figure out what to do," McKay said. "But certainly not the whole place."[32]

Nobody in the community wanted Rocky Flats to be a permanent nuclear waste dump. The DOE and EG&G floated this notion in early 1995 when they suggested burying solar pond waste. The response was universally negative. "The only question is a values one: Do we want to have waste permanently disposed at Rocky Flats?" asked Ken Korkia of the Citizens Advisory Board. Then the DOE and its new contractor, Kaiser-Hill, began altering the plant's cleanup timetable and costs at an astonishing pace. A 1995 DOE study concluded the plant's cleanup would take fifty years and cost $36.6 billion. In October 1995 Kaiser-Hill proposed an "accelerated" plan taking seven years and costing just $6 billion. This plan also contained the permanent dump idea. Kaiser-Hill said Rocky Flats should release most of its buffer zone for unrestricted use and raze and bury its contaminated buildings. "If this is a sneaky way to do a 'dirty closure' and walk away from it, it's not going to have public support," local Sierra Club's chairman Eugene De Mayo said, voicing a typical reaction.[33]

Kaiser-Hill and the DOE then backed off from public proposals about on-site waste burial. Both stressed that plutonium and other nuclear waste would be shipped off the site before its closure. In 1996 the DOE cut its estimate of the plant's cleanup costs to $17.3 billion. In July of that year Kaiser-Hill said the work could be completed by the year 2015. The Citizens Advisory Board questioned the DOE's decision-making process, particularly after the agency canceled its work on a "site-wide" environmental impact study of Rocky Flats. Department of Energy officials claimed the study had become meaningless because the plant's mission had changed so much since the study began in 1991.[34]

In August 1997 Energy Secretary Federico Peña dramatically accelerated the cleanup schedule for Rocky Flats. Peña, a former Denver mayor and U.S. transportation secretary who took over the Energy post at the beginning of President Clinton's second term, said the site would be closed in 2006 at a cost of $7 billion. "If, compared to the 1995 estimate, we can save $29 billion at Rocky Flats and shave forty years off the time it takes to do the job, we must be doing something right," he said at a Jefferson County commissioners' forum in suburban Lakewood.[35]

Peña did qualify his prediction by saying his accelerated timetable depended on stable funding from Congress and the opening of the controversial Waste Isolation Pilot Plant (WIPP) nuclear waste facility in New Mexico. What he didn't mention were assessments about the profound difficulty in decontaminating Rocky Flats' old plutonium production buildings, demolishing them, and then removing plutonium from the soil.

At the same time Peña was making his optimistic projections about cleanup, workers in airtight suits and respirators were toiling away in Room 3549 inside Building 371 at Rocky Flats. The room was one of thirteen concrete chambers at the site so heavily contaminated with plutonium that radiation levels couldn't be measured with standard equipment. The needles went off the scale, toward infinity. Thus the chambers were called "infinity rooms." They had been locked and sealed off with plastic and duct tape during the plant's production era. By the end of August 1997 specially clad workers had removed sixty bags of radioactive trash from the room, used acid to dissolve bits of plutonium, scoured surfaces with high-pressure hoses, and then painted the plutonium-laced concrete walls and floor with epoxy to reduce radiation levels enough for equipment to be removed.[36] The infinity room cleanup reflected a small part of the rigor and danger involved in dismantling this defunct nuclear weapons plant. Several accidents had already occurred, including the irradiation of two workers cleaning sludge tanks in August 1996. By the end of 1997 only a few relatively minor buildings had been razed out of more than four hundred buildings and structures slated for demolition. The first one, a small building mildly contaminated with uranium, had been torn down in June 1996 at a cost of $1.7 million. The cleanup experiences at Rocky Flats confirmed one government study's earlier prediction that nuclear weapons production had left "a legacy of environmental contamination that is unprecedented in scope and complexity." That study, by the Office of Technology Assessment, warned that cleanup workers at Rocky Flats and the other thirteen facilities in the U.S. nuclear weapons complex would face enormous safety hazards.[37]

By early 1998, in some sections of Rocky Flats a few structures were being readied for demolition and drums of contaminated low-level waste were being hauled away. Cleanup work was proceeding much more slowly in the fenced-in, high-security former plutonium production area. Workers had just recently finished the time-consuming process of draining plutonium solutions from holding tanks in Building 771, the processing building that the DOE had declared its most dangerous structure in 1995. The building's dozens of miles of ductwork, pipes, and glove boxes were contaminated with plutonium, and an unknown amount of plutonium had seeped through the concrete floors into the ground beneath it.

The DOE's accelerated cleanup plan called for Building 771 and the other seven major plutonium buildings to be demolished by the year 2006 so Rocky Flats could be closed. But some experts said the DOE's plans didn't go far enough. They worried that plutonium, with its radioactive half-life of 24,065 years, would be left to poison the ground under the plutonium buildings. "I believe you have to take the whole thing, including the [foundation] slab," said Jack Weaver, now working for a private contractor on Building 771's cleanup. "The current plan doesn't call for that. It calls for taking the roof and the walls down to the slab and then pouring a cap over the slab. I believe there's too much stuff under 771 and even 776 Building that has the potential someday to leach out into the rest of the world. I don't believe that's acceptable."[38]

On January 28, 1998, DOE and Kaiser-Hill executives sponsored what they described as the "first annual" State of the Flats Meeting. More than a hundred people filled the conference room at a local community center. Many familiar faces were in the audience, including Ken Korkia of the Citizens Advisory Board, Tom Marshall of the Rocky Mountain Peace and Justice Center, and Jim Stone, whose lawsuit against Rockwell was still pending. Department of Energy and company officials presented an upbeat assessment of their recent and future cleanup activities. They emphasized that the plant's predicted closure in the year 2006 was realistic. "We're drumming up Rocky Flats and sending it elsewhere," said Kaiser-Hill president Robert Card. Many in the audience were skeptical.[39]

Epilogue

On January 6, 1998 Charlie McKay got up at 4:00 a.m. to plow eight inches of fresh snow off the road leading into his new, nearly complete warehouse and office complex. The one-story buildings are built with tasteful brown concrete block that resembles stone. They sit on Church Ranch land his family homesteaded more than a century ago. After plowing the road McKay checked on his cattle pastured three miles west near Rocky Flats and then prepared for his regular business day. Wearing a gray tweed sport coat over an open-collared shirt and looking a little tired, he came out of a mid-morning meeting to greet a visitor. "You want to go for a little ride?" he asked jovially. He guided his faded green Lincoln Continental down Church Ranch Boulevard and past the ever-expanding U.S. Homes sub-division. McKay said he wished his late uncle Marcus Church could see this area now. He stopped to point out his next development project on land near the heavily traveled Denver-Boulder turnpike. A large commercial real estate company had agreed to pay $6 million to become his partner on a $200 million joint venture project including a luxury Westin Hotel.[1] Three years later, in early 2001, the hotel is operating, as is the new Westminster Promenade office complex next door along with a twenty-four-screen AMC theater and the Rock Bottom Restaurant and Brewery just down the street.

McKay and other developers cashing in on the booming commercial and residential growth along Colorado's Front Range don't realize how close this land came to being turned into a nuclear wasteland. The 1969 fire at the Rocky Flats nuclear weapons plant nearly made this prime real estate as unusable as the irradiated countryside around Chernobyl. Despite the fire, and the subsequent civil disobedience, public commissions, scandals, and environmental disputes, Cold War "national security" ideology and vested interests enabled Rocky Flats to continue processing plutonium and building bombs for twenty more years. The FBI's extraordinary June 1989 raid on the plant occurred at a time that, thanks to news media coverage, the public and the politicians they elected had become more aware of the troubled plant's operations. This knowledge converged with the abrupt end of the Cold War to halt Rocky Flats' direct participation in nuclear weapons production in January 1992. During its four decades of production, the plant manufactured about 70,000 nuclear bombs and processed more than 150 tons of plutonium. The amount of processed plutonium exceeded the estimated 100 tons of weapon-grade plutonium produced in U.S. nuclear reactors because Rocky Flats recycled plutonium from old weapons to fabricate new ones.[2]

Its deadly products still exist in the 10,500 nuclear warheads in the current U.S. arsenal.[3] If the nation's leaders make the unfortunate decision to resume plutonium processing and bomb manufacturing, the DOE has guaranteed this would occur at other DOE facilities and not at Rocky Flats. At a bare minimum, perhaps the public will learn a lesson from Rocky Flats and insist on genuine independent oversight of any such operations.

With bomb production terminated, Rocky Flats itself no longer poses the global threat it once did, but it remains a local hazard to the environment and to worker and public health. Government reports such as the plutonium vulnerability assessment conclude there is a low probability of events such as earthquakes, plane crashes, or tornados that would have high consequences outside the plant boundaries. But the risk exists, particularly until the remaining tons of plutonium stored at the site are removed. Charlie McKay is among those who minimize the potential risk. He continues to haggle with the DOE over his right to mine gravel on a section of the plant site where contaminated water was sprayed. And he talks about building a new home on his pasture adjacent to the plant.

But at least one local development company took no chances about incurring liability should anything go awry at Rocky Flats. The sprawling, upscale Rock Creek subdivision, consisting of thousands of homes and condominiums, lies just a mile-and-a-half northeast of the Rocky Flats boundary. Homebuyers were told about the plant in the purchase agreements they signed. "Purchaser(s) are advised to conduct their own independent investigation as to the nature and scope of any potential risk posed by Rocky Flats," stated one document from the mid-1990s. "Purchaser(s) understand that any potential risks associated with the Property's proximity to

Rocky Flats are hereby assumed by Purchaser(s)."[4] Home sales were brisk. And just east of the subdivision an expansive new regional mall called Flatiron Crossing began operating in August 2000.

Debates continue today over the plant's cleanup, health effects, legacy, and the future use of the land. Although these issues are closely intertwined, the local news media often cover them as discrete questions and don't provide context. "Study: Flats Neighbors Safe" trumpeted a 1998 banner headline in the *Boulder Daily Camera*. The story reported Colorado State University researchers' findings that plant neighbors "have no more plutonium in their bodies than people who live far from the site." The finding pleased local real estate agents and developers. While the story quoted one scientist as saying the results should be interpreted cautiously, it didn't mention any risks from the tons of plutonium still stored on the site and gave short shrift to concerns about possible accidents occurring during the demolition of contaminated buildings.[5]

A July 1998 *Denver Post* story reported that a local "task force" wanted Rocky Flats cleaned up enough to be used as an industrial park, not just open space. The story referred to the defunct plant's plutonium production area, but didn't mention DOE's plans for this area, which were restated in a DOE document a month earlier. "Approximately 100 acres of the site will be capped where complete remediation is technically or economically infeasible," according to the DOE report. "The caps will reduce water infiltration and direct runoff in the area, thereby preventing migration of contaminants. Additional cleanup may be conducted should technological advances or increased funding allow." Neither had occurred by early 2001 — cleanup simply does not mean completely clean in DOE's lexicon.[6]

Some citizens, through the Citizens Advisory Board and local activist organizations, have vigorously contested DOE's cleanup procedures, including the agency's guidelines for soil cleanup. They became outraged when it was revealed that the DOE's proposed standards would allow plutonium contamination as high as 650 picocuries per gram of dry soil, a concentration forty times higher than allowed in the DOE's cleanup of former nuclear test sites Johnston Island and Rongelap Atoll in the Pacific Ocean. Citizens also are worried about radionuclides migrating off the plant site. Local governments and citizens groups successfully pushed for an independent analysis of soil cleanup standards by Risk Assessment Corp., which in February 2000 recommended the significantly more stringent standard of less than 35 picocuries per gram of dry soil.[7]

Site cleanup standards have also been part of the dispute over the ultimate use for the ten square miles of Rocky Flats land. By 1999 the disagreement boiled down to whether the land would be designated primarily as an open space wildlife refuge or freed up for multiple uses, including commercial and industrial. While most of the surrounding communities favored open space, the town of Arvada adjacent to the site held out for some industrial redevelopment, which could have contributed to its tax base. In addition, however, Arvada officials pointed out that under federal rules an open space designation required weaker cleanup standards than if the land were eligible for redevelopment. Democratic Congressman Mark Udall drafted an open space bill in 1999 and then collaborated with Republican Senator Wayne Allard to draft another bill that both men introduced in Congress in September 2000 to create a Rocky Flats National Wildlife Refuge. Arvada agreed to back the refuge but insisted that the land be decontaminated to the greatest extent possible.[8]

The pace of the cleanup depends partly on the speed with which DOE can transport nuclear waste from Rocky Flats and that, too, has been a source of controversy. The argument has focused on transuranic waste — nuclear waste containing high concentrations of plutonium and other elements with an atomic number greater than uranium. Opponents of transportation include LeRoy Moore of the Rocky Mountain Peace and Justice Center, who blasted DOE's "ill-conceived plan to put nuclear waste on the nation's highways and to bury it at the Waste Isolation Pilot Plant (WIPP) near Carlsbad, New Mexico." He and other activists argue that transporting nuclear waste is too dangerous, WIPP is a deeply flawed facility, and a more sensible alternative exists. Moore favors storing the waste at Rocky Flats "in a state-of-the-art facility that isolates it from the environment so that it can be monitored and retrieved if problems arise or if a method for neutralizing it is developed."[9]

WIPP, which has been controversial since first proposed in the 1970s, finally opened its doors and accepted its first shipment of nuclear waste — from Los Alamos — on March 26, 1999. Rocky Flats trucked its first shipment to WIPP in June 1999. Despite occasional suspensions of shipments due to safety violations, Rocky Flats shipped 42 truckloads, containing 279 cubic meters of transuranic waste to WIPP in fiscal year 2000. This was much less than the plant had scheduled. Plant officials plan to send some 15,000 cubic meters of waste to the New Mexico facility by 2006. Another 175,000 cubic meters of low-level radioactive waste and mixed waste are slated to be sent to the Nevada Test Site Waste Repository and Envirocare of Utah by that date. In addition, waste with high levels of recyclable plutonium is being shipped to the Savannah River site.[10]

Even with regular Rocky Flats shipments to WIPP, however, many doubt that DOE will meet its self-imposed deadline to close the plant by 2006. A May 1998 report from the congressional General Accounting Office concluded DOE had already fallen behind in its cleanup schedule.[11] Safety problems appearing in the accelerated Kaiser-Hill cleanup program are contributing to the delay. From 1996 to the end of 2000, that company was fined $700,000 for safety violations. More fines are likely. For example, DOE may fine Kaiser-Hill for two serious problems that surfaced in December 2000. The first was the revelation that ten workers cleaning Building 771, the highly contaminated former plutonium processing facility, had tested positive for radiation exposure. Plant officials could not immediately identify the precise source of the contamination. Then, in January 2001, officials disclosed that on two occasions in December workers overstuffed drums containing classified bomb parts and uranium, raising the possibility of a chain reaction "criticality" at the site.[12]

As the cleanup of Rocky Flats has lurched ahead, its costs have risen. The DOE in 1998 estimated the cost at $6.3 billion, but added, "these costs will continue to be refined." In 2000, DOE refined the costs upward to $7.7 billion. Still, this figure is a pittance compared to the tens of billions of dollars taxpayers paid during the Cold War to produce nuclear weapons at Rocky Flats. And even this enormous amount is just a small portion of the estimated $5.5 trillion the nation has spent for nuclear weapons and delivery systems since World War II, according to a 1998 Brookings Institution study.[13]

Regardless how long the Rocky Flats cleanup takes, members of United Steelworkers of America Local 8031 will participate in it under a contract renewal signed with Kaiser-Hill in January 2001 covering about 1,400 union workers. But continued employment isn't the only concern of workers, said Jerry Harden, a past president of the union local. "There's still a stigma attached to working at the plant," said Harden, a lanky Denver native who has been employed at Rocky Flats since 1967. "People ask me if I glow, I say 'only in the daytime.'" Joking aside, Harden knows that during the Cold War the federal government placed a much higher priority on weapons production at Rocky Flats than on worker health and safety. He and his fellow workers desperately want to know how the plant's working conditions affected their health.[14]

To date the clearest work-related illness at Rocky Flats has been suffered by employees who worked with beryllium, a light, silver-gray metal that was used to make nuclear weapons components at this and other facilities. When beryllium is machined, it creates dust that can cause chronic beryllium disease, an incurable disease similar to the Black Lung disease suffered

by underground coal miners. By the end of 2000, more than 115 Rocky
Flats workers had contracted chronic beryllium disease — and some had
already died. Nearly 200 were "sensitized to beryllium," and at risk of
developing the disease, according to Dr. Lee Newman, director of the
Division of Environmental and Health Services at National Jewish Medical
and Research Center in Denver.[15]

The causes of radiation-related diseases such as cancer are much more
difficult to pin down than the illness caused by beryllium. The plant's poor
record keeping, the long lag time that often occurs between exposures to
radioactive materials and the onset of disease, and disagreement over data
interpretation all make firm answers elusive, according to James Ruttenber,
a physician and University of Colorado epidemiologist who is supervising a
workers' health study at the plant. Similar problems exist in determining
health damage at the thirteen other major facilities and laboratories and
dozens of smaller facilities that made up the nation's nuclear weapons production complex. But the federal government took a step toward compen-
sating workers in April 2000 when Energy Secretary Bill Richardson admitted for the first time that the department's nuclear weapons production
plants had exposed workers to radiation and chemicals that made many of
them sick, sometimes fatally. Reversing the DOE's decades-long policy
of contesting claims from sick employees or their survivors, Richardson
sketched out a program that could aid thousands of the 600,000 workers
nationwide who had been recruited to fight the Cold War by producing
nuclear weapons. Congress failed to fund a full compensation program. In
January 2001, just before the Clinton Administration left office, Secretary
Richardson announced new steps to identify people with nuclear work-
related illnesses and urged Congress to pass legislation.[16]

Assessing the environmental legacy of Rocky Flats' operations on the
surrounding community has been even more daunting than calculating the
plant's impact on worker health. The most concerted effort was the two-
phase study overseen by the Colorado health department and the Health
Advisory Panel and funded by DOE. During the first phase, from 1990 to
1994, the ChemRisk division of McLaren/Hart Environmental Engineering conducted a technological review and dose reconstruction study that
concluded the plant's operations had little or no impact on the adjacent
community.[17]

For the second phase, intended to provide another opinion, the state
health department in 1992 hired Radiological Assessments Corp. (later
renamed Risk Assessment Corp.), a private company run by health physi-

cist John Till. This company's scientists analyzed incidents such as the 1957 and 1969 fires along with the plant's past routine operations. They didn't find significant offsite contamination. On a weekday morning in May 1998 Paul Voilleque, one of the Radiological Assessments scientists, presented his latest findings on the 1957 fire at a public meeting at a Sheraton hotel in suburban Denver. A pleasant, unflappable man, Voilleque wasn't perturbed when a perennial questioner suggested he was "intellectually dishonest." Voilleque patiently explained he had pieced together the plant's technical past as best he could given data that are sketchy, often inaccurate, and sometimes missing entirely. Horse rancher and plant neighbor Bini Abbott was at this session, as she has been at almost all of them over the years. She continues her quest to understand the plant's effects as thoroughly as possible.[18]

Abbott didn't attend a reunion and workshops held at the Rocky Mountain Peace and Justice Center in Boulder in April 1998. She considers herself an "environmentalist" rather than a peace activist. The reunion celebrated the twentieth anniversary of the anti-nuclear activists' first large civil-disobedience demonstration at the plant in 1978. Dan Ellsberg, who gained fame by leaking the Pentagon Papers' history of the Vietnam War and later directed his attention to the nuclear arms race, was present. So were Judy Danielson, the former American Friends Service Committee organizer, and many other local activists. They reflected on the importance of the anti-nuclear movement and the intensity of the struggle against Cold War militarism. "We really thought they were going to blow up the world," recalled Mary Hey, whose infant daughter's picture adorned a peace poster in the 1970s. LeRoy Moore said, "I think we have had an enormous influence on what has happened." He reminded the audience that "at the same time there's a lot to be done."[19]

Activists promoting nuclear disarmament have gained influential allies since the Cold War's end. They include retired air force Gen. Lee Butler, who until 1994 headed the U.S. Strategic Air Command, which controls the nation's intercontinental nuclear forces. "A world free of the threat of nuclear weapons is necessarily a world devoid of nuclear weapons," Butler said in a December 1996 news briefing. His position was endorsed by retired army General Andrew Goodpaster, a former NATO commander, and sixty other former military commanders from around the world. Added later to those voices was that of Paul Nitze, a top arms control negotiator under President Reagan. In an October 1999 *New York Times* opinion piece, Nitze called on the United States to unilaterally get rid of nuclear weapons.

He concluded, "It is the presence of nuclear weapons that threatens our existence."[20]

Unfortunately, the sane logic of disarmament hasn't led to an end to nuclear weapons, either in the United States or abroad. In year 2000, the five largest nuclear weapons states possessed 31,535 nuclear warheads broken down as follows: Russia, 20,000; United States, 10,500; United Kingdom, 185; France, 450; and China, 400. An unknown number of nuclear weapons are possessed by Israel, India, and Pakistan.[21] The latter two countries joined the nuclear "club" in May 1998 when each set off a series of nuclear weapons tests. Joyful newspaper headlines in both countries were reminiscent of the *Denver Post*'s banner headline on March 23, 1951: "There's Good News Today: U.S. to Build $45 Million A-Plant Near Denver." A few hawks in Congress reacted to the Indian and Pakistani tests by urging the United States to restart nuclear weapons production lines. President Clinton responded to the tests by soberly observing that, "I cannot believe that we are about to start the 21st century by having the Indian subcontinent repeat the worst mistakes of the 20th century."

Rocky Flats epitomizes those mistakes, which rest on the myopic notion that nations can preserve their security by building weapons of mass destruction — placing incalculable numbers of men, women, and children at risk — and then threatening to use them. Still, many people, including congressional representatives and senators and members of the George W. Bush Administration, deny the risks inherent in nuclear weapons by promoting ostensible technical fixes such as nuclear missile defense. Despite the end of the Cold War, the history of the nuclear weapons age persists and is bleeding into the future. That Rocky Flats played a major role in this continuing history was highlighted in January 1998 when the U.S. National Park Service added the plant to the National Register of Historic Places for "making a significant contribution to the broad patterns of U.S. history."[22] In September 2000 the possibility that a physical museum might be established to preserve and interpret the Rocky Flats historical contribution was signaled when Sen. Allard and Rep. Udall included such a facility in their wildlife refuge bill. Whether or not a museum is built, disagreements over the real historical legacy of Rocky Flats are bound to continue.

Notes

Charlie McKay's archive contains a wealth of information about the Church family's history and its relationship with Rocky Flats, both the mesa and then the nuclear weapons plant. The archive consists of several filing cabinets filled with correspondence, business documents, and copies of documents. It is largely located in the basement of McKay's Westminster, Colorado, home. McKay's prolific late uncle Marcus Church filed the bulk of the material, which includes carbon copies of the letters he wrote to family members, business associates, and government officials over many decades. This archive is identified in the endnotes as "McKay Files."

I conducted research in three units of the National Archives and Records Administration. The Denver office, located in the Federal Center west of the city, was a source for old land records, federal court cases, and some material from the Rocky Flats plant. The National Archives headquarters building in Washington, D.C., holds the files of the congressional Joint Committee on Atomic Energy (JCAE). Many of the JCAE documents relevant to my research were still classified. Indeed, even their existence was classified until the early 1990s, when the archives declassified the "Finding Aid" index to the classified documents. Since Congress exempted itself from the federal Freedom of Information Act, I filed requests for "Mandatory Review," seeking declassification of a number of documents, as indicated in the endnotes. The archives' own file numbers and boxes where documents are located sometimes have undergone changes; thus the precise location of some documents may be confusing. The National Archives branch in College Park, Maryland, holds some Atomic Energy Commission (AEC) documents although others have been shipped to the U.S.

Department of Energy (DOE) archive in Germantown, Maryland. I obtained some AEC records under Freedom of Information Act requests filed with the DOE. Beginning with the administration of former energy secretary James Watkins and then accelerated under former secretary Hazel O'Leary, the DOE has itself declassified many documents.

I conducted other archival research at the Truman Library in Independence, Missouri; the Western history archives at Norlin Library at the University of Colorado at Boulder; and the Records Management offices at the Rocky Flats plant site. Many lawsuits have been filed regarding Rocky Flats. Two were particularly useful for historical information. First was the suit filed in October 1975 by Marcus Church et al. against the U.S. government and Rocky Flats contractors. Some records for this suit, identified in the endnotes as *Church v. U.S. et al.*, are at the National Archives in Denver. This suit was preceded in April 1975 by Church's injury claim against the U.S. Energy Research and Development Administration, the DOE's predecessor, and records of this action, identified in the endnotes as *Church Claim*, also reside at the archives. The second lawsuit providing useful information was filed by real estate developer Ken Good against Church in 1975 and is identified in the text as *Good v. Church*. Some documents from this case are at the archives. In addition, journalist Ryan Ross provided me with copies of several depositions taken in the case, including the one from Dow Chemical Company's first Rocky Flats plant manager.

For purposes of distinguishing newspaper and magazine headlines from the actual text of articles, I have capitalized their headlines even though the new convention among some publications is to use lowercase headlines. Also, the *Boulder Daily Camera* has taken "Boulder" off its name, but I cite the entire name for clarity. Other organizations have changed their names. For example, the Colorado Department of Health is now the Colorado Department of Public Health and Environment; the Rocky Mountain Peace Center is now the Rocky Mountain Peace and Justice Center, and the *Denver Rocky Mountain News* is that newspaper's new name. I used the contemporary names in the text and endnotes. Similarly, the dollar amounts in the book are contemporary figures rather than current dollars adjusted for inflation.

Finally, because this book rests so heavily upon primary source documents and interviews, I am not providing an extensive bibliography although specific secondary sources are cited in the endnotes. A bibliography could not do justice to the large number of articles and books, including Martin Sherwin's *A World Destroyed*, Paul Boyer's *By the Bomb's Early Light*, Patty Limerick's *The Legacy of Conquest*, and Charles Wilkinson's *Crossing the Next Meridian: Land, Water, and the Future of the West,* that have influenced my thinking about the nuclear arms race and the nuclear West.

CHAPTER ONE

1. The biographical information on the Churches comes from Sarah (Miller) Church's reminiscences and her 1903 statement to Hilda Lindley. McKay Files. See also "George Henry Church," in *Colorado* (Chicago: S. J. Publishing Co., 1918), 535–40.

2. Sarah Church wrote her reminiscences in longhand at various times, and they were later transcribed to typewriter by family members or friends. This quote is from "Church's Ranch, Dec. 1913, by Mrs. Geo. Henry Church, Written for the Children." The originals and transcriptions are in the McKay Files.

3. This and the following citations from Sarah Church in this chapter are from her "Recollections of My Trip Across the Plains in 1861," 1907, transcribed and typewritten. McKay Files.

4. Carl Abbott, Stephen J. Leonard, and David McComb, *Colorado, A History of the Centennial State,* 3d ed. (Niwot: University Press of Colorado, 1994), 36, 75.

5. The quote comes from Thomas H. Leflorge, as told by Thomas B. Marquis, *Memoirs of a White Crow Indian* (1928; Lincoln: Univ. of Nebraska Press, 1974), 171. In Patricia Limerick, *The Legacy of Conquest* (New York: W. W. Norton & Co., 1988), 220.

6. Stephen J. Leonard and Thomas J. Noel, *Denver: Mining Camp to Metropolis* (Niwot: University Press of Colorado, 1990), 8, 12.

7. On the Churches and Millers and the naming of Lafayette, Colorado, see James D. Hutchison, *Survey and Settlement: Lafayette, Colorado* (Lafayette: Morrell Graphics, 1994), 31, 43–47, 77.

8. Denver Land Office, Tract Book 159, Township 2, Range 69, Section 14. In the U.S. National Archives and Record Center, Denver.

9. Limerick, *Legacy,* 60, 82.

10. Failure rates from Fred A. Shannon, *The Farmer's Last Frontier* (New York, 1935), 55. In Wallace Stegner, *Beyond the Hundredth Meridian* (Boston: Houghton Mifflin, 1954, republished by Penguin Books, 1992), 220–21.

11. Marcus Church, deposition, July 28, 1975, vol. 1, pp. 9–10. This deposition was taken pursuant to Church's *Claim for Damage, Injury, or Death, v. the U.S. Energy Research and Development Administration,* 2 April 1975. (Hereafter *Church Claim.*) In Civil Action 75-x-29, folder 2, U.S. National Archives and Records Administration, Denver. Wheat, a grass like rye, barley, and corn, has a grain consisting of a hard, thin shell covering a tiny, vitamin-rich embryo surrounded by carbohydrates, a small amount of protein, and minerals. This cereal grain, like rice, fits the role of the staff of life, which explains why it was one of the first plants cultivated by humans more than 7,000 years ago.

12. "George Henry Church," 536. Sarah Church reminiscences. McKay Files.

13. *Denver Post*, 24 July 1908. In Leonard and Noel, *Denver*, 331.

14. Charlie McKay, interview by author, tape recording, Westminster, Colo., 21 November 1995.

15. Much of the detail in this section comes from Marcus Church's correspondence in the McKay Files. Other details come from his depositions taken on several occasions between 25 July 1977 and 7 December 1977 in the *Good Fund, Ltd. — 1972 et al. v. Marcus F. Church et al.* (Hereafter *Good v. Church.*) The long and complex history of this litigation is set forth in detail in *Good Fund, Ltd. — 1972 v. Church*, 540 F.Supp. 519 (D.Colo. 1982).

16. Leonard and Noel, *Denver*, 220.

17. Ad copy in memo from W. W. MacGruder, Inc., advertising agency to Church Ranch, 27 August 1947. McKay Files. Cattle and horse figures from Marcus Church, Deposition, *Church Claim*, 20.

18. Charles Beise, of Fairfield and Woods law firm, letter to Sen. Johnson, 22 April 1949. McKay Files.

19. Timberlake's complaint described in a letter from Church's attorney Beise to Sen. Johnson, 18 August 1949. McKay Files.

20. Major General Lewis A. Pick, Chief of Engineers, letter to Sen. Johnson, 10 October 1949. McKay Files.

CHAPTER TWO

1. Unbylined, "Big Ed Compiled Fantastic Record," *Pueblo (Colo.) Star-Journal and Sunday Chieftain*, 2 March 1969. Patrick Fargo McCarty, "Big Ed Johnson of Colorado — A Political Portrait" (master's thesis, University of Colorado at Boulder, 1958). Despite Johnson's prominence, little has been written about him, perhaps because he didn't want his early personal records archived. "Majority of his papers destroyed at his request," a U.S. Senate report notes: *Guide to Collections of Former United States Senators 1789–1982*, 97th Cong., 2d sess. (Washington: U.S. Senate), 142. The following biographical details come from the Pueblo newspaper and McCarty's thesis unless otherwise noted.

2. Unbylined AP story, "Former Governor 'Big Ed' Johnson Dies," *Boulder Daily Camera*, 30 May 1970. Leonard and Noel, *Denver*, 190–200. Phyllis Smith, *A Look at Boulder: From Settlement to City* (Boulder: Pruett Publishing Company, 1981), 166–69.

3. Lee Casey, "He Read Horatio Alger," *Rocky Mountain News*, 17 October 1942.

4. On the highway network, see Casey, "He Read." On jackrabbit hunts, see *Pueblo Chieftain*, 2 March 1969. On invaders, see *The Literary Digest* 121:18, 2 May 1936, 5. In McCarty, "Big Ed Johnson," 57.

5. Limerick, *Legacy*, 28. Leonard and Noel, *Denver*, 71.

6. Leonard and Noel, *Denver*, 220, 226.

7. Gerald D. Nash, *World War II and the West* (Lincoln: University of Nebraska Press, 1990), 3.

8. Quoted in Leonard and Noel, *Denver,* 352.

9. Associated Press Biographical Service, "Sketch 3940, issued 15 April 1955, Eugene D. Millikin." In clippings file, Carnegie Library, Boulder, Colo. Douglass Cater, "Mr. Conservative — Eugene Millikin of Colorado," *The Reporter,* 17 March 1953.

10. Edwin Johnson, "Statement Released to Press on Mon., Nov. 29, 1954, Re. Proposed Censure of Senator McCarthy." Carnegie Library, clippings, 1941–54.

11. The Committee for the Compilation of Materials on Damage Caused by the Atomic Bombs in Hiroshima and Nagasaki, *Hiroshima and Nagasaki: The Physical, Medical, and Social Effects of the Atomic Bombings* (New York: Basic Books, 1981), 344–69. This authoritative study explains the basis for the casualty estimates.

12. Gar Alperovitz was the major proponent of the thesis about the Soviet Union. See his *American Diplomacy: Hiroshima and Potsdam: The Use of the Atomic Bomb and the American Confrontation with Soviet Power* (New York: Penguin, 1985). Also his *The Decision to Use the Atomic Bomb and the Architecture of an American Myth* (New York: Alfred A. Knopf, 1995). For a contextual review of Truman's decision, J. Samuel Walker, *Prompt and Utter Destruction: Truman and the Use of Atomic Bombs Against Japan* (Chapel Hill: University of North Carolina Press, 1997).

13. Paul Boyer, *By the Bomb's Early Light* (New York: Pantheon Books, 1985), 111–12.

14. Alice Kimball Smith, *A Peril and a Hope* (Chicago: University of Chicago Press, 1965), 130. Einstein quoted in Otto Nathan and Heinz Norden, eds., *Einstein on Peace* (New York: Simon & Schuster, 1960), 376.

15. Richard Wayne Dyke, *Mr. Atomic Energy: Congressman Chet Holifield and Atomic Energy Affairs, 1945–1974* (New York: Greenwood Press, 1989), 24. Smith, *Peril and Hope,* 128. Johnson's argument in Phil J. Rodgers, " 'Big Ed' Johnson," *Denver Post,* 20 October 1946.

16. Harold P. Green and Alan Rosenthal, *Government of the Atom* (New York: Atherton Press, 1963), 2. Johnson also had his eye on moving industries from Connecticut to Colorado. See Bill Lanouette, *Genius in the Shadows: A Biography of Leo Szilard, the Man Behind the Bomb* (Chicago: University of Chicago Press, 1992), 299.

17. Richard G. Hewlett and Francis Duncan, *Atomic Shield, 1947/1952,* vol. II, *A History of the United States Atomic Energy Commission* (University Park: The Pennsylvania State University Press, 1969), 3.

18. Green and Rosenthal, *Government,* 30. Their emphasis.

19. *Bulletin of the Atomic Scientists,* August 1, 1946, 1.

20. Cater, "Mr. Conservative."

21. Hewlett and Duncan, *Atomic Shield,* 19.

22. U.S. Atomic Energy Commission, "Report to the President of the United States from the Atomic Energy Commission January 1 — April 1, 1947," 3 April 1947, 1 (declassified from Top Secret). In President's Secretary's files, Harry S. Truman Library. Hewlett and Duncan, *Atomic Shield,* 47–48. In July 1946 the arsenal consisted of just nine nuclear bombs, none of which was assembled. David

Alan Rosenberg, "The Origins of Overkill: Nuclear Weapons and American Strategy, 1945–1960," *International Security* 7, no. 4 (spring 1983): 15.

23. Daniel Yergin, *Shattered Peace: The Origins of the Cold War and the National Security State* (Boston: Houghton Mifflin, 1977), 336–38.

24. Rosenberg, "Overkill," 9–11. As the AEC's demanding customer, the Defense Department placed officers from its Armed Forces Special Weapons Project at AEC weapons laboratories to help set up routines for assembling, testing, and maintaining nuclear weapons. Hewlett and Duncan, *Atomic Shield*, 131–35.

25. Hewlett and Duncan, *Atomic Shield*, 145.

26. Leona Marshall Libby, *The Uranium People* (New York: Charles Scribner's Sons, 1979), 51.

27. Henry DeWolf Smyth, *Atomic Energy for Military Purposes, The Official Report on the Development of the Atomic Bomb under the Auspices of the United States Government, 1940–1945* (Princeton: Princeton University Press, 1948), 52, 65. A memorandum noted that enough plutonium could, through a chain reaction, release energy at "an explosive rate which might be described as a 'super bomb.'"

28. Glenn T. Seaborg and Walter D. Loveland, *The Elements Beyond Uranium* (New York: John Wiley & Sons, 1990), 14.

29. *Nuclear News*, "Special Section: ANS/ENS International Meeting," January 1993.

30. Lanouette, *Genius*, 227–28.

31. Smyth, *Atomic Energy*, p. 37. Committee to Provide Interim Oversight of the DOE Nuclear Weapons Complex, *The Nuclear Weapons Complex: Management for Health, Safety, and the Environment* (Washington, D.C.: National Academy Press, 1989), 118–22.

32. Smyth, *Atomic Energy*, 92–94. U.S. Department of Energy, Office of Environmental Management, *Linking Legacies: Connecting the Cold War Nuclear Weapons Production Processes to Their Environmental Consequences* (Washington, D.C.: DOE, January 1997), 18. Thomas B. Cochran, William M. Arkin, and Milton M. Hoenig, *Nuclear Weapons Databook*, vol. I, *U.S. Nuclear Forces and Capabilities* (Cambridge: Ballinger Publishing Co., 1984), 31–32.

33. Hewlett and Duncan, *Atomic Shield*, 148–49.

34. Ibid., 148.

35. Ibid., 148–49.

36. Rosenberg, "Overkill," 14.

37. Ibid., 16. Hewlett and Duncan, *Atomic Shield*, 178.

38. Boyer, *Bomb's Early Light*, 53–58. Rosenberg, "Overkill," 12.

39. David E. Lilienthal, *The Journals of David E. Lilienthal, 1945–1950* (New York: Harper & Row, 1964), 386. Cited in David McCullough, *Truman* (New York: Simon & Schuster, 1992), 650.

40. Morton Halperin, *Nuclear Fallacy* (Cambridge: Ballinger Publishing Co., 1987), 6–7.

41. Fred Kaplan, *The Wizards of Armageddon* (New York: Simon & Schuster, 1983), 26–32.

42. Michael Krepon, personal communication to author, 16 February 1998. Rosenberg, "Overkill," 12. The literature on deterrence is extensive. See the bibliography in McGeorge Bundy's *Danger and Survival: Choices about the Bomb in the First Fifty Years* (New York: Random House, 1988).

43. Joint Committee on Atomic Energy, "The Scale and Scope of Atomic Production: A Chronology of Leading Events," 30 January 1952, 8 (declassified from Top Secret), RG 128, Box 510. (Hereafter: JCAE, "Chronology.") National Archives, Washington, D.C. The meeting in question occurred on 16 March 1949. This annotated forty-page chronology is useful in itself and for identifying other documents.

44. Rosenberg, "Overkill," 16.

45. JCAE, "Chronology," 9–10.

46. Hewlett and Duncan, *Atomic Shield*, 181.

47. JCAE, "Chronology," 12.

48. Robert Young, "Millikin — Mild Mannered Militant," *Chicago Tribune* magazine, 31 August 1947. Rosenberg, "Overkill," 21–22. President Eisenhower in June 1953 transferred a number of nuclear weapons to the military for deployment. By 1961 less than ten percent of the stockpile was under civilian control. Halperin, *Nuclear Fallacy*, 9–19.

49. Halperin, *Nuclear Fallacy*, 9, argues that Truman is responsible for deciding to use nuclear weapons to promote U.S. interests instead of holding them solely to deter others and that President Eisenhower created the structure that treated the devices as weapons.

50. Richard Rhodes, *Dark Sun: The Making of the Hydrogen Bomb* (New York: Simon & Schuster, 1995), 379.

51. Gerald Marsh, "Details, Details," a review of *The Swords of Armageddon*, by Chuck Hansen, *Bulletin of the Atomic Scientists*, July/August 1997, 54. In retrospect, Teller's intuition was apparently correct, Marsh writes.

52. Rhodes, *Dark Sun*, 404.

53. Later revelations showed that the Soviet bomb program had been given a two-year boost by atomic spying, not scientific discourse. David Holloway, *Stalin & the Bomb* (New Haven: Yale University Press, 1994), 222.

54. *Court of Current Issues* (television program), "Is There Too Much Secrecy in Our Atomic Program?" Dumont Television Network, New York, 1 November 1949. Transcript excerpts in Papers of Harry S. Truman, Official File, Box 1523, File 692, Truman Library.

55. Hewlett and Duncan, *Atomic Shield*, 394.

56. Copies of Johnson and Truman letters are in Papers of Harry S. Truman, Official File, Box 1523, File 692, Truman Library. Hewlett and Duncan, *Atomic Shield*, 406.

57. Hewlett and Duncan, *Atomic Shield*, 408. Truman quote from McCullough, *Truman*, 763.

58. *Congressional Record*, 81st Cong., 2d sess., 25 May 1950, 9766. Hewlett and Duncan, *Atomic Shield*, 448.

59. Unbylined, "Millikin Urges Domestic Self-Sufficiency of Ore," *(Pueblo) Chieftain and Star-Journal*, 17 August 1950. In Scrapbook 7 of Millikin Files, Archives, U. of Colorado at Boulder Libraries. (Hereafter: CU Archives.) Internal documents backed up Millikin. The commission's FY 1946 budget was $320 million, about 5 percent of which went to the procurement of uranium ore. JCAE, "Chronology," 1.

60. JCAE, "Chronology," 17, 22. On new reactors, see Hewlett and Duncan, *Atomic Shield*, 522. The budget was still not enough, in McMahon's opinion. "I am convinced that, dollar for dollar, an investment in atomic weapons gives more security than any other defense outlay," McMahon wrote Truman on August 3, 1950. He added that "in the fiscal year just ended, the American public paid twice as much for television sets, twice as much for cosmetics, and almost twice as much for candy and confections as it paid for atomic weapons. Since our strategy both for peace and for war has those weapons as its final and strongest material premise, I suggest that a treasury outlay of a billion-and-a-half or two billion dollars per year is now necessary." Letter in President's Secretary's Files, Truman Library.

61. Truman, Memo, 19 August 1950, initialed by Truman. President's Secretary's Files, Truman Library.

62. Bob Lloyd, " 'Hydrogen Bomb' Plant in San Luis Valley?" *Alamosa Courier*, 14 August 1950. CU Archives, Millikin Scrapbook #7.

63. James Daniel, "Senators Warn Colorado of H-Bomb Plant Dangers," *Rocky Mountain News*, 13 August 1950.

64. Lloyd, " 'Hydrogen Bomb' Plant."

65. Daniel, "Senators Warn Colorado."

66. JCAE, Executive Session transcript, 24 August 1950 (declassified from Secret), 9, Record Group 128, Document #1414. National Archives, Washington, D.C.

67. William Lanouette, "Weapons Plant at 40: Savannah River's Halo Fades," *Bulletin of the Atomic Scientists*, December 1990, 27–38.

68. Associated Press, "Senator Ed Johnson Takes Rap at Carroll," *Trinidad Free Press*, 28 October 1950, reported that at a rally of 1,100 Democrats in Trinidad, Johnson said that some of Carroll's votes in the House had been "disappointing." He urged voters to scrutinize Carroll's record closely. CU Archives, Millikin Scrapbook #8.

69. Unbylined, "Colorado Members Will Retain Important Posts in Congress," *Chieftain and Star-Journal*, 10 November, 1950. CU Archives, Millikin Scrapbook #8.

70. George Sanford Holmes, "Senator Johnson of Colorado Becomes Pivotal Figure in Close Senate Division," Grand Junction *Daily Sentinel*, 12 November 1950.

71. Phil J. Rodgers, "State Gets Air Defense Hq.: Colorado Springs Made Permanent Command Post," *Denver Post*, 16 November 1950.

CHAPTER THREE

1. Marcus Church, letter to R. C. Chamberlain, 10 February 1951. McKay Files.

2. Watson A. Bowes, Appraisal of Church Ranch, 8 December 1951. McKay Files.

3. Jean Woodis (formerly Zehnder), interview by author, tape recording, Arvada, Colo., 13 July 1995.

4. Frank Carey, "New Bomb-Making Technique Hinted for Denver A-Plant," *Rocky Mountain News*, 24 March 1951. Joseph Givando, "Denver A-Plant Plans Shrouded in Strict Secrecy," *Denver Post*, 24 March 1951.

5. JCAE, "Discussion of Policy and Accomplishments," 20 December 1950 (declassified from Top Secret), 12, RG 128, Box 5. National Archives, Washington, D.C.

6. National Security Council, "Memorandum for the President," 10 October 1950 (declassified from Top Secret). President's Secretary's Files, Truman Library.

7. Indeed, by the end of the fiscal year, on 30 June 1951, Congress had approved four appropriations totaling $2.032 billion. U.S. Atomic Energy Commission, "Major Activities in the Atomic Energy Programs, January-June 1951" (U.S. Government Printing Office, July 1951), 52.

8. JCAE, Executive Session transcript, 11 November 1950 (declassified from Top Secret), 20–24, RG 128, Box 5. National Archives, Washington, D.C. Thomas B. Cochran, William M. Arkin, Robert S. Norris, and Milton M. Hoenig, *Nuclear Weapons Databook*, vol. II, *U.S. Nuclear Warhead Production* (Cambridge: Ballinger Publishing Co., 1987), 15.

9. Cochran et al., *Databook*, vol. I, *U.S. Nuclear Forces and Capabilities* (Cambridge: Ballinger Publishing Co., 1984), 24–26, 32. Chuck Hansen, *U.S. Nuclear Weapons: The Secret History* (New York: Orion Books, 1988), 32. The *Databook* authors describe critical mass as "the minimum mass of material necessary to sustain a chain reaction." While the critical mass of a bare sphere of uranium 235 is about 114.4 pounds (fifty-two kilograms) and of plutonium 239 is about twenty-two pounds (ten kilograms), the critical mass in bombs can be lowered by reflectors and high compression of the fissile core. The other approach to nuclear weapons design is the gun assembly technique, using two subcritical masses of uranium 235 that achieve supercriticality when one is fired into the other. The Hiroshima bomb typifies this kind of bomb.

10. Hansen, *Nuclear Weapons*, 32, 35. John McPhee, *Curve of Binding Energy* (New York: Ballantine Books, 1975), 160.

11. Theodore B. Taylor, "Circles of Destruction," *Bulletin of the Atomic Scientists*, January-February 1996, 4. The superalloy bomb was tested on Eniwetok atoll in the Pacific on 15 November 1952. Cochran et al., *Databook*, vol. I, 34.

12. Cochran et al., *Databook*, vol. I, 27. Hansen, *Nuclear Weapons*, 32, 35.

13. JCAE, Executive Session transcript, 11 November 1950, 44.

14. History Associates, Inc., "History of the Production Complex: The Methods of Site Selection," prepared for U.S. Department of Energy, Assistant Secretary for Defense Programs, Office of Nuclear Materials, September 1987, 64. U.S. Department of Energy, *Linking Legacies: Connecting the Cold War Nuclear Weapons Production Processes to Their Environmental Consequences* (Washington, D.C.: DOE Office of Environmental Management, 1997), 197.

15. Gordon Dean, letter to McMahon, 5 February 1951 (declassified from Secret at author's request), Rocky Flats, Project Apple, File #1898. National Archives, Washington, D.C.

16. JCAE, "Second Supplemental A.E.C. Budget Review, Fiscal '51," Executive Session transcript, 14 December 1950 (declassified from Secret), 9, RG 128, File #1808. National Archives, Washington, D.C.

17. F. G. Gosling and Terrence R. Fehner, *Closing the Circle: The Department of Energy and Environmental Management, 1942–1994*, Draft #3, History Division, Executive Secretariat (DOE: Washington, D.C., March 1994), 5–6.

18. Director of Military Application, "AEC Selection of Operating Contractor for Project Apple," 8 January 1951 (declassified from Confidential after author's Freedom of Information Act request to DOE), AEC/394 (Germantown, Md.: DOE).

19. Don Whitehead, *The Dow Story* (New York: McGraw-Hill Book Co., 1968), 176, 222.

20. Hewlett and Duncan, *Atomic Shield*, 428, 494, 512. *Bulletin of the Atomic Scientists*, May 1953, 135–36. Francis Henry Langell, deposition, *Good v. Church*, 20 June 1978, 128–29.

21. Langell, deposition, 88, 185. Director of Military Application, "AEC Selection," 8 January 1951. On 3 January, AEC chairman Dean wrote Dow Chemical to confirm the deal. "We believe it will not be necessary to emphasize to you the high urgency and importance of this operation to the national security." Letter attached to 8 January document.

22. History Associates, "History," 16–20.

23. Langell, deposition, 30. History Associates, "History," i–ii.

24. WPB (Wayne P. Brobeck) and ELH (Edward L. Heller) of the JCAE staff, "Memo for the File," 23 February 1951 (declassified from Secret at author's request), Rocky Flats, Project Apple, File #1950. National Archives, Washington, D.C.

25. History Associates, "History," 69, notes, "The Santa Fe Operations Office inspected eight other areas, which confirmed their original judgment that the Denver area convincingly outshone the competition." Langell, deposition, 24, said Dow was not involved in the original site survey.

26. Director of Military Application, "Selection of a Site for Project Apple" (declassified from Secret after author's FOIA request to DOE), 3, AEC 394/4 (Germantown, Md.: DOE, 19 March 1951). Langell, deposition, 31–2.

27. The information and quotes from Cornelison in this section are from interview by author, tape recording, Wheatridge, Colo., 26 June 1995.

28. Kalman Seigel, "Remington Guilty on Perjury Count; Sentencing Today," *New York Times*, 8 February 1951. Victor S. Navasky, *Naming Names* (New York: Viking Press), 9–11, 29.

29. Unbylined, "Ed Keating to Join Staff of Sen. Johnson," *Boulder Daily Camera*, 12 February 1951.

30. Phil J. Rodgers, "Giant Arms Lab Urged for Boulder," *Denver Post*, 22 August 1949. Wayne P. Brobeck and Edward L. Heller, "Memorandum for the File," 16 January 1951 (declassified from Confidential at author's request), Bureau of Standards Lab, File #1858. National Archives, Washington, D.C. The contract was executed by the AEC's Los Alamos office. The capacity of each of these cryogenic plants was conservatively rated at two hundred liters, or sixty gallons, an hour. Robert L. Perkin, "Second Huge Atomic Plant in Denver Area Reported," *Rocky Mountain News*, 28 March 1951 and 5 May 1951. Unbylined, "Ground Broken for Atom Research Lab," *Boulder Daily Camera*, 8 May 1951.

31. Director of Military Application, "Site Selection for Project Apple" (declassified from Secret after author's FOIA request to DOE) (Germantown, Md.: DOE, 5 March 1951). Whitehead, *Dow Story*, 223. The Austin Co., "Survey and Report for the Santa Fe Operations Office of the United States Atomic Energy Commission on the Location and Site for Project Apple," 27 March 1951, 4–8. Langell, deposition, 33–34.

32. Austin Co., "Engineering Survey," 4–5, 4–6. The incorrect wind calculations were pointed out in a pretrial motion filed in *Marcus F. Church and Marcus F. Church, Trustee v. United States of America, Dow Chemical Co., and North American Rockwell Corp.*, CA 75–1162, U.S. District Ct., 30 October 1975. (Hereafter *Church v. U.S. et al.*) The motion was filed on 11 July 1978 (vol. 1), 77–80. National Archives, Denver.

33. Gosling and Fehner, *Closing*, 1, 5. Hewlett and Duncan, *Atomic Shield*, 362–409, 521–72, 586–87, 669.

34. Director of Military Application, "Selection of a Site," 19 March 1951, 8–9. The report noted that the Rocky Flats site's major disadvantages are that the land is privately owned and that it is located twenty-seven miles by highway from Stapleton Airport. However, these objections "are more than compensated by its advantages."

35. Unbylined, "Boulder Leaders Cheer Atom Plant," *Boulder Daily Camera*, 27 March 1951. Tom Gavin, "State and City Leaders Pleased Atom Production Plant Is Slated," *Rocky Mountain News*, 24 March 1951. A battle of headlines erupted between Denver and Boulder newspapers claiming Rocky Flats for their respective communities. "Boulder Gets $45,000,000 Atomic Plant," read the *Daily Camera* banner. "Denver Gets Atom Plant: $45 Million Project to Be Rushed," the *News* proclaimed. A column in the Boulder paper cheerfully concluded that maps proved that its town was just half as far from the new plant as Denver. "Viewing the site on a nationwide basis, it is certainly correct to say it is near Denver. Locally, it is more

correct to say it is near Boulder." Unbylined, "Boulder and Denver Both Claim New Atomic Plant," *Boulder Daily Camera*, 24 March 1951.

36. Sam Lusky, "Atom Plant Workers to Increase State's Housing Problems," *Rocky Mountain News*, 25 March 1951.

37. Tom Gavin, "State and City Leaders Pleased Atom Production Plant Is Slated," *Rocky Mountain News*, 24 March 1951.

38. Associated Press, "Denver's Atomic Plant Makes That City Bomb Target," *Boulder Daily Camera*, 29 March 1951. This headline is darkly humorous after the earlier competition between the Boulder and Denver papers to claim the plant.

39. Unbylined, "Boulder Leaders Cheer Atom Plant," *Boulder Daily Camera*, 24 March 1951.

40. Washington Bureau, "CF&I Did Not Figure in Picking Boulder for Atomic Bomb Project," *(Pueblo) Chieftain and Star-Journal*, 3 April 1951. Newspaper stories in later years mentioned the role of Johnson and Millikin, sometimes with odd twists. Keating's role was described several years later by the Boulder newspaper. "Mr. Keating assisted the Colorado senators in securing the Rocky Flats plant [and] the National Bureau of Standards laboratories for the Boulder Region," the *Boulder Daily Camera* exaggerated in an unbylined 6 August 1955 article about the town's native. But the article caught the flavor of Keating's job. "He also performed many other services for residents of Boulder on their mission in Washington for which 'all in the know' are very grateful."

41. Director of Military Application, "Selection of Site," 19 March 1951, 8.

42. Marcus Church, *Church v. U.S. et al.*, deposition (vol. 6), 5 October 1977, 59. Marcus's mother, Katherine, owned all the land in 1951–52 and he had a leasehold interest for which he paid her $1,200 per year.

43. Katherine Church, letter to the Corps of Engineers, 9 July 1951. McKay Files. Robert L. Perkin, "Denver Gets Atom Plant," *Rocky Mountain News*, 24 March 1951.

44. Katherine Church, letter to AEC, 9 July 1951. McKay Files.

45. The ownership of land surface is distinguished from ownership of the subsurface, where valuable minerals may exist. In the American West, mining was regarded as a good use of public lands, and the 1872 Mining Law gave miners and mining corporations access to most federal land virtually free of charge to extract gold, silver, copper, and other "hardrock" minerals. The Homestead Act, which privatized some public land, deeded over both surface and mineral rights. Landowners could retain title to both or sell off or lease either. Over the decades, mining and oil and gas companies bought the rights to considerable subsurface holdings potentially containing extractable resources.

46. Edward A. Putzier, "The Past Thirty Years at Rocky Flats Plant," November 1982, 112. Putzier was a health sciences manager for contractor Rockwell International at the plant. Marcus Church, *Church Claim*, deposition, 28 July 1975 (vol. 1), 3. Church said he held title to oil, coal, and gas under AEC land.

47. Church, *Church Claim*, deposition, 28 July 1975, 9–10, 23. Also undated draft

letter in McKay Files. Church said he ran 200 to 250 head on 4,200 acres on Rocky Flats.

48. *The United States of America v. Church et al.*, "Petition in Condemnation," Civil Action 3624, U.S. District Court for the District of Colorado, 10 July 1951.

49. Church, *Church Claim*, deposition, 28 July 1975, 25–26.

CHAPTER FOUR

1. Whitehead, *Dow Story*, 223.

2. All of Langell's quotes in this section come from his deposition, *Good v. Church*, 20 June 1978.

3. The buildings at Rocky Flats were first designated by letters, then were given two numbers, and in the 1970s were designated by three numbers, which is how they are known today. In an effort to reduce confusion, the current three-number designation will be used in most references.

4. Unbylined, "A-Plant Building Firm Old Hand at Business," *Rocky Mountain News*, 25 March 1951. Don Sterling, "Rocky Flats A-Weapons Center, AEC Hints," *Denver Post*, 12 October 1951.

5. Robert L. Perkin, "$2,500,000 Denver Atom Plant Contracts Let," *Rocky Mountain News*, 1 September 1951.

6. The quotes from Jim Stone in this section are from an interview by author, tape recording, Lakewood, Colo., 10 May 1995.

7. Cornelison interview. Unbylined, "Rocky Flats Gets Security Chief," *Rocky Mountain News*, 25 August 1952.

8. Unbylined, "Building of A-Plant to Start This Month," *Denver Post*, 14 June 1951.

9. Don Sterling, "Many Details Disclosed on Rocky Flats A-Plant," *Denver Post*, 12 October 1951.

10. The Austin Co., Site Map, 16 October 1951 (declassified from Official Use Only at author's request), attached to Rocky Flats, File #2446. National Archives, Washington, D.C. ChemRisk, *Rocky Flats History, Rocky Flats Toxicological Review and Dose Reconstruction Task*, report prepared for the Colorado Department of Health, February 1992 draft, 47. (Hereafter: ChemRisk, *History*.) Robert L. Perkin, "PSC Expected to Get $45 Million Atomic Plant Contract," *Rocky Mountain News*, 28 October 1951.

11. On completion date and materials see Langell, deposition, 23. Gordon Dean, letter to Sen. McMahon of the JCAE, 9 January 1952 (declassified from Secret), RG 128, File #2546. National Archives, Washington, D.C.

12. Rosenberg, "Overkill," 22, writes: "The growth of the nuclear stockpile was linked to escalating target estimates, just as expansion of SAC [the air force's Strategic Air Command] was linked to the stockpile." On the targets, "Memorandum for the President," 17 January 1952, summarizing the National Security Council Spe-

cial Committee on Atomic Energy meeting at which he presided (declassified from Top Secret). President's Secretary's Files, Truman Library. JCAE, "Expansion Report," 23 January 1952 (declassified from Top Secret), RG 128, Box 11, includes a memo from the executive director saying that a "comparatively cheap US victory could be obtained with nuclear weapons." It also stated that the United States should have 100,000 nuclear weapons when Russia had 10,000. National Archives, Washington, D.C.

13. The quotes and information about Chuck Arnbrecht in this section come from an interview by author, Parachute, Colo., 19 March 1995.

14. Whitehead, *Dow Story*, 159–60. Langell, deposition, 11.

15. The Cornelison quotes here and below are from the interview by author.

16. Marcus Church, letter to Hoover, 17 November 1952. McKay Files.

17. All of Langell's quotes in this section come from his deposition, *Good v. Church*, 20 June 1978.

18. Stone interview.

19. ChemRisk, *History*, 72.

20. Ibid., 67, 72, 77.

21. Ibid., 67.

22. Dow Chemical, Rocky Flats Division, "A Report on Radiation Problems Related to Plutonium Fabrication Operations at the Rocky Flats Plant," January 1968. It states on page 8, "The first plutonium feed solution arrived from Hanford and was moved into Building 71 [771] during April. Actual attempts at processing the nitrate feed were started during May."

23. The reports were technically inaccurate since the Soviets had exploded a "boosted" weapon that wasn't a hydrogen bomb, but the reports contributed to the AEC's desire to have Rocky Flats in full production.

24. Unbylined, "Fence Contracts for Rocky Flats A-Plant Awarded," *Boulder Daily Camera*, 10 November 1951.

25. The quotes from Pat Kelly in this section are from an interview by author, tape recording, Broomfield, Colo., 7 July 1995.

26. Putzier, "The Past Thirty Years," 93–94.

27. Herrick Roth, *Local 8031: Its Struggles and Its Victories* (Denver: A. B. Hirschfeld Press, 1989), 13–14. AEC, "Major Activities, January-June 1951" (Washington, D.C.: U.S. Government Printing Office), 49. These biannual, public AEC reports contained a section on the agency's labor relations dealings.

28. Edward L. Heller, "Memorandum to the Files," 2 October 1952 (declassified from Secret at author's request), Rocky Flats File #3018. National Archives, Washington, D.C. Heller, a JCAE staff member, described his visit to Rocky Flats. He wrote, "The construction job is approaching completion and the force is now down to some 1500 men." He said the production workforce is estimated "to run from 1,000 to 1,300 people." The *Rocky Mountain News* reported that as of 1 January 1953, there were 1,061 personnel employed by Dow, twenty-two AEC employees,

and one military person at the plant. Unbylined, "There's No Atomic Blast Danger at Rocky Flats," *Rocky Mountain News*, 1 June 1954.

CHAPTER FIVE

1. Marcus Church, letter to Ruth McKay, 20 December 1953. McKay Files. *U.S. v. McKay et al.*, C.A. #3624, "Petition in Condemnation," July 10, 1951, and subsequent filings. National Archives, Denver. The Church case was resolved on April 22, 1955. On the lake, Church, letter to Buckman, 29 November 1954. McKay Files.

2. Lyle Borst was the U. of Utah chairman. Catherine Caufield, *Multiple Exposures* (Chicago: U. of Chicago Press, 1989), 111.

3. William R. Sturges, Jr., "Public Relations Conference Concerning Mercury," 20 December 1950. Cited in Barton Hacker, *Elements of Controversy: The Atomic Energy Commission and Radiation Safety in Nuclear Weapons Testing, 1947–1974* (Berkeley: U. of California Press, 1994), 43.

4. Hacker, *Elements of Controversy*, 127–29.

5. The *News* front-page headline was followed inside by a story. Henry Still, "Radioactive Particles Bathe Colorado," *Rocky Mountain News*, 3 March 1955.

6. Unbylined, "Angry Ed Rips Report, Says Arrest Authors," *Denver Post*, 13 March 1955. This controversy was pointed out by Linda Vollan, "To the Village Square: Early Activism Against Rocky Flats Nuclear Weapons Plant" (master's thesis, University of Colorado at Boulder, 1994), chap. 3.

7. Langell, deposition, 52–53. Barton Hacker, *The Dragon's Tail: Radiation Safety in the Manhattan Project, 1942–1946* (Berkeley: U. of California Press, 1987), 31.

8. For a more complete, fairly nontechnical discussion of ionizing radiation, see Len Ackland, "The Radiation Question," *Science Year 1996*, World Book Annual Science Supplement (Chicago: World Book, 1995), 133–43.

9. Hacker, *Dragon's Tail*, 10. On the committee see "Radiation Protection and the Human Radiation Experiments," *Los Alamos Science*, no. 23 (1995), 118.

10. On radon see "Radiation Protection," *Los Alamos Science*, 31. Hacker, *Dragon's Tail*, 21–22, notes that United States Radium apparently employed no more than three hundred workers at a time. Thus the number of exposed workers was probably more than three hundred and could be considerably more if there were a high turnover rate. The radium dial industry as a whole employed more than 2,000 workers, mainly young women.

11. Energy is the most distinctive feature of radiation, either ionizing or non-ionizing. The energy is measured in electron volts (eV). A particle, or photon, of visible light carries 2 eV and of ultraviolet radiation, 3 to 124 eV. An alpha particle of plutonium, by contrast, has 5 million electron volts (MeV) of energy. Although alpha particles contain extremely high energy, they travel just 1.4 inches in air and are too bulky to penetrate materials easily. The particles, consisting of two protons

and two neutrons — the nucleus of a helium atom — can be blocked by thin barriers such as paper or skin. But once alpha particles enter the human body, their high energy can damage cells. Damage also can be caused by beta particles, or electrons, gamma rays, and neutrons. Although possessing less energy than alpha particles, they are able to penetrate thicker barriers. Beta particles emitted by tritium, a radioactive isotope of hydrogen, average 5,000 eV, or 1,000 times less than plutonium alpha particles. If a radiation source is outside a human body, the main threat is from gamma radiation. "Radiation Protection," *Los Alamos Science*, 3, 15, 21. Hacker, *Dragon's Tail*, 65, notes that plutonium was the first major radioactive element whose hazard was primarily detected through its alpha activity.

12. Radioactivity and its effects are confusing and controversial subjects. An element's radioactivity is inversely proportional to its half-life and atomic weight. (The half-life is the time it takes for a radioactive source to lose half its radioactivity. Plutonium 239, the isotope used in the nuclear bomb cores made at Rocky Flats, has a half-life of 24,065 years.) In determining radioactivity, for example, iodine 131's half-life (eight days) is a million times shorter than plutonium 239's and its atoms weigh half as much. Thus iodine 131 is 2×10^6, or two million times, more radioactive per gram. But the story doesn't end with this calculation of radioactivity. In calculating radiation doses, health physicists must determine whether a single organ, such as the thyroid in the case of iodine 131, or the whole body received the dose. In a whole body dose, for example, the energy from the iodine's gamma radiation emissions is dispersed, so that no single cell of an exposed person receives a large amount. In contrast, once plutonium is inside the body, its focused alpha particle emissions deliver one hundred times more energy to each gram of irradiated tissue than does iodine 131. In calculating a radiation dose, scientists need to know how many particles the radioactive source is emitting each second, the energy of each emission, and the biological features of the exposed organism. See "Radiation Protection," *Los Alamos Science*, 22–27, 119.

13. Chuck Hansen, *U.S. Nuclear Weapons: The Secret History* (New York: Orion Books, 1988), 28 (note 15).

14. Hacker, *Dragon's Tail*, 64–68. "Radiation Protection," *Los Alamos Science*, 132, 150.

15. "Radiation Protection," *Los Alamos Science*, 113.

16. Eileen Welsome, "The Plutonium Experiment," *Albuquerque Tribune* series, 15–17 November 1993. Philip J. Hilts, "Secret Radioactive Experiments to Bring Compensation by U.S.," *New York Times*, 20 November 1996.

17. Hacker, *Dragon's Tail*, 63.

18. "Radiation Protection," *Los Alamos Science*, 126.

19. Putzier, "The Past Thirty Years," 11.

20. Langell, deposition, 66.

21. Ibid., 84.

22. Ibid., 100–101. On waste shipments, Paul Voillequé, "Estimated Airborne

Releases of Plutonium During the 1957 Fire in Building 71," May 1995, 6–7. He presented this report to the Health Advisory Panel, Colorado Department of Health.

23. Gosling and Fehner, *Closing*, 4, 7, 11.

24. Langell, deposition, 73–74, 95.

25. The biographical information and quotes from Thielsen in this section are from an interview by author, tape recording, Golden, Colo., 6 August 1992.

26. Industrial Treatment Record, 31 March 1958. Thielsen provided the author with copies of his medical records.

27. C. W. Piltingsrud, "Plutonium Exposure—M. C. Thielsen (2503)," 27 February 1967. In medical records Thielsen provided the author. Hacker, *Dragon's Tail*, 38–39. "Radiation Protection," *Los Alamos Science*, 119, 229, 232.

28. This translation of Thielsen's body burden was confirmed by James Ruttenber and David McClure of the University of Colorado Health Sciences Center, using modern dosimetry models, 1 July 1998. The estimate for U.S. residents is from the National Council on Radiation Protection and Measurements. Of the total 0.36 rem, or 360 millirem, dose, the largest single amount, fifty-five percent, comes from radon gas released by the disintegration of uranium in rock and soils. A typical diagnostic chest x ray equals ten millirem. International standards are recommended by the International Commission on Radiological Protection. William H. Hallenbeck, *Radiation Protection* (Boca Raton: Lewis Publishers, 1994). Several other radiation measures exist, including "radiation absorbed dose," or rads, which equal rems for external radiation. For the sake of simplicity this book will use rems.

CHAPTER SIX

1. The information and quotes from Jim Kelly in this section are from an interview by author, tape recording, Local 8031 union hall, Golden, Colo., 27 June 1995.

2. E. J. Bloch, director of production, memorandum re "PU Fire in 234–5 Facility—Final Report," to AEC general manager K. D. Nichols, 15 November 1954 (declassified from Secret), RG 326. National Archives, College Park. This includes the investigation report of the July 27, 1954, plutonium fire at the Hanford nuclear facility. Page 3 notes, "The actual extinguishment of a fire in plutonium or other pyrophoric materials is practically impossible."

3. AEC, Serious Accidents report, "Plutonium Chip Fire," issue no. 92, 14 December 1955. In AEC, *Report on Investigation of Fire, Building 776–777, Rocky Flats Plant*, vol. II-B (This Secret report was not fully declassified and was called a "deleted version"), August 1969, appendix J-1. (Hereafter: AEC, *Report on Investigation—1969 Fire*.) Rocky Flats site, Records Management.

4. AEC, Accident and Fire Prevention Information, "Plutonium Fires," issue no. 21, 28 October 1955. Washington, D.C.: DOE.

5. Putzier, "Past Thirty Years," vi. ChemRisk, *History*, 61.

6. Dow Chemical, Rocky Flats Division, "A Report on Radiation Problems Related to Plutonium Fabrication Operations at the Rocky Flats Plant," January 1968, 8. (Hereafter: Dow, "Radiation Problems.") Putzier, "Past Thirty Years," 37–39.

7. Putzier, "Past Thirty Years," 37. ChemRisk, *History*, 65. The first line was called the West Chem Line. The second line, the East Chem line, was capable of producing larger "buttons."

8. DOE, *Linking Legacies*, 196–97. Putzier, "Past Thirty Years," vi. Thomas B. Cochran et al., *Nuclear Weapons Databook*, vol. II, *U.S. Nuclear Warhead Production* (Cambridge: Ballinger, 1987), 38–40. Rosenberg, "Overkill," 49–50, describes another feature of the weapons: "Through the mid-1950s, the fission cores used to fuel atomic weapons and to initiate the fusion reaction in "two stage" thermonuclear bombs could be inserted only immediately before takeoff, or in flight. This problem was solved by the perfection of a new "sealed pit" advanced bomb design that, among other things, contained smaller amounts of high explosives and fissionable material. Sealed pit weapons were efficient, lightweight, high-yield thermonuclear bombs, equipped with safety devices that reduced the risk of inadvertent detonation to near zero." By 1959 most nuclear bombs were sealed pit.

9. Los Alamos weapons scientists had recognized the potential of hollow fissile cores as early as 1950, but other design changes and the H-bomb took precedence. Panel on Military Objectives in the Field of Atomic Energy, chaired by J. Robert Oppenheimer, "Military Objectives in the Use of Atomic Energy," 29 December 1950 (declassified from Top Secret), RG 128, Box 8. National Archives, Washington, D.C. ChemRisk, *History*, 45.

10. The AEC hired Catalytic Construction Co. of Philadelphia as architect-engineer and Swinerton and Walberg Co. of Denver and San Francisco as the builder. The agency gave both companies its typical cost-plus-fixed-fee contract. Joint Committee on Atomic Energy, letter from R. W. Cook to Clinton P. Anderson, 10 September 1955 (declassified from Official Use Only), RG 128, Box 646. National Archives, D.C. ChemRisk, *History*, 51, 79.

11. AEC, "Proposed Extension of Dow Chemical Company Contract," report to the general manager by the director of Military Application, and "Memorandum: Extension of Dow Chemical Company Contract,"18 April 1958 (declassified from Secret), RG 326, National Archives, College Park. Rosenberg, "Overkill," 52.

12. John Epp et al., *Report of Investigation of Serious Incident in Building 71 on September 11, 1957*, 7 October 1957 (declassified from Secret), 23. (Hereafter: Epp, *Report of Investigation — 1957 Fire*.) This document was released by Energy Secretary Hazel O'Leary at her 7 December 1993 news conference. Putzier, "Past Thirty Years," 41–43.

13. Epp, *Report of Investigation — 1957 Fire*, 9, 10, 17. Room 180 was 2,500 square feet.

14. Langell, deposition, 110–12.

15. Paul Voillequé, "Rocky Flats Plutonium Releases," 3 March 1997, overheads,

9. Presentation to Health Advisory Panel, Colorado Department of Public Health and Environment.

16. Epp, *Report of Investigation — 1957 Fire*, 11.

17. The chronology and details of the fire come primarily from Epp, *Report of Investigation — 1957 Fire*. This report contains extensive interviews with participants. Additional fire details come from an unpublished manuscript by former plant fireman William D. Dennison, "The Fires of Rocky Flats," 1990.

18. Paul Voillequé, "Estimated Airborne Releases of Plutonium During the 1957 Fire in Building 71," May 1995 draft, Colorado Department of Public Health and Environment. On filters see Epp, *Report of Investigation — 1957 Fire*, 10.

19. Paul Voillequé, "Further Analysis of the 1957 Fire," Source Term Workshop, Health Advisory Panel Meeting, 26 May 1998, overheads, 7. Colorado Department of Public Health and Environment. Voillequé arrived at this conclusion after consulting with a fire protection engineer and finding information about filter dust buildup in two AEC documents: "Fifth Atomic Energy Commission Air Cleaning Conference," 24–27 June 1957, and "Sixth AEC Air Cleaning Conference," 7–9 July 1959. Idaho National Engineering Laboratory technical library.

20. Epp, *Report of Investigation — 1957 Fire*, 18.

21. Dennison, "Fires of Rocky Flats," 31.

22. Epp, *Report of Investigation — 1957 Fire*, 77.

23. J. B. Owen, "Review of the Exhaust Air Filtering and Air Sampling, Building 71," 8 May 1963, 5. Records management office, Rocky Flats site.

24. Paul Voillequé, "Rocky Flats Plutonium Releases," 3 March 1997. Colorado Department of Health. He confirmed this range of releases in a telephone interview with author on 5 August 1998.

25. See notes 27 and 28 of chap. 5 above.

26. This and Jim Kelly's other quotes about the fire come from an interview by author, tape recording, Golden, Colo., 27 June 1995.

27. Epp, *Report of Investigation — 1957 Fire*, 7.

28. Another colleague described Venable as firm but sensitive. Putzier, "Past Thirty Years," 92.

29. Epp, *Report of Investigation — 1957 Fire*, 8. R. W. Cook, letter to Carl T. Durham (JCAE), 21 November 1957 (declassified from Secret), RG 128, JCAE #5385. National Archives, Washington, D.C. AEC, *Report on Investigation — 1969 Fire* (vol. 2-B), 97. Putzier, "Past Thirty Years," 83.

30. AEC, "Small Metallic Plutonium Fire Leads to Major Property Damage Loss," Serious Accidents report, issue no. 130, 27 November 1957. Washington, D.C.: DOE.

31. Unbylined, "$21,000,000 Addition Done at Rocky Flats Atomic Plant," *Boulder Daily Camera*, 2 January 1958. The lack of a byline on this story suggests the paper simply printed a news release from the plant.

32. U.S. Rep. Chet Holifield of California, chairman of the JCAE, criticized the

AEC for a conflict of interests because it was in charge of both producing nuclear weapons and evaluating the risks of fallout. Yet he and other committee members didn't question the AEC's production priority. In a 3 August 1957 article in *Saturday Review*, a month before the Rocky Flats fire, he praised the AEC for "doing a good job" in weapons development. H. Peter Metzger, *The Atomic Establishment* (New York: Simon & Schuster, 1972), 15–17, describes AEC officials lying to the JCAE during 1957 hearings about the safety of nuclear testing and how committee members bought the story.

33. Mark Bearwald, "Sprawling Rocky Flats Keeps Its AEC Secret," *Denver Post*, 16 January 1958. Louisa Ward Arps, *Denver in Slices* (Denver: Sage Books, 1959), 40. Leonard and Noel, *Denver*, 416–17.

34. Leonard and Noel, *Denver*, 410, 414.

35. Marcus F. Church, draft testimony for *Church Claim*, 21 May 1975. McKay Files. Also Church, deposition, *Church Claim*, 28 July 1975. National Archives, Denver.

36. Marcus Church, letter to Father Robert F. Chamberlain, 29 December 1958. McKay Files.

37. AEC, "Safety Considerations in the Operations of the Rocky Flats Plutonium Processing Plant," March 1970. In Senate Subcommittee of the Committee on Appropriations, *Public Works Appropriations for Fiscal Year 1971: Atomic Energy Commission*, 91st Cong., 2d sess., 21 April 1970, 903.

CHAPTER SEVEN

1. "Church Property and Industrial District," Marcus Church, brochure, undated. McKay Files.

2. Photo caption, "Allott Speaks at Jefferson Airport," *Denver Post*, 2 August 1959.

3. The quotes from Charlie McKay in this chapter are from interviews by author, tape recording, Westminster, Colo., 4 March and 6 June 1994.

4. Marcus Church letter to Ruth McKay, 21 May 1961. McKay Files.

5. Marcus Church letter to Ruth McKay, 30 May 1963. McKay Files. The description of Church's office is from Charlie McKay in the interviews cited in note 2 above.

6. David Halberstam, *The Fifties* (New York: Villard Books, 1993), 699–700.

7. Ibid., 700.

8. Jim Kelly interview, 25 June 1995.

9. Voillequé, "Estimated Airborne Releases," May 1995, 3. In terms of radioactivity, Voillequé writes that a gram of Rocky Flats weapons-grade plutonium contained .37 curie of plutonium 241 and just .072 curie of plutonium 239 and plutonium 240 combined. For a discussion of radioactivity, see chap. 5, notes 11 and 12.

10. Dow, "Radiation Problems," 23.

11. Ibid., 26.

12. Ibid., 11–12, 22, 26, 27.

13. Ibid., 27. In 1955, after a request by AEC commissioner Lewis Strauss, the National Academy of Sciences founded the Biological Effects of Atomic Radiation (BEAR) committee. In 1956 the committee recommended a limit of 5 rems per year for workers. Caufield, *Multiple Exposures*, 135–36.

14. Roth, *Local 8031*, 9, 14.

15. Ibid., p. 14.

16. Joint Committee on Atomic Energy, Subcommittee on Research and Development, *Employee Radiation Hazards and Workmen's Compensation*, 86th Cong., 1st sess., 10–12, 17–19, March 1959, 251–52.

17. Pat Kelly interview.

18. Roth, *Local 8031*, 11. Langell, deposition, 58–62, 163.

19. Jack Weaver, interview by author, tape recording, Boulder, Colo., 6 February 1998.

20. Putzier, "Past Thirty Years," 111.

21. Gene Lindberg, "Rocky Flats Plant Open to Press for 1st Time," *Denver Post*, April 11, 1963. Lindberg and the reporters and editors at the other papers all seem to have forgotten the 1951 tour. The body counter was an eight-foot-by-nine-foot steel room with six-inch walls. The body counter actually used the americium–241 gamma rays as a tracer for plutonium. So three detectors counted the gamma rays emitted by the americium. Exposed workers would have two detectors positioned over their chests and a third over their livers. The fraction of americium in the plutonium had to be known for the body counter to provide an accurate measure. Putzier, "Past Thirty Years," 17.

22. The quotes from Jim Kelly in this section are from an interview by author, tape recording, Golden, Colo., 9 February 1996.

23. *The Kennedy Tapes: Inside the White House During the Cuban Missile Crisis*, ed. Ernest R. May and Philip D. Zelikow (Cambridge: Belknap Press of Harvard University, 1997), 694.

24. In November 1957, for instance, the development schedule was accelerated to produce a deployed Polaris submarine missile system by 1961. Rosenberg, "Overkill," 55. The Rocky Flats structure with the incomplete roof was Building 883. ChemRisk, *History*, 72.

25. Voillequé, "Estimated Airborne Releases," 6–7. He noted that Rocky Flats didn't make serious attempts to measure the amount of plutonium in waste drums and boxes until a 1964 analysis of plutonium losses.

26. Ibid., 17. In one plutonium recovery process, combustible residues such as plastic bags were incinerated to reduce the bulk of materials and convert plutonium to an oxide form. ChemRisk, *History*, 65. Bini Abbott, who lives east of the plant near Standley Lake, recalled seeing occasional smoke. Interview by author, tape recording, Westminster, Colo., 8 July 1997.

27. Putzier, "Past Thirty Years," 67. ChemRisk, *History*, 182.

28. ChemRisk, *History*, 187–90. Putzier, "Past Thirty Years," 113.

29. Edward Putzier, "A Summary of On-site Radioactive Waste Disposal," 22 April 1970, 1–2. Rocky Flats site, Records Management. Putzier, "Past Thirty Years," 64–65. ChemRisk, *History*, 190, 222.

30. J. R. Seed et al., "Committee Evaluation of Plutonium Levels in Soil Within and Surrounding USAEC Installation at Rocky Flats, Colorado," 1971, 5–8. Rocky Flats site, Records Management. ChemRisk, "History," 224.

31. ChemRisk, *History*, 174–76, 202–3. Putzier, "Past Thirty Years," 66.

32. Putzier, "Past Thirty Years," 65. ChemRisk, *History*, 80.

33. Seed, "Committee Evaluation of Plutonium Levels,"6. Edward Putzier, "903 Oil Drum Storage Area," 14 April 1970, 1–4. Rocky Flats site, Records Management. ChemRisk, *History*, 22.

34. Putzier, "Past Thirty Years," 65.

35. Seed, "Committee Evaluation of Plutonium Levels," 5–8. ChemRisk, *History*, 221–27.

CHAPTER EIGHT

1. Paul Wilkes, "Uncommon Tour of Closely-Guarded Plant: Rocky Flats Unveils New Facilities," Boulder *Daily Camera*, 19 May 1965.

2. Dow, "Radiation Problems," 23–24.

3. While the AEC transferred the plant's highly enriched uranium-manufacturing jobs to Oak Ridge, it retained some uranium R&D work at Rocky Flats. AEC, "Announcement," 29 January 1965, RG 128, Box 646. National Archives, Washington, D.C. Among the stainless steel parts, previously made in the South Albuquerque Works, Rocky Flats produced the small steel "reservoirs" that contained tritium injected into the pit's center to boost the fission chain reaction. The pit fabrication equipment in Hanford's plutonium-finishing plant was removed and buried between 1975 and 1976. DOE, *Linking Legacies*, 185.

4. DOE, *Linking Legacies*, 194. Dow, "Radiation Problems," 29.

5. Dow Chemical Co., "Discussion of Shielding Requirements," 10 November 1967, contained in AEC, *Report on Investigation — 1969 Fire*" (vol. 4), appendix L-3. For more than two years the new processing techniques had been exposing workers to higher radiation doses. Yet the report concluded, "Studies will be made before shielding designs are finalized to indicate whether or not it is economically more attractive to add shielding or to buy new equipment for americium milking," a technique for extracting americium from weapons-grade plutonium.

6. The quotes from Jim Kelly in this section are from the interview by author, 9 February 1996.

7. A majority of the plant's 1,711 production workers voted out the AFL-CIO's Denver Metal Trades Council. Pat Kelly interview. Dow quote from Dow, "Radiation Problems," 9.

8. Roth, *Local 8031*, 31–32. The International Board of the Mine Workers ex-

pelled District 50 in March 1968. Roger Rapoport, "Secrecy and Safety at Rocky Flats," *L.A. Times West* magazine, 7 September 1969, 13–14.

9. William Turnbull, letter to Rufus Klein, 29 January 1968. McKay Files.

10. Lee Hancock, "Personnel Exposure to Ionizing Radiation at the Rocky Flats Plant," Memorandum to Seth R. Woodruff, Jr., Area Manager, Rocky Flats Office, 8 November 1967. In AEC, *Report on Investigation — 1969 Fire* (vol. 4), appendix L-5.

11. Dow, "Radiation Problems," 61–62.

12. AEC, *Report on Investigation — 1969 Fire* (vol. 1), 7, 14. Building 776–777 was 211,000 square feet, but 776 was two story.

13. The description of the chainveyors comes from the author's observation and discussions with workers who used them.

14. Dow, "Radiation Problems," 65.

15. Ibid.

16. Ibid., 9. C. W. Barrick, "Past Accidental Releases of Radioactivity from the Rocky Flats Plant," 14 January 1981, pp. 23–25. Rocky Flats site, Records Management.

17. ChemRisk, *History*, 235. AEC, *Report on Investigation — 1969 Fire* (vol. 1), 97.

18. "Fire Experience 1966-May 1969," in AEC, *Report on Investigation — 1969 Fire* (vol. 2-B), appendix J-2 (p. J-7), appendix H-2 (p. H-34). When larger pieces of plutonium such as ingots caught fire, workers were instructed to cover the burning metal with magnesium oxide sand, place it on the glove box floor, and cool the underside of the glove box by spraying it with carbon dioxide. This efficiently removed heat from the fire and extinguished it. Ibid. (vol. 2-B), appendix H-2 (p. H-36).

19. "Ignition and Burning Characteristics of Plutonium," in AEC, *Report on Investigation — 1969 Fire* (vol. 2-B), appendix H-2 (pp. H-29–34).

20. AEC, *Report on Investigation — 1969 Fire* (vol. 1), 65; (vol. 2-A), appendix B-1. As nuclear weapons designers at the Los Alamos and Lawrence Livermore laboratories came up with new warhead designs, older warhead models in the weapons arsenal were returned to the Pantex plant in Texas or another AEC facility for disassembly. The plutonium components were then trucked back to Rocky Flats and broken or cut up on the 777 side and the plutonium placed in steel cans and sent to the small foundry furnaces in 776 to be cast into fifteen-to-eighteen-pound (seven-to-eight-kilogram) feed ingots. Ingots meeting plutonium assay specifications went to the molten salt facility for americium removal. If not, they were sent to Building 771 for "chemical purification" and returned to the foundry as fresh buttons.

21. The building's general layout and operations are taken primarily from AEC, *Report on Investigation — 1969 Fire* (vol. 1), Background Information, 8–44, and (vol. 2-A), appendix B-1.

22. David E. Patterson, "Trip Report — Rocky Flats Plant — March 11–15, 1969." In AEC, *Report on Investigation — 1969 Fire* (vol. 4), appendix O1.

23. AEC, *Report on Investigation — 1969 Fire* (vol. 4), 22.

24. Jim Kelly, interview, 9 February 1996.

25. AEC, *Report on Investigation — 1969 Fire* (vol. 1), 38–39.

26. "Fire Experience," in AEC, *Report on Investigation — 1969 Fire* (vol. 2-B), appendix J-2; (vol. 1), 39. Rowland E. Felt, "Fire Safety at Rocky Flats," briefing at Rocky Flats, 24 January 1996, author's tape recording.

27. Felt, "Fire Safety." He said, "As a result of this — now this is not in the literature, this never came into view before today — they had an oily rag fire in the press box." Felt, a nuclear materials specialist with the DOE in Idaho Falls, Idaho, was a member of the 1969 fire investigation team. His account fills in holes left in the original AEC investigation report.

28. AEC, *Report on Investigation — 1969 Fire* (vol. 2-B), appendix E-7, table E-74; (vol. 1), 65–66.

29. Ibid. (vol. 1), 44. AEC, "Fire — Rocky Flats Plant — May 11, 1969," Serious Accidents report, no. 306, 1 December 1969.

30. AEC, Serious Accidents report, 1 December 1969, p. 4.

31. Ibid., AEC, *Report on Investigation — 1969 Fire* (vol. 3), 5–6. Felt, "Fire Safety."

32. This and the following account of the fire have been pieced together primarily from AEC, *Report on Investigation — 1969 Fire* (vol. 1), 45–59; AEC, Serious Accident Report, 1 December 1969; Felt, "Fire Safety," and Dennison, "Fires of Rocky Flats." Felt described the fire as out of control.

33. Scientists had hypothesized that burning plutonium would decompose the water and cause hydrogen explosions. AEC, *Report on Investigation — 1969 Fire* (vol. 1), 68. Felt, "Fire Safety," said that Jesser disobeyed every rule in the book but used his knowledge of the situation, which far exceeded that of the criticality experts.

34. Dennison, "Fires of Rocky Flats," 76.

35. The direction and spread of the fire were largely controlled by the continued operation of booster system #1. AEC, *Report on Investigation — 1969 Fire* (vol. 1), 110. Felt, "Fire Safety," said the fireman told investigators he hit the utility pole by accident.

36. The information and quotes from Jim Kelly in this section are from the interview by author, 9 February 1996.

37. J. F. Willging, "Possible Origins of the Smoke Seen Evolving from Bldg. 776 on May 11, 1969," Dow Chemical Co., 3 October 1969, 2. AEC, *Report on Investigation — 1969 Fire* (vol. 1), 55; (vol. 2-A), appendix D.

38. R. E. Giebel et al., "Building 776 Roof Burning Tests," 21 July 1969, 1. In Willging, "Origins of the Smoke," appendix A.

39. Dennison, "Fires of Rocky Flats," 78–79, 92.

40. Felt, "Fire Safety."

41. AEC, *Report on Investigation — 1969 Fire* (vol. 1), 89–94.

42. Ibid. (vol. 1), 57.

43. Ibid. (vol. 1), 2, 74. AEC, report, 1 December 1969.

44. Ibid., 10, 102–3. Paul Voillequé, "Rocky Flats Plutonium Releases," 3 March

1977, overheads, 19. Presented at public meeting sponsored by Colorado health department.

45. AEC, *Report on Investigation — 1969 Fire* (vol. 5), "Management Conclusions," 1–5.

46. AEC, Serious Accidents report, 1 December 1969, 4. Felt, "Fire Safety."

47. AEC, *Report on Investigation — 1969 Fire* (vol. 4), 35–36.

48. Ibid. (vol. 3), 2.

49. House Committee on Appropriations, Subcommittee on Public Works, *Hearings on Supplemental Appropriations Bill, 1971, U.S. Atomic Energy Commission*, 91st Cong., 2d sess., 1 October 1970, 295.

CHAPTER NINE

1. John Primack and Frank von Hippel, *Advice and Dissent* (New York: New American Library, 1974), 165–66. The Colorado Committee on Environmental Information (CCEI) began as an evening discussion group attended by as many as two dozen scientists from the University of Colorado at Boulder and nearby government laboratories. After revelations in 1968 that sheep in Utah had been poisoned during nerve gas experiments at the army's Dugway test facility, the group released a short fact sheet raising questions about the nerve gas produced and stored at the Rocky Mountain Arsenal on the northeast edge of Denver. The group organized itself formally as the CCEI in early 1969.

2. The quotes and biographical information from Ed Martell in this chapter are from an interview by author, tape recording, Boulder, Colo., 26 February 1992.

3. Martell graduated from West Point in 1942 and commanded a combat engineering unit in World War II, achieving the rank of lieutenant colonel. Afterward, while still in the army, he received a doctorate in nuclear chemistry from the University of Chicago, where his mentor was Willard Libby, a Manhattan Project physicist who soon became an AEC commissioner. On returning to the Pentagon in 1951, Martell was assigned to the Armed Forces Special Weapons Project, later renamed the Defense Nuclear Agency, which collaborated with the AEC and Los Alamos laboratory in conducting nuclear weapons tests.

4. Primack and von Hippel, *Advice*, 169–70. Metzger, *Atomic Establishment*, 148–50. Ed Giller, interview by author, tape recording, Boulder, Colo., 22 September 1995. Giller didn't recall the details of his conversation with Martell or meetings in Denver. For him Rocky Flats paled beside other events of his time at the AEC, particularly the controversies surrounding underground nuclear testing.

5. Detailed descriptions of the sampling technique are given in S. A. Poet and E. A. Martell, "Plutonium-239 and Americium-241 Contamination in the Denver Area," *Health Physics* 23 (1972): 537–48.

6. LeRoy Moore et al., *Citizen's Guide to Rocky Flats* (Boulder: Rocky Mountain Peace Center, 1992), 52.

7. AEC, *Operational Accidents and Radiation Exposure Experience Within the United States Atomic Energy Commission, 1943–1975* (Washington, Fall 1975) 118–45. Rocky Flats site, Records Management. This report listed just four "reportable" fires at the plant from June 1969 to January 1975.

8. Primack and von Hippel, *Advice*, 173. The ACLU filed its complaint in U.S. District Court in Denver on August 22. A district judge denied it on August 27, and his ruling was upheld on September 2. Hacker, *Elements of Controversy*, 242–44.

9. E. A. Martell et al., "Fire Damage," *Environment* 12, no. 4 (1970): 16–18. Metzger, *Atomic Establishment*, 148–50.

10. Martell et. al., "Fire Damage," 20–21.

11. Roy L. Cleere, letter to Lloyd Joshel, 3 March 1970. In *Church v. U.S. et al.*, Pre-trial Statement, 11 July 1978, vol. 3, 479. National Archives, Denver. Cleere sent copies of his letter to Colorado governor John A. Love and AEC chairman Glenn Seaborg, the scientist who had discovered plutonium in 1941.

12. Martell et al., "Fire Damage," 15–20. Martell interview. Poet and Martell, "Plutonium-239," *Health Physics*, explain their system of dated soil sampling. AEC, "Safety Considerations, 893–931.

13. Senate Subcommittee, *Public Works Appropriations FY 1971*, 888–91.

14. Charles J. Beise, *Good v. Church*, deposition, 29 March 1977, 98, 109, 112.

15. Jean Woodis, interview by author, tape recording, Arvada, Colo., 18 July 1995.

16. Bini Abbott interview.

17. Jim Kelly interview, 9 February 1996.

18. Weaver interview. Several memoranda and letters about the problems between Dow and the union and the glove-slitting incident are located in RG 128, Box 646, National Archives, Washington, D.C. They include: Col. Seymour Shwiller, "Rocky Flats Union—Dow Problem," Memorandum to File, 24 October 1969; Shwiller, "Meeting with Members of District 50 United Mine Workers of America," Memorandum to File, 5 November 1969; John V. Vinciguerra, letter to Edward J. Bauser, "Use of Polygraph at Rocky Flats," 5 November 1969, which said thirty-five employees had agreed to polygraph examinations; Vinciguerra, letter to Bauser, "Damage to Gloves in Building 777 at Rocky Flats," 28 January 1970, which said, "Neither the investigation by the FBI which is currently in an inactive status, the polygraph examinations conducted during November 10–19, 1969, nor the interviews of the week of January 12, 1970, resulted in the identification of the person or persons responsible."

19. *Dow Corral*, "Special Issue," 24 March 1970, p. 3. Rocky Flats site, Pat Buffer files. Edward Giller, letter to Edward Bauser (JCAE), 20 April 1970 (declassified from Official Use Only), RG 128, Box 646. National Archives, Washington, D.C.

20. On the size of the complex: Senate Subcommittee of the Committee on Appropriations, *Public Works Appropriations for Fiscal Year 1973: Atomic Energy Commission*, 92nd Cong., 2d sess., 26 April 1972, 238. Frank Graham, *Since Silent Spring* (Boston: Houghton Mifflin, 1970), 13, cites Carson: "I suppose my thinking began to be affected soon after atomic science was firmly established. Some of the thoughts

that came were so unattractive to me that I rejected them completely, for the old ideas die hard, especially when they are emotionally as well as intellectually dear to one. It was pleasant to believe, for example, that much of Nature was forever beyond the tampering reach of man: he might level the forests and dam the streams, but the clouds and the rain and the wind were God's."

21. Roth, *Local 8031*, 38. Labor leaders claimed, for example, that Dow was trying to bust the union. And union claims that Dow was operating unsafely prompted JCAE chairman Holifield to send four inspectors to the plant in July. They concluded that the plant was safe.

22. Judy Danielson, interview by author, tape recording, Denver, Colo., 14 March 1992. The soil-sampling campaign was organized by Chester McQueary, Duane Gall, and Tom Rauch of Clergy and Laity Concerned About Vietnam.

23. Pam Solo, "Rocky Flats Campaign History," unpublished paper for the American Friends Service Committee, September 1977, p. 1. AFSC files.

24. Ibid. Pam Solo, *From Protest to Policy: Beyond the Freeze to Common Security* (Cambridge: Ballinger Publishing Co., 1988), 29–30.

25. Roth, *Local 8031*, 51.

26. Jim Kelly interview, 9 February 1996. Kelly said the television journalists were Bob Nelson, Bob McNichols, and Dave Minshall.

27. AEC, "Investigation of the Tritium Release Occurrence at the Rocky Flats Plant," 26 November 1973, 14–19. Rocky Flats site, Records Management.

28. Ibid. (exhibit 5), 59.

29. Ibid. The September 14 letter noted that the maximum tritium concentration was observed in Walnut Creek on May 24. It amounted to "3,000,000 picocuries" (trillionths of a curie) per liter, which was equal to the maximum permissible concentration in the state's rules. The Department of Health wrote, "Should concentrations of this magnitude have been anticipated for the recent detonation of Project Rio Blanco, the Board of Health and the Department would have taken all steps within their authority to preclude the occurrence of any such potential general population exposure." Community and realtors' concern was raised by articles such as Tony Stroh, "Permanent Diversion of Walnut Creek Is Sought by Broomfield," *Boulder Daily Camera*, 25 September 1973.

30. "Buechner to Meet Governor to Discuss Communications," Boulder *Daily Camera*, 25 September 1973, reported that John Buechner, a Republican state representative from Boulder, complained that the state should have provided local officials with the tritium report on a more timely basis. Barrick, "Past Accidental Releases," 32.

31. Unbylined, "Rocky Flats Work to Cost $130 Million," *Denver Post*, 4 January 1972.

32. Jim Kelly, interview, 9 February 1996.

33. Beise, letter to members, 28 December 1970. McKay Files.

34. Frank R. Komatz Co., letter to Robert E. Hollingsworth, 25 August 1970. McKay Files. Church, "Effort to Sell Property," draft deposition in *Church Claim*,

27 May 1975. McKay Files. Church said that Komatz "came back when the buffer zone got publicity and wanted a listing and I refused them."

35. E. J. Walko, "Briefing for Local Landowners," memo to AEC manager, 12 March 1971. McKay Files. Charles Beise, letter to J. F. Willging, 29 March 1971. McKay Files.

36. Alan Cunningham, "Putzier: Press Plagues Rocky Flats," *Rocky Mountain News*, 16 December 1971.

37. Church, letter to Ruth McKay, 27 January 1972. A day after a local official met with Church on January 25, the AEC released an environmental impact statement (EIS) regarding $8 million for acquisition of the buffer zone and a second EIS about a $113 million new plutonium recovery facility (Building 371). Robert Threlkeld, "AEC Planning Buffer Zone for Rocky Flats Plant," *Rocky Mountain News*, 26 January 1972.

38. House Committee on Appropriations, *Public Works for Water and Power Development and Atomic Energy Commission Appropriation Bill, Fiscal Year 1973*, 92nd Cong., 2d sess., 20 April 1972, 197. Senate Subcommittee, *Public Works Appropriations*, 26 April 1972, 279–80.

39. James Crawford, "Radiation Unit Undecided on Flats Housing," *Rocky Mountain News*, 17 March 1973.

40. On Beise quote, State Board of Health hearing, "Hearing on Proposed Regulation Relative to Permissible Level of Plutonium in Soil," 14 February 1973. Martell quoted in James Crawford, "Strict Land Development Radiation Proposal Eased," *Rocky Mountain News*, 22 March 1973.

CHAPTER TEN

1. Lamm-Wirth Task Force on Rocky Flats, "Final Report" (Denver: self-published, 1 October 1975), 1.

2. Jack Olsen, Jr., "EPA Reverses Finding on Rocky Flats Cattle," *Rocky Mountain News*, 27 January 1975.

3. *Church Claim*, exhibit A, 7. Church, *Good v. Church*, deposition (vol. 3), 19–20 September 1977, 365.

4. Church, *Church Claim*. The filing claimed property damage of $4,996,250 and exemplary damages of $15 million, citing "negligence, nuisance, dangerous instrumentality, strict liability."

5. Among the expert witnesses was controversial California health physicist John Gofman. A former employee of the government's Lawrence Livermore nuclear weapons laboratory, Gofman became an outspoken critic of government assessments of radiation hazards, which he contended underestimated the real risk. On September 16, 1975, he prepared a technical report for Church and his attorneys titled "The Habitability of the Environs of the Rocky Flats Plant." McKay Files.

6. Lamm-Wirth, "Final Report," 4–7. The task force report was written by

Robert Damrauer, a chemist at the University of Colorado at Denver, who was hired as the group's technical staff member.

7. This and the following quotations from Weaver are from the interview by author, 6 February 1998.

8. Roth, *Local 8031*, 62–65.

9. This and the following statements by Danielson are from the interview by author.

10. Robert S. Norris and William Arkin, "Nuclear Notebook," *Bulletin of the Atomic Scientists*, November 1989, 53, and December 1989, 52. In 1975 the United States arsenal amounted to 6,800 megatons (million tons of TNT) and the Soviet arsenal totaled 16,200 megatons.

11. Martell interview.

12. Carl Johnson, letter to Jefferson County commissioner Joanne Paterson, 30 December 1974. In Bryan Abas (later Ryan Ross), "Rocky Flats: A Big Mistake from Day One," *Bulletin of the Atomic Scientists*, December 1989, 21. Martell's opinions about Johnson are from the author's interview with him, 26 February 1992. Niels Schonbeck, a colleague of the late Martell, provided more details about Johnson's soil sampling in a telephone interview by author, 9 August 1998.

13. Johnson's work included "Evaluation of the Hazard to Residents of Areas Contaminated with Plutonium," a paper given at the International Congress of the Radiation Protection Association in Paris, April 1977. Several other papers and studies are cited in notes 141–47 in LeRoy Moore et al., *Citizen's Guide*, 71–72. For a critique of Johnson's epidemiology, see L. Hamilton, "Alternative Interpretation of Statistics of Health Effects of Low Level Radiation," *The American Statistician* 37 (1983), 422–58. In Abas, "Rocky Flats: Mistake." According to Schonbeck, a chemist at Metro State College in Denver, members of the Rocky Flats Environmental Monitoring Council analyzed Johnson's epidemiological work and found that the evidence could not support his conclusions. Schonbeck, personal communication with author, 12 August 1998.

14. Pam Solo, interview by LeRoy Moore, tape recording transcript, 9 January 1998. Moore is working on a book about activists and workers at Rocky Flats.

15. Abbott interview.

16. This and the following quotes are from the Jim Kelly interview by author, 9 February 1996.

17. Solo, "Rocky Flats Campaign History," 5.

18. Ibid., 6–7.

19. Solo, *From Protest to Policy*, 31. On DOE, Gosling and Fehner, *Closing*, 25.

20. Solo interview by Moore.

21. Paul Wehr, *Conflict Regulation* (Boulder: Westview, 1979), 111–22. John J. Kennedy, Jr., "Annihilation Beckons: A Brief History of Colorado's Nuclear Bomb-Trigger Factory," *Colorado Heritage* (spring 1994), 27.

22. Solo interview by Moore.

23. Ibid. Solo, *From Protest to Policy*, 63.

24. Joe Seldner, "Ellsberg Trespass Nets $1,000 Fine," *Denver Post*, 14 July 1979. Mike Patty, "Ellsberg Fined $1,000 for Flats Trespass," *Rocky Mountain News*, 14 July 1979. The trial judge was U.S. District Court judge Richard Matsch, who presided in the Oklahoma City bombing trials in 1997.

25. Roth, *Local 8031*, 66.

26. Charlie McKay, interview by author, tape recording, Westminster, Colo., 31 January 1998.

CHAPTER ELEVEN

1. Charlie McKay, interview by author, tape recording, Westminster, Colo., 11 May 1998.

2. Jonathan Schell, *The Fate of the Earth* (New York: Alfred A. Knopf, 1982). An example of the PSR symposia was a two-day session titled "The Medical Consequences of Nuclear Weapons and Nuclear War," held in Chicago on 19–20 June 1981. Australian physician and activist Helen Caldicott was the keynote speaker.

3. Pam Solo, personal communication with author, 14 October 1998.

4. James W. Spensley and Guy M. Burgess et al., *Blue Ribbon Citizen's Committee Final Report on the Department of Energy Long Range Rocky Flats Utilization Study* (Washington, D.C., Federal Emergency Management Agency, December 1983), preface, 72.

5. Department of Energy, *Final Environmental Impact Statement: Rocky Flats Plant Site* (Washington, D.C., April 1980), 1–17, 1–18. The second study is Battelle Columbus Laboratories, *The Social and Economic Impacts of Changing Missions at the Rocky Flats Plant*, to Rockwell International and the DOE (Columbus, Ohio: 15 December 1981), xxiv. *Long-Range Rocky Flats Utilization Study*, prepared for Albuquerque Operations Office and Office of Military Application, United States Department of Energy (Washington, D.C., February 1983), 104.

6. David Skaggs, interview by author, tape recording, Westminster, Colo., 15 April 1992. Pat Buffer, "Highlights in Rocky Flats History," a selected chronology by year. Rocky Flats site, Records Management. The contract went to Commercial Industrial Construction of Denver.

7. William J. Broad, *Teller's War* (New York: Simon & Schuster, 1992). Solo, *From Protest to Policy*, 134–35. The late Bernard Feld made his comment to the author on several occasions during the mid-1980s.

8. The quotes and information from Tom Rauch in this section are from an interview by author, Denver, Colo., 31 July 1991.

9. Ginsberg, "Plutonian Ode," 17.

10. Weaver interview.

11. House Subcommittee, *Public Works Appropriations, FY 1971*, 1 October 1970, 286. House Committee, *Public Works Appropriation Bill, FY 1973*, 20 April 1972, 211–12.

12. Senate Subcommittee, *Public Works Appropriations, FY 1973*, 26 April 1972, 286.

13. Weaver interview. Buffer, "Highlights," for 1980. Fred Gillies, "Rocky Flats Dedicates Plutonium Recovery Facility," *Denver Post*, 11 April 1980.

14. The quotes from Weaver in this section are from the interview by author. The radiation increase occurred because the tiny quantities of plutonium 241 in the mostly plutonium-239 pits had decayed to americium, which emits gamma rays.

15. The quotes and information from Thielsen are from the interview by author and Thielsen's medical records.

16. C. W. Piltingsrud, "Plutonium Exposure — M. C. Thielsen (2503)," 27 February 1967.

17. Barry Meier, "The Dark Side of a Magical Metal," *New York Times*, 25 August 1996. On Anderson, see Len Ackland, "Dawn of the Atomic Age," *Chicago Tribune* magazine, 28 November 1982. By the early 1980s Anderson's lungs had deteriorated so much that he always had an oxygen tank with him. He then had been working at Los Alamos for many years.

18. The plant's beryllium operations are described in ChemRisk, *History*, 74–75, appendix B Building Summaries for Buildings 444 and 883.

19. The layout was described by former beryllium workers Thielsen, Carlo Peper, and I. K. Roberts, interview by author, tape recording, Golden, Colo., 17 August 1992.

20. E. A. Putzier, "Internal Letter to Medical File," 8 March 1976.

21. Meier, "The Dark Side."

22. Putzier, "Past Thirty Years," 106–7. He says the first publicized hearing was the case of Joseph Sykes in August 1970. Other cases include that of Don Gabel, detailed in Tad Bartimus and Scott McCartney, *Trinity's Children: Living Along the Nuclear Highway* (New York: Harcourt Brace Jovanovich, 1991), 198–202.

23. Gosling and Fehner, *Closing*, 42.

24. Department of Energy, *Final Environmental Impact Statement: Rocky Flats Plant Site*, 1–16, stated, "If Plant operations were to continue for seventy years, with no changes, the radiological impact on persons living within fifty miles of the Plant for that period would be imperceptible, both compared to doses received from natural background radiation and based on risk of cancer mortality and genetic defects."

25. Congress passed the Resource Conservation and Recovery Act (RCRA) to discourage companies from producing hazardous wastes and to encourage advanced recycling. The Environmental Protection Agency was responsible for setting standards and regulating hazardous waste from "cradle to grave." The agency could issue "permits" allowing some levels of pollution. It also was given the authority to delegate hazardous waste management to state agencies that had established programs at least as stringent as the EPA's program. When, during the Love Canal controversy, it became clear that RCRA didn't require the cleanup of hazardous sites, Congress in 1980 passed the law popularly known as "Superfund." The Natural Resources Defense Council filed suit in 1983 over DOE activities in Oak Ridge and won the case against the DOE on April 13, 1984. While the DOE didn't appeal,

in an EIS for the Savannah River Plant in May 1984, it argued that mixed waste (hazardous plus radioactive) is not subject to RCRA. In a related development, Congress passed the Hazardous and Solid Waste Amendments (HSWA) of 1984, listing five categories of waste and telling the EPA to promulgate regulations specifying standards and methods of treatment for each category. The DOE continued to try to evade RCRA and HSWA regarding mixed waste and tried to expand the Atomic Energy Act definition from "radioactive material" to "waste substance containing radioactivity." Gosling and Fehner, *Closing*, 33–39. Stephen Dycus, *National Defense and the Environment* (Hanover: University Press of New England, 1996).

26. U.S. District Court, Colorado, "Findings of Fact and Conclusions of Law," *Church v. U.S. et al.*, C.A. 75-M-1162, 3 July 1985. National Archives, Denver. The settlement agreement was executed on 14 December 1984, but Judge Richard P. Matsch temporarily sealed the "Findings of Fact and Conclusions of Law" on 15 February 1985. On payments, U.S. District Court, Colorado, "Order Directing Payment of Funds," *Church v. U.S. et al.*, C.A. 75-M-1162, 8 July 1985. National Archives, Denver.

27. Albert Hazle, director, Radiation Control Division, certificate on McKay land, 8 July 1985. McKay Files. The document certified that the land was tested and that the concentrations were below the state standard of two disintegrations per minute per gram of dry soil.

28. Proposed NPL listing cited in Colorado Department of Health et al., "Compliance Agreement," July 30, 1986, p. 8. Senator John Glenn's statement in "Senators Warn DOE Over Cleanups of Mixed Waste and Nuclear Facilities," *Inside Energy*, March 31, 1986, p. 5. In Gosling and Fehner, *Circle*, 46.

29. Gosling and Fehner, *Circle*, 46.

30. Although Rocky Flats created large amounts of nuclear, hazardous, and mixed waste, it had never been intended as a disposal site. The plant's low-level nuclear waste, such as nitrate salts, were shipped to the Nevada Test Site for burial. Its transuranic waste was shipped by train to the government site in Idaho. The government planned in 1976 that all transuranic waste eventually would go to a disposal site near Carlsbad, New Mexico, called the Waste Isolation Pilot Project (WIPP). But WIPP, originally scheduled to open in 1985, had encountered both technical and political difficulties. Gosling and Fehner, *Circle*, 31.

31. "Briefing for Mary L. Walker," assistant secretary for DOE's Environment, Safety, and Health Division, July 14, 1986, 4.

CHAPTER TWELVE

1. The quotes and information about Jim Stone in this section are from the interview by author.

2. Weaver interview.

3. Colorado State Legislature, Joint Resolution, in *Congressional Record-Senate*, 100th Cong., 1st sess., vol. 133, part 14, 7 July 1987, 18804–5.

4. John Isaacs, "Using Summitry to Thwart Congress," *Bulletin of the Atomic Scientists*, December 1986, 4–5. Ibid., Leon V. Sigal, "Getting Over the Summit," January/February 1987, 12–13.

5. David Skaggs, interview by author, tape recording, Westminster, Colo., 1 May 1992.

6. Skaggs interview.

7. Lou Chapman, "Rockwell Admits 1981 Test Burn of Radioactive Waste," *Denver Post*, 19 March 1987. On tabling of the plans, see Janet Day, "Plant to Burn Maximum Amount of Plutonium," *Rocky Mountain News*, 29 April 1987. Activist Jan Pilcher played a central role in organizing opposition to the incinerator.

8. ABC's program quoted in Tom Shales, "ABC's Alarming 'Bomb Factories,'" *Washington Post*, 24 April 1987. Joan Lowy, "Government OK's Flats Cleanup to Deflect Scrutiny, Memo Says," *Rocky Mountain News*, 29 April 1987.

9. House Committee on Science, Space, and Technology, *Environmental Crimes at the Rocky Flats Nuclear Weapons Facility: Hearings Before the Subcommittee on Investigations and Oversight*, 102nd Cong., 2d sess., September and October 1992, 399–400.

10. House Committee on Government Operations, *The Costs of Inadequate Oversight and Control; A Review of Production of Gifts, Mementos, and Personal Items at Rocky Flats Nuclear Facility: Hearing Before Subcommittee on Environment, Energy, and Natural Resources*, 100th Cong., 1st sess., 11 December 1987, 10.

11. House Committee, *Costs of Inadequate Oversight*, 233. Martin Connolly, "Rocky Flats Fraud: Seventeen-Year Secret," *Boulder Daily Camera*, 23 August 1987. While the original False Claims Act was passed in the nineteenth century, Congress had amended and strengthened it in 1986. On the settlement, Sally McGrath, "Rockwell, Livermore to Pay $450,000 in Whistleblower Case, *Boulder Daily Camera*, 17 July 1993.

12. Martin Connolly, interview by author, Kansas City, Mo., 18 May 1992.

13. House Committee, *Costs of Inadequate Oversight*, 2, 335.

14. Michael Krepon, "INF Agreement in Principle," *Bulletin of the Atomic Scientists*, November 1987, 5–6. The *Bulletin* turned back the hands of its symbolic Doomsday Clock in January 1988.

15. Federal Bureau of Investigation, *Application and Affidavit for Search Warrant*, for Rocky Flats, U.S. District Court, case 89-730M, attachment C, 36–40, 50–4. Waste treatment included "spray irrigation" of wastes on open fields and "use of a fluid bed (or chemical process) incinerator."

16. On DOE concession, see Gosling and Fehner, *Circle*, 39. The DOE published a rule change in the May 1, 1987, Federal Register acknowledging that RCRA covered mixed waste. On Romatowski, see FBI, *Affidavit*, 56–57.

17. House Committee, *Costs of Inadequate Oversight*, 304–5. On the award see Janet Day, "DOE Blasted for Award Given to Flats Overseer," *Rocky Mountain News*, 24 February 1988.

18. Gosling and Fehner, *Circle*, 48. Keith Schneider, "Operators Got Millions in Bonuses Despite Hazards at Atom Plants," *New York Times*, 26 October 1988. For

his performance the DOE had awarded Romatowski bonuses of $13,950 on top of his $77,500 salary.

19. Janet Day, "Possibility of Closure Stuns Flats," *Rocky Mountain News*, 1 April 1988.

20. Skaggs interview. Gary Schmitz, "Government May Abandon Rocky Flats Nuclear Plant," *Denver Post*, 1 April 1988. Cleanup estimates changed frequently over the years.

21. General Accounting Office, *Problems with Cleaning Up the Solar Ponds at Rocky Flats* (Washington, GAO), RCED-91–31, January 1991, 4. House Committee, *Environmental Crimes*, 575–6.

22. GAO, *Solar Ponds*, 1–5.

23. FBI, *Application for Search Warrant*, 9. Martin Hestmark, interview by author, Denver, Colo., 8 August 1992.

24. Hestmark interview. FBI, *Application for Search Warrant*, 63.

25. The editorial was based on this news story: Gary Schmitz, "Concerns Over Safety Nearly Shut Down Rocky Flats," *Denver Post*, 1 September 1988.

26. Keith Schneider, "2D Nuclear Plant Is Ordered Closed by Energy Department," *New York Times*, 11 October 1988.

27. House Committee, *Environmental Crimes*, 400.

28. Ibid., 404, 1017–18, 1312. Norton said that his office took on the Rocky Flats investigation in August 1988.

29. Romer's quote in Bill Scanlon, "DOE Offers No Solution for N-Waste," *Boulder Daily Camera*, 17 November 1988. The "Ship Out . . ." headline is from the *Denver Post* on the same day.

30. FBI, *Application for Search Warrant*, 83–84, 99. House Committee, *Environmental Crimes*, 770–72. The photos were interpreted by Al Divers at the Environmental Photographic Interpretation Center in Las Vegas, Nevada. A second expert disagreed. The infrared photo was the main evidence for the incinerator portion of the affidavit.

31. In Gosling and Fehner, *Circle*, 55.

32. Ibid., 57, 60–61.

33. FBI, *Application for Search Warrant*, 65.

34. *U.S. v. Rockwell International Corporation*, "Plaintiff's Sentencing Memorandum," U.S. District Court for the District of Colorado, 92-CR-107, 20 March 1992, 3.

CHAPTER THIRTEEN

1. Janet Day and Sue Lindsay, "U.S. Agents Raid Rocky Flats," *Rocky Mountain News*, 7 June 1989.

2. Janet Day presentation to journalism class, University of Colorado at Boulder, and interview by author, Boulder, Colo., 5 March 1992.

3. Unbylined, "Romer Angry State Kept in Dark About Probe," *Denver Post*, 7 June 1989.

4. Colorado Council on Rocky Flats, *The Handbook on Rocky Flats* (Denver, 1993). The Environmental Monitoring Council, renamed the Colorado Council on Rocky Flats in August 1992, was a citizens' advisory committee appointed by Skaggs and Romer. It was to perform a function similar to the Rocky Flats Monitoring Committee, established by Governor Lamm and Representative Wirth in 1976 as recommended by the Lamm-Wirth Task Force. That committee lost its federal funding in 1981 and became relatively inactive.

5. The grand jury was impaneled by Chief Judge Sherman G. Finesilver in August 1989.

6. On Skaggs and Schroeder: Unbylined, "Romer Angry State Kept in Dark about Probe," *Denver Post*, 7 June 1989. On Kelly: Janet Day, "Investigation Numbs Rocky Flats Workers," *Rocky Mountain News*, 8 June 1989.

7. Gosling and Fehner, *Circle*, 63.

8. Ibid.

9. Jay Grelen, "Doctors Call for Shutdown of Rocky Flats," *Denver Post*, 18 June 1989. J. Sebastian Sinisi, "Doctors Reverse Stand on Flats," *Denver Post*, 20 June 1989. LeRoy Moor et al., *Citizen's Guide*, 52–54, describes many protest activities.

10. LeRoy Moore, interview by author, Boulder, Colo., 13 March 1992; personal communication, 8 July 1998. Moore et al., *Citizen's Guide*, 54.

11. The information and quotes from Charlie McKay in this section are from the interview by author, 11 May 1998.

12. Gosling and Fehner, *Circle*, 67.

13. Benjamin Weiser, "Manager Threatened to Close Rocky Flats," *Washington Post*, 25 July 1989. Mathew Wald, "Rockwell Threatens to Close Nuclear Weapons Plant," *New York Times*, 16 September 1989, noted that the three civilians at Aberdeen were sentenced the previous May to three years' probation and $15,000 in fines. Gosling and Fehner, *Circle*, 64.

14. Rick Wartzman, "Rockwell Bomb Plant Is Repeatedly Accused of Poor Safety Record," *Wall Street Journal*, 30 August 1989. Karen Dorn Steele, "Hanford: America's Nuclear Graveyard," *Bulletin of the Atomic Scientists*, October 1989, 15–23.

15. Matthew L. Wald, "Rockwell Is Giving Up Rocky Flats Plant," *New York Times*, 23 September 1989. On the EG&G fee, Unbylined, "EG&G Will Manage Nuclear Arms Plant in $2.5 Billion Contract," *Wall Street Journal*, 12 October 1989.

16. Thomas Graf, "Plutonium in Flats Ducts Enough to Spark Radiation," *Denver Post*, 7 October 1989. Later inspections found a total of sixty-four pounds of plutonium in ducts. But criticalities require that the plutonium be configured in a certain way for a chain reaction to begin. Criticalities have occurred at other nuclear weapons facilities, but the DOE contends no such accident has ever occurred at Rocky Flats.

17. Skaggs told reporters at a news conference before learning of the suspension,

"To me it comes down to the simple question: How do we compare the health and safety risk to Rocky Flats workers and to people in the Denver metropolitan area if we continue regular operations at the plant, versus the risk to our national security if we temporarily suspend Rocky Flats plutonium operations?" Keith Schneider, "U.S. Temporarily Shutting Down Nuclear Plant for Safety Problems," *New York Times*, 30 November 1989.

18. Mark Obmascik, "Illegal Burn Didn't Occur, Officials Say," *Denver Post*, 30 November 1989.

19. Keith Schneider, "Energy Secretary Says Rocky Flats Will Be Closed Indefinitely," *New York Times*, 2 December 1989.

20. Senate Committee on Energy and Natural Resources, *Hearing on the Nomination of James D. Watkins to Be Secretary of Energy*, 101st Cong., 1st sess., 22 February 1989, 39–41.

21. William Lanouette, "James D. Watkins: Frustrated Admiral of Energy," *Bulletin of the Atomic Scientists*, January–February 1990, 36–42. Mathew Wald, "Promise of Change in Bomb Program Not Yet Fulfilled," *New York Times*, 7 December 1989.

22. Robert Nelson interview by author, tape recording, Rocky Flats, 10 December 1991.

23. Gosling and Fehner, *Closing*, 76–77.

24. EG&G Community Relations and DOE Public Affairs, "Economic Impact of Rocky Flats," information sheet, August 1991. Most of the information for this release came from Tucker Hart Adams, *The Impact of Rocky Flats Operations on Colorado and the Denver Metropolitan Area* (Colorado Springs: The Adams Group, February 1991). Footnote 1 reads: "As of July 1, ongoing contracts with additional firms increase total plant employment to more than 8,000." On 1989 figures, see Dominick J. Sanchini, president, Rockwell International, Rocky Flats Plant, statement to the FBI, June 1989. In House Committee, *Environmental Crimes*, 644. At the time the plant employed 5,300 Rockwell employees and 700 subcontract employees, mostly in construction. Quote from Ginger Swartz, personal communication to author, 20 July 1998.

25. Secretary Watkins said public participation was a priority when he released the DOE's first national five-year plan in August 1989. Through public participation in its planning process, the DOE officially hoped to "establish public confidence in its ability to operate its facilities without posing a threat to public and worker health and the environment." In Gosling and Fehner, *Circle*, 69.

26. The quotes from David Albright in this section are from an interview by author, tape recording, Boulder, Colo., 27 May 1998.

27. David Albright, Tom Zamora, David Lewis, "Turn Off Rocky Flats," *Bulletin of the Atomic Scientists*, June 1990, 12–19.

28. Abbott interview.

29. Caryn Shetterly, States News Service, "Watkins: Flats May Lose 2,000 Jobs," *Denver Post*, 3 March 1991. Mark Obmascik, "Summer Date Envisioned for Resum-

ing Flats Work," *Denver Post*, 13 March 1991, cited DOE undersecretary John Tuck as saying the plant still had some safety problems but should reopen in the summer. Mark Obmascik, "Foes of Flats Rule Forum on Closing Plant," *Denver Post*, 4 April 1991.

30. Frank Scandale, "Meeting on Flats Almost Free-for-all as Sides Get Vocal," *Denver Post*, May 3, 1991. The author interviewed several activists who attended.

31. The quotes and information from this meeting are from author's notes.

32. The quotes and information from this news conference are from author's notes and tape recording.

33. Terence Hunt, "Bush Wants Tax Breaks, Military Cuts," *Boulder Daily Camera*, 29 January 1992.

CHAPTER FOURTEEN

1. Eugene Tanner photograph accompanying Gregory Todd, "Flats Workers Angrily Listen to Speech," *Boulder Daily Camera*, 29 January 1992.

2. Jim Zane, "PA on Response to Watkins' Budget Briefing," 29 January 1992, fax from Community Relations. Rocky Flats site. William J. Weida, "Regional Employment Impacts from Nuclear Waste Cleanup at Rocky Flats," unpublished paper, 14 May 1993. Weida is an economics professor at Colorado College.

3. Gregory Todd, "Comments from Plant Workers," *Boulder Daily Camera*, 29 January 1992. Job multiplier and spending figures from Adams, *Economic Impact of Rocky Flats*, section V. Dinah Zieger, "Gradual Layoffs at Rocky Flats May Blunt Economic Impact," *Boulder Daily Camera*, 29 January 1992.

4. Quotes and information about Thielsen and Roberts from the interview by author, 6 August 1992.

5. Ibid. Len Ackland, "Who the Hell Will Insure Us?" *Bulletin of the Atomic Scientists*, November 1992, 27.

6. John Mossman, "Flats Demonstrators Rejoicing in Changes," AP story in the *Denver Post*, 2 February 1992.

7. The January 23 Interagency Agreement to clean up contaminated sites was the first such agreement under the 1986 Superfund amendments (SARA). Gosling and Fehner, *Circle*, 83.

8. Many small activist groups engaged in the Rocky Flats debate. Among them was the Environmental Information Network, run by two sisters, Paula Elofson-Gardine and Susan Hurst, who regularly attended public meetings and vigorously challenged DOE, contractor, and health department officials to provide more complete and accurate information.

9. The five felonies included four violations of the Resource Conservation and Recovery Act and one of the Clean Water Act. The five misdemeanors all involved the Clean Water Act. Government prosecutors noted that this was the second-largest fine ever for environmental damage, exceeded only by the Exxon Corporation's $125 million fine for the *Exxon Valdez* oil spill in Alaska. Still, the federal judge

in the Rocky Flats case delayed his acceptance of the plea bargain for a few weeks to ensure that the deal was fair. Mark Obmascik, "Flats Plea Bargain on Hold," *Denver Post*, 27 March 1992. *U.S. v. Rockwell*, "Plea Agreement and Statement of Factual Basis," U.S. District Court for the District of Colorado, 26 March 1992.

10. Janet Day, "Dismay, Content Pepper Activists' Reactions," *Denver Post*, 27 March 1992.

11. Kelly Richmond, "Congressional Panel to Open Flats Hearing," States News Service in the *Denver Post*, 23 September 1992.

12. Wes McKinley, public statement at "Return to the Nuclear Crossroads" reunion, Rocky Mountain Peace and Justice Center, Boulder, Colo., 25 April 1998, author's notes and tape recording.

13. Bryan Abas, "The Secret Story of the Rocky Flats Grand Jury," *Westword*, 30 September–6 October 1992, 15–26. Schroeder's demand in Peter G. Chronis, "Schroeder Demands Investigation of U.S. Attorney," *Denver Post*, 3 October 1992. House Committee, *Environmental Crimes*. Rep. Howard Wolpe, chairman of the Subcommittee on Investigations and Oversight, also released a subcommittee report on its review, which began in June. Wolpe, "The Prosecution of Environmental Crimes at the Department of Energy's Rocky Flats Facility," 4 January 1993. The principle of grand jury secrecy was supported by some people critical of the DOE and the plant's operations. Rep. David Skaggs, for example, urged that the grand jury remain gagged. "I simply do not believe that this oversight [of Rocky Flats] requires undercutting the long-standing, critical practice of maintaining secrecy about grand jury activities," Skaggs wrote in a letter. In Adriel Bettelheim, "Gag Flats Grand Jury, Skaggs Says," *Denver Post*, 17 November 1993.

14. Michael D. Lemonick, "Sometimes It Takes a Cowboy," *Time*, 25 January 1993, 58.

15. In the negotiated "Plea Agreement" the Justice Department agreed to state publicly that "the investigation has not revealed that hazardous or mixed wastes were burned in the Building 771 incinerator during the period October 1988 to January 1989 or at any time in the Building 776 fluidized bed incinerator." *U.S. v. Rockwell*, "Plea Agreement and Statement of Factual Basis." Allegations of such burning had been central to the FBI's affidavit for a search warrant. The Building 771 incinerator was installed in 1959 and upgraded and modified over the years. It operated under the Colorado Clean Air Act with an emissions permit, according to an affidavit by Rockwell official William F. Weston. Prior to 1980 the incinerator had burned more than five hundred tons of combustibles, and plutonium had been recovered from the ash in significant amounts on an ongoing basis. Regarding the ash, a regulatory dispute existed over whether residues were regulated under RCRA. That dispute wasn't resolved until Judge Babcock ruled in the Sierra Club suit in April 1990 that the incinerator was a RCRA-regulated unit. Investigators found that the DOE had "in no uncertain terms" told Rockwell to hold on to the residues. In House Committee, *Environmental Crimes*, 1504, 1173–74.

16. House Committee, *Environmental Crimes*, 1382, 1485, 1550–1. Investigators went through 3.5 million pages of documents. Fimberg noted that the Resource Conservation and Recovery Act exempted "any activity or substance which is subject to the Atomic Energy Act of 1954."

17. *U.S. v. Rockwell*, "Plaintiff's Sentencing Memorandum," 20 March 1992, 8, 13. Fimberg elaborated in his congressional testimony. He said investigators didn't find evidence that DOE officials had told Rockwell to "go out and bury this stuff on the back 40. This is not what we found. What we found, which was in some ways equally shocking, was that here was a nuclear defense facility that for all intents and purposes the Government had abdicated to a private contractor. Rockwell ran that plant, not DOE. Rockwell turned the valves, pushed the buttons, made pondcrete, operated spray irrigation." In House Committee, *Environmental Crimes*, 1592. On the DOE in charge, *U.S. v. Rockwell*, "Defendant's Sentencing Memorandum," 6–7. Also, two Rockwell attorneys had spelled out the company's position in an April 22, 1991, letter to the government. "In our view, what 'happened' at Rocky Flats has a simple explanation: the Department of Energy's foremost and overriding priority was the production of nuclear warheads. As a result, DOE failed for many years — consciously and admittedly — to devote the money, personnel, and effort needed to bring an antiquated weapons complex into compliance with the rapidly expanding body of federal and state environmental laws. . . . Consequently it now takes little effort to identify, retrospectively, possible areas where Rocky Flats was not in conformance with RCRA and other environmental laws during the 1980s." The letter continued, "We believe, however, that none of the potential 'violations' identified by the grand jury warrants *criminal* prosecution." Reprinted in House Committee, *Environmental Crimes*, 1354–55. Rockwell's interpretation of its relationship with the government was also supported in the historical record explaining the way government-owned, contractor-operated nuclear weapons production plants were managed. The Atomic Energy Commission's Edward Giller described the relationship at a 1972 congressional hearing. "Dow Chemical runs our plant in Rocky Flats, Colo., for instance. The AEC (the Government) pays all the salaries, buys all the material, and the contractor gets a fee for operating the plant but we control their budget. We discussed this with the committee a couple of years ago. Very precisely, it is Government owned and controlled, but contractor operated. . . . Now, the AEC's employees, which are civil service, monitor it, control it, manage it." Senate Subcommittee, *Public Works Appropriations, FY 1973*, 26 April 1972, 243.

18. House Committee, *Environmental Crimes*, 1018, 1481–1485.

19. In a supplemental memorandum addressing Rockwell's argument that none of the "sensational" accusations had been proven, the prosecutors wrote that Rockwell hadn't just admitted to technical violations. "Simply put, Rockwell has pled guilty to serious crimes involving 330 instances of *knowing felonious conduct*, and eighty instances of *criminal negligence* from 1987 to 1989." *U.S. v. Rockwell*, "Plaintiff's Supplemental Sentencing Memorandum," 28 May 1992.

20. *Denver Post* reporter Mark Obmascik commented insightfully on the grand jury situation in a July 3, 1997, column after jurors met with a federal judge in another unsuccessful attempt to go public. "For five years, the runaway grand jurors and their spotlight-craving Washington lawyer, Jonathan Turley, have been whispering that they and they alone know some deep, dark secret about our notorious neighborhood nuclear weapons plant," Obmascik wrote. "After nearly a decade of reporting on Rocky Flats, I understand how grand jurors got angry and outraged — angry that our own government converted part of Colorado into one of the most toxic places on Earth, outraged that we federal taxpayers are being stuck with the multibillion-dollar cleanup bill. When an ordinary citizen sees such massive malfeasance, you want to scream for justice and secure the harshest possible punishment. But there's a big catch. In America you can only dole out punishment under the strict requirements of the law." Obmascik noted that the grand jurors aren't trained environmental experts knowledgeable about the law's fine points. He wrote that "at least eleven separate investigatory agencies — including the Colorado Health Department, several congressional committees, and the Defense Nuclear Facilities Safety Board — searched for the same prosecutable lawbreaking outlined in the renegade 124-page report. They found none."

21. Other appointees included Bob Alvarez, a former environmental and antinuclear activist and then staffer to Sen. John Glenn of Ohio; Tara O'Toole, a physician and former nuclear researcher at the congressional Office of Technology Assessment; and James Werner, a former EPA employee and NRDC scientist. Keith Schneider, "Disclosing Radiation Tests Puts Official in Limelight," *New York Times*, 6 January 1994. Gosling and Fehner, *Circle*, 134.

22. Schneider, "Disclosing Radiation Tests." Eileen Welsome won the 1994 Pulitzer Prize for her *Albuquerque Tribune* series.

23. Department of Energy, "Openness Press Conference Fact Sheets," 7 December 1993, 21, 28. The total figure was subsequently boosted to one hundred tons.

24. O'Leary used the slogan, for example, at a slide-show presentation to the national Society of Environmental Journalists meeting in Utah on 7 October 1994. These studies and hearings brought to light some of the details about Rocky Flats operations that appear in this book.

25. Romer and Skaggs, who appointed the members of the Colorado Council on Rocky Flats, concurred with the organization's board that the council should be phased out to make way for the Citizens Advisory Board. Colorado Council on Rocky Flats, *Final Report to the Citizens of Colorado* (Denver, January 1994), 9. The CAB became self-selecting and supported by a paid staff, funded by the DOE. Unlike the defunct council, the CAB doesn't report directly to the elected governor and congressional district representative.

26. Len Ackland, "The Permanence of Plutonium," *Boulder Daily Camera*, 6 October 1994.

27. Mark Obmascik, "Russians Get Tour of Flats," *Denver Post*, 22 July 1994, and

Carol Chorey, "Welcome Mat: Russians Get Tour at Flats," *Boulder Daily Camera*, 22 July 1994. On worker's comment, author's notes from plant visit 25 July 1994.

28. Thomas Graf, "Security Firm Hired for Flats," *Denver Post*, 27 July 1990. Wackenhut, based in Coral Gables, Florida, already provided security at the Nevada Test Site and Savannah River. Security issues came up several other times. See Judith Brimberg, "3 Guards at Flats Suspended Over Drugs," *Denver Post*, 27 October 1990; Kelly Richmond, "Flats Security at High Risk, GAO Says," States News Service in *Denver Post*, 2 February 1993; Jim Carrier, "Flats Security Lax, Ex-officials Warn," *Denver Post*, 20 May 1997.

29. L. L. Zodtner and R. F. Rogers, "Study of Unaccounted For Plutonium Losses" (censored version), 6 January 1964. Rocky Flats Site, Records Management. MUF figures from Secretary O'Leary's news conference 27 June 1994. DOE. Chris Roberts, "Missing Flats Plutonium in Idaho, Manager Says," *Boulder Daily Camera*, 22 February 1996. Voillequé, "Rocky Flats Plutonium Releases," 3 March 1997.

30. The two Kaiser-Hill partners were ICF Kaiser International Inc. and CH2M Hill Companies Ltd. See Janet Day, "Rolling the Dice at Rocky Flats," *Denver Post*, 9 April 1995. The DOE had put the plant contract out for bid in 1994 under its "contract reform initiative." Budget details in Rocky Flats news release, 30 June 1995. Rocky Flats site, Kaiser-Hill communications.

31. DOE Rocky Flats manager Mark Silverman described the site in an October 20, 1995, letter to stakeholders. Rocky Flats site, DOE communications office. Bonnie Lavelle (EPA Region 8), presentation to U. of Colorado journalism class and interview by author, Boulder, Colo., 11 October 1995. Gary Gerhardt, "Rocky Flats 'Refuge' Opens for Visitors," *Rocky Mountain News*, 23 March 1997.

32. McKay interview, 11 May 1998.

33. The DOE estimates are contained in DOE, *The 1996 Baseline Environmental Management Report* (Washington: DOE), vol. 2, 52. Bill Scanlon, "Rocky Flats Proposes Burying Waste On-site," *Rocky Mountain News*, 27 January 1995. Chris Roberts, "Flats Plan: Raze, Bury Site," *Boulder Daily Camera*, 2 November 1995.

34. Patrick O'Driscoll, "Flats Impact Study Dumped," *Denver Post*, 26 February 1997.

35. Camera staff and wire services, "Designation to Speed Rocky Flats Cleanup," *Boulder Daily Camera*, 8 August 1997.

36. Berny Morson, " 'Infinity' Painters Trap Plutonium," *Rocky Mountain News*, 28 August 1997. Katy Human, "Off-the-Meter Radiation Cleaned Up," *Boulder Daily Camera*, 28 August 1997.

37. *Camera* staff, "Plutonium Exposure Reported by Rocky Flats Contractor," *Boulder Daily Camera*, 7 November 1997. On first demolition, see Mark Obmascik, "Razing Building Raises Bill," *Denver Post*, 18 June 1998. Office of Technology Assessment, *Hazards Ahead: Managing Cleanup, Worker Health and Safety at the Nuclear Weapons Complex* (Washington, U.S. Government Printing Office, 1993).

38. Weaver interview.

39. Author's notes.

EPILOGUE

1. Charlie McKay, interview by author, Westminster, Colo., 6 January 1998. For details of the real estate deal see John Rebchook, "Etkin Joins Turnpike Boom," *Rocky Mountain News*, 30 December 1997.

2. David Albright, Frans Berkhout, and William Walker, *Plutonium and Highly Enriched Uranium 1996: World Inventories, Capabilities and Policies* (New York: Oxford University Press, 1997) 40. David Albright, et al., "Plutonium by the ton," *Bulletin of the Atomic Scientists*, June 1990, 15. Warhead figure from Robert S. Norris of the Natural Resources Defense Council in Washington, D.C., personal communication with author, 18 August 1998. The DOE has not yet released actual Rocky Flats production figures. Since 1965 Rocky Flats was the nation's only plant manufacturing large numbers of plutonium components for pits primarily used to detonate hydrogen bombs. The Los Alamos laboratory in New Mexico, in its TA-55 facility built in 1978, retains the capacity to fabricate relatively small numbers of pits. DOE announced in the mid-1990s that Los Alamos would continue to provide the contingency for pit production.

3. Robert S. Norris and William M. Arkin, "NRDC Nuclear Notebook," *The Bulletin of the Atomic Scientists*, March/April 2000, 79.

4. Richmond Homes Inc., II, "Rock Creek Ranch Purchase Agreement Addendum No. 1," 7 April 1995.

5. Katy Human, "Study: Flats Neighbors Safe," *Boulder Daily Camera*, 29 June 1998.

6. Jessica Gleich, "Future of Flats Debated," *Denver Post*, 9 July 1998. U.S. Department of Energy, *Accelerating Cleanup: Paths to Closure*, Office of Environmental Management (Washington, D.C.: June 1998), 3–7.

7. Marc Fioravanti and Arjun Makhijani, *Containing the Cold War Mess: Restructuring the Environmental Management of the U.S. Nuclear Weapons Complex* (Takoma Park, Md.: Institute for Energy and Environmental Research, October 1997, 3, 55. In Arjun Makhijani, Stephen I. Schwartz, and William Weida, "Nuclear Waste Management and Environmental Remediation," *Atomic Audit: The Costs and Consequences of U.S. Nuclear Weapons Since 1940* (Washington, D.C.: Brookings Institution Press, 1998), 356. LeRoy Moore, "Migration of Plutonium in the Soil at Rocky Flats: Narrative of a Controversy and the Case for Public Oversight," Rocky Mountain Peace and Justice Center, 28 April 1998. Katy Human, "Cleaning up Flats," *Boulder Daily Camera*, 11 February 2000.

8. Kevin Flynn, "Arvada Backs Flats as Refuge," *Rocky Mountain News*, 29 August 2000.

9. LeRoy Moore, "*Camera* was wrong about WIPP," op-ed column in the *Boulder*

Daily Camera, 13 June 13 1998. The Rocky Mountain Peace Center's name was changed by adding "and Justice" in the mid-1990s.

10. Ed Bodey "Flats Tops All DOE Sites in Waste Shipments," *Rocky Flats Envision*, Kaiser-Hill, vol. 6, #23, 4 December 2000.

11. Michael Romano, "Report Skeptical of Finishing Flats Cleanup on Time," *Rocky Mountain News*, 3 June 1998.

12. Stacie Oulton, "Flats Cleanup Violations Cited," *Denver Post*, 9 January 2001. Michael Janofsky, "Workers Cleaning Nuclear Arms Site for Wildlife Preserve Test Positive for Radiation," *New York Times*, 8 December 2000.

13. DOE, *Accelerating Cleanup*, 3–8. Stephen I. Schwartz, ed., *Atomic Audit*, 3.

14. Beth Wohlberg, "Flats Workers Will Stay Till It's Done," *Boulder Daily Camera*, 5 January 2000. Jerry Harden, interview by author, Lakewood, Colo., 26 May 1998.

15. Len Ackland, "Deadly Metal," *Denver Post*, 7 May 2000. The updated totals are in Unbylined, "Feds' Plan to Aid Nuclear Workers," *Boulder Daily Camera*, 12 January 2001.

16. Ibid. Berny Morson, "Nuke Workers May Get Lost Pay," *Rocky Mountain News*, 12 January 2001. James Ruttenber, interview by author, Boulder, Colo., 16 June 1998. On workforce, see Chapter 9 above.

17. ChemRisk, *Historical Public Exposures*, Volumes for Tasks 1–12, 1992–94, Colorado Department of Public Health and Environment.

18. Paul Voilleque at Radiological Assessments Corp., "Technical Work Session," Lakewood, Colo., author's notes, 26 May 1998.

19. Author's notes.

20. Slobodan Lekic, "Retired Generals Urge Nuclear Disarmament," *Denver Post*, 5 December 1996. George Lee Butler, "Time to End the Age of Nukes," *The Bulletin of the Atomic Scientists*, March/April 1997, 33–36. Paul H. Nitze, "A Threat Mostly to Ourselves," *New York Times*, 28 October 1999.

21. Robert S. Norris and William M. Arkin, "NRDC Nuclear Notebook," *The Bulletin of the Atomic Scientists*, March/April 2000, 79.

22. Katy Human, "Blast from the Past," *Boulder Daily Camera*, 17 January 1998.

Index

and, 113; Project Apple and, 58; radiation poisoning and, 197; radiation report by, 146–47, 148, 150, 151; safety issues and, 144–45, 167; secrecy and, 70; suit against, 179, 235; tritium incident and, 172, 173, 176; union relations with, 167, 171, 277n21; waste issues and, 141, 167

Dugway Proving Grounds, 275n1

Du Pont Company, 30, 57

Earth Day, demonstrations on, 168. *See also* Environmentalists

EG&G, Inc.: cleanup and, 223, 229, 230; contract for, 220–21; criticism of, 224; replacement of, 239, 240–41; temporary shutdown and, 221

Einstein, Albert, 32, 37

Eisenhower, Dwight D.: Gaither Committee and, 129; nuclear weapons and, 115, 257nn48, 49

Ellender, Allen J., 165

Elliott, Dick: on Rocky Flats, 52

Ellsberg, Daniel, 248; arrest/conviction of, 187–88; civil disobedience by, 186

Elofson-Gardine, Paula, 287n8

Eminger, Verle "Lefty": fire and, 117, 118

Encirclement, described, 193–94

Energy Research and Development Administration (ERDA), 176; Church claim against, 178–79; DOE and, 185

Engstrom, Wally, 66

Eniwetok, 60; bomb test on, 259n11

Environmental Action of Colorado, 170

Environmental impact statement (EIS), 200, 240, 278n37, 282n23

Environmental Information Network, Rocky Flats debate and, 287n8

Environmental issues, 126, 141, 197, 200, 210, 214, 218; concern for, 3, 173, 182, 183, 217, 224, 231, 232, 233, 235; DOE and, 201; waste and, 139

Environmentalists, 177, 181, 218; nuclear weapons/nuclear power and, 186; and peace activists compared, 169–70, 185; protests by, 168, 170–71, 190, 204

Environmental laws, 168, 214, 200, 201, 202, 205, 220, 240, 278n37, 281–82n25, 287nn7, 9, 288n15. *See also* Resource Conservation and Recovery Act

Environmental Monitoring Council, 285n4

Environmental Protection Agency (EPA), 168; buffer zone and, 178; Church suit and,

200–202; cleanup and, 231, 239; DOE and, 200, 201, 209, 220, 223, 234; environmental compliance and, 220; investigation by, 206, 208, 212, 215, 216, 217; mobile investigation unit of, 92 (photo), 215; ongoing violations and, 220; Rocky Flats and, 168, 177, 203, 205; standards/regulation by, 281–82n25; tritium incident and, 172; waste operations and, 190

EPA. *See* Environmental Protection Agency

Epp, John: waste disposal group and, 106

ERDA. *See* Energy Research and Development Administration

Exposure, 143–44, 148, 194, 197, 198, 225, 266n11; cancer and, 230; concern about, 221, 231; decrease in, 148; guidelines for, 121, 132. *See also* Radiation; Health issues

Exxon Corporation, fine for, 287n9

False Claims Act, 207, 283n11

Fallout shelters, 135–36

Fate of the Earth, The (Schell), 190

FBI: environmental crimes and, 234; investigation by, 70, 200, 206, 207, 212, 216, 218, 244; polygraph examinations by, 276n18; Stone and, 204

Federal Center, Denver, 52

Federation of American Scientists, 182, 224; nuclear energy control and, 32

Feld, Bernard, 280n7; on Star Wars, 193

Felt, Rowland E., 274n27; on fire, 156, 158

Fermi, Enrico, 38, 198

Fernald uranium foundry, closing of, 221

Filtering systems, 117–18, 119, 120, 122; radiation and, 131

Fimberg, Kenneth: on mixed waste violations, 234; on RCRA, 289n16; testimony of, 289n17

Fires, 178, 195, 204; cleanup following, 121–23, 157; containing, 119, 159; described, 75, 117–19; impact of, 122–23, 126, 146–48, 165–66, 243–44; investigation of, 156, 163–65; media coverage for, 163; Mother's Day, 152–54, 163–65; plutonium and, 112–13, 116–17, 119–20, 123, 148, 149, 153; risks following, 119–21, 165; routine, 148–49, 152

Fission, 37, 43, 52, 272n3. *See also* Nuclear weapons

Fission bombs, 114, 268n8; core components of, 53; yield from, 54

Fitzsimmons Army Hospital, 29